First published in 2019. This edition published in 2025
Copyright © Chris Bates 2025
Tarot Images Copyright © Digitaln

The right of Chris Bates to be identified as the Author of the Work has been asserted by him in accordance with the Copyright, Designs and Patent Act 1988.

All rights reserved. This book and copyright material must not be copied, reproduced, transferred, distributed, leased or licensed in any way except when specifically permitted in writing by the publisher. Any unauthorized distribution or use of this text may be a direct infringement of the author's and publisher's rights.

ebook ISBN:978-1-7638824-1-6
Paperback ISBN:978-1-7638824-0-9

BOOKKOOP
PO Box 172, Imbil Qld 4570
ABN 91 296 420 733
www.bookkoop.co

LOST IN TRANSIT

A romantic misadventure about love, loss, excess baggage and karma.

CHRIS BATES

For my mother, Lynette...
who kept the fire burning and the path lit.

"Sometimes," said Pooh, "the smallest things take up the most room in your heart."
'Winnie-the-Pooh'—*A.A. Milne*

Author's Note

Let me set something straight right from the start: I know absolutely nothing about magical mysticism, divine providence or spiritual serendipity. And yet I've decided to punctuate several chapters of this book with imagery from the otherworld. The world of the tarot, to be specific.

Now, for the sake of design aesthetics, these tarot card pictures have all been placed *upright*. To the average reader this is of no relevance whatsoever. But to tarot card freaks —and you know who you are!—this kind of casual flippancy could trigger an OCD episode that will turn their world upside down.

To address this I've included both positive (*upright*) and negative (*reversed*) definitions below each card. If you're a tarot tragic you'll know exactly what that oddball sentence actually means. If you're not, just think of these pics as a literary commercial break that will remind you to grab another cup of coffee, or another glass of wine. Or even another book.

Of course, if you're a cynical reader, you could, quite rightly, view the tarot illustrations as a cheap marketing gimmick to fool people into believing that this book might actually be spiritually enlightening.

It isn't.

Also, while I'm here, a warning: there is swearing and blasphemy in this book. Both of which are used to re-create my 'authentic' voice. Tellingly, this adherence to realism doesn't necessarily extend elsewhere in the book. In fact, the opposite is true, since I've compressed timelines, merged scenes and deliberately altered names, physical descriptions, locations and dates. I've also fictionalized parts of emails and other conversations in an effort to protect the innocent. And myself, I guess.

I should also advise readers that this book is written in a mishmash of languages. These are: colloquial Australian English, British English, American English and my native gibberish. So sometimes there are words like 'Mum' instead of 'Mom', and 'bloke' instead of 'guy/fella/man'. Not to mention many other deviations from the expected forms of proper English spelling and grammar. Suffice to say, I'm assuming most people are smart enough to figure things out. And, really, if you can decipher auto-correct text messages written by drunk ex-partners or daft friends, you should be able to read a book penned by a lazy Australian who types Tourette's-like sentences.

And lastly, despite keeping copious notes and re-reading old travel emails, I can't for the life of me recall each and every line of pointless rambling dialogue that was uttered during the time-span of this story (which, by the way, is mostly set before the wholesale adoption of digital technologies). So, in an effort to craft a readable version of events that won't bore readers to death, I have selectively edited many spoken interactions. I've also pretty much gone and made up a whole load of crap as well—in particular, the occasional connecting banter between people.

What isn't made-up, however, is the emotional truth that lies at the core of these exchanges (admittedly, crafted from my own selective memory). That stuff is real, as is the questionable actions and thoughts I've documented throughout this memoir. All that is real.

Even the really dumb stuff.

Unfortunately.

UPRIGHT - Passionate, spontaneous and fun ... That's me.
REVERSED - Naive, misguided and idiotic ... Yep, still me.

Prologue

I'M A FOOL.

I'm standing in an establishment called *Tea and Tarot,* and I've just been given some bad news: the tea leaf reader has cancelled my appointment.

This is not good. Not good at all.

"Jade called in sick," explains the woman behind the counter. "I can do a tarot reading for you. Or were you specifically wanting her for a tea-leaf reading?"

I'm too embarrassed to explain just how specific my psychic needs are right now, so rather than elaborate or reschedule, I agree to an unwanted tarot reading.

The woman gives me a sympathetic smile, introduces herself, then, in a rustle of silk and chiffon, sashays past a wall decorated with Native American dream catchers, astrology charts, and other mystical items that elude my comprehension.

"Is this your first time?" Celeste asks, stopping in front of an ornate wooden jewelry box.

My cheeks flush. "Yeah."

"I thought so," she says, already reading my mind. She extracts a deck of tarot cards from the box, then gestures toward the shop entrance. "Shall we sit outside?"

Beyond the doorway, several vacant cafe tables are shaded by a rustic iron awning—all are in full view of the passing inner-city public. Reluctantly, I follow the fortune-teller to one of the settings and, in an effort to avoid the mocking gaze of any judgmental passerby, choose a chair that faces *away* from the sidewalk. We sit and Celeste begins to cut and shuffle her cards like a Las Vegas casino dealer. Once done, she instructs me to do the same. I do as I'm told, then slide the tarot deck back.

"So, what would you like to know?" she asks. "It can be a specific question, or something general like love, career, or family."

The skeptic in me stirs. I've always considered horoscopes and fortune-tellers to be the exclusive domain of fragile women and vague men, so I decide to play my cards close to my chest. After all, if Celeste really *can* read the future, she should know why I'm here. Which means she should know about Emma and the tea leaf reader's prediction of true love.

My arms cross involuntarily. "How about all of the above?"

Celeste's lips tighten in a show of slight exasperation. "Sure, we can do a general reading."

And with that, she places the card stack at the centre of the table, and begins a spiel that introduces me to the art of tarot reading. It sounds neither scientific nor remotely plausible. Sensing my disbelief, Celeste flips the first card over to reveal…

DEATH

The grim figure instantly spooks me and a nervous laugh escapes my lips.

"Wow, this is off to a good start…"

A wry smile creases Celeste's face. "Don't stress. First impressions are often misleading. In this case, Death is symbolic, not literal. We'll come back to it later and I'll explain."

She turns the next card over and places it cross-wise over the first…

THE LOVERS

The contrast couldn't be greater. My heart skips a beat because this is *exactly* why I'm here.

Celeste continues on, carefully laying a selection of cards into a pattern she calls the *Celtic Cross*. There are cards illustrated with cups, swords, and big sticks. But nothing surpasses the naked lovers or the deathly figure they partially obscure. Eventually, the last card appears. On its face is an image of a man, woman, and child standing in separate coffins. Floating above the figures is an angel beckoning the family to heaven. Pretty cheery stuff. A single word on the card states:

JUDGEMENT

I have no idea what any of this means, but apparently Celeste does.

"This is a *really* interesting spread," she says thoughtfully. "Lots of conflict and uncertainty." She takes a moment, probably to summon the spirits—obviously the ones she hasn't already drunk—then tilts her head in my direction. "Do you work in a creative field by any chance?"

The question catches me off-guard. It's either a lucky guess or… or what? Can this woman really read my future?!

I take the bait.

"I'm *supposed* to be a writer."

Celeste acknowledges the self-deprecation with a forced smile. "Okay, that makes sense. Because these cards"—she waves a hand over a section of the spread—"suggest a strong creative interest or career. But these three"—her palm hovers over *The Lovers* and a pair of *cup* cards—"relate to affairs of the heart. And in this instance, they indicate that there are two women in your life. Two loves. Does that sound right?"

I nod my little freaked-out noggin in the affirmative.

"But neither of these relationships are resolved," she states emphatically.

"There was a messy breakup with one," I admit, casting any previous divinity doubts aside. "And the other one is…complicated."

"Ah, that explains all the wands and swords. There's lots of turmoil and misdirection here."

I stare at the snitching cards, wondering how they could possibly know my life is in crisis. Maybe they don't. Maybe Celeste is simply reading me like an open book, particularly the most recent chapters of my life—the ones titled Claire, Success, Emma, and Distress. Oddly enough, her uncomfortable insight makes me feel seen. And for a second, I'm willing to accept that Celeste and I live in the same universe, possibly even on the same planet.

"These two loves are draining your emotional resources and

causing a creative block." She raises her gaze to meet mine. "Is this something you're experiencing at the moment?"

I nod my head. "Absolutely."

"I think one of these women will help you heal," she continues. "But the other one," her hand shadows a card with three swords piercing a heart, "the other one is in a lot of pain." She pauses briefly again to study the spread in its entirety. Suddenly, her demeanor shifts uncomfortably as if a resident evil has channeled her. "This is really *really* important," she says, her tone shifting. "This other woman—" Celeste's eyes break free of the cards and lock onto mine. "This other woman, you *must not* hurt."

I'm unsure of which woman she is referring to—Emma or Claire—but her emphasis on the last words make them sound like an accusation, and for a terrifying moment I wonder if Celeste can read both my future *and* my past.

"I don't want to hurt anyone," I say, defensively. My voice sounds weak and unconvincing.

Celeste studies me for a long moment as if weighing the sincerity of my words against the truth of her cards. Her silent judgement makes me uneasy.

"Okay, let's go back to the beginning," she says, finally releasing me. "Let's go back to *Death*."

UPRIGHT - A new start. Your transformation begins now.

REVERSED - Stuck in limbo. Ruin is coming, sucker.

The Beginning

MY GIRLFRIEND IS SCREAMING at me.

"God, why am I so dependent on you?" She hammers the air with frustrated fists. "I don't even know who I am anymore. Look at me." She points to her flushed face. Her pale skin is marked with red blotches induced by cries of self-loathing. "This is not me. This is not who I am."

Cue Mr. Sensitivity. "So what the fuck do you want me to do, Claire?"

"I want you to make a decision so I know where I stand."

"Are we seriously going to go through this again?"

"Just tell me," she pleads, "are we together or not?"

"It's not that simple."

Frustration creases her brow. "It is that simple! It's YES or NO."

I sigh audibly. "I don't know, okay? I'm not even focused on *you* or *us*. I'm trying to get *my* life sorted." I spot the familiar look of hurt on my lover's face. It's a vision that usually fills me with guilt, but now it triggers disdain. "Why do we always have to go over this?"

The veins in Claire's neck pulse a warning. "Go over *what*, Chris?! Tell me what *this* even is? It's not a relationship because one minute you say we're not right for each other, and the next you say you love me." Her tone is hostile and accusatory. "And it's not a partnership because *you* control every part of it."

I turn my back on her and open the fridge door. The usual comfort food is gone, leaving only 'good' food, which is the last thing a guy like me ever wants to be fed. I pause, exhale sharply, then pivot back to Claire.

"You know what? I don't want to talk about this right now."

"Well, I *do*," she blasts.

"There's nothing to talk about. I can't give you whatever it is you want from me, okay, because I don't even know what I want." I slam the fridge door. "I need more than this, Claire."

"So where does that leave me?"

"I don't know."

She shakes her head, refusing to accept my response. "Yes, you do."

"No. I really don't."

"Just tell me," she begs.

"Claire, just STOP." My aggressive bark startles her, and I see a flicker of fear in her eyes. I hesitate, then lower my voice. "Fuck this." I begin to retreat from the kitchen. "I need to get out of here and get a new life."

"So what's stopping you?" Claire challenges. "I never said you have to stay here with me."

I spin on my heels, incredulous. "What's stopping me? Are you serious? *Everything* is stopping me. I'm stopping me. You're stopping me. Having no money is stopping—"

"I AM NOT STOPPING YOU," yells Claire. "When have I *ever* stopped you from doing *anything*? Name one time?"

I wave her off. "Forget it. I'm done."

"Good," she says, marching past me towards the bedroom.

She makes it five paces before I fire another angry shot. "You know what I really want?"

Claire doesn't break stride. "I don't care anymore."

"Exactly, because you don't care about *anything* I say."

Suddenly, she stops. Her shoulders tense, and she turns on me.

"WHAT?!!" Her voice is guttural and her face is crimson with rage. "My whole life revolves around caring about you. I listen to your problems *every single day*. Then I tip-toe around you because I don't know if you're happy, or angry, or depressed, or if I'm going to be frozen out because life isn't going your way. But you don't see any of that. Because you only care about yourself."

"Bullshit."

An exasperated expression appears on Claire's face. "Then tell me why you're with me."

Her challenge wrong-foots me for a second.

"Go on," she presses. "Tell me one thing you actually *like* about me. There obviously isn't anything, because you question everything I do."

"I never question anything you do…unless you do something stupid."

Claire throws her hands in the air. "See?! You hate *everything* I do. You hate the plants I buy, the music I listen to, the way I shelve my books." She counts each item on her fingers. "You hate going out, you hate staying in, you hate my friends, you even hate *your* friends." She pauses to compose herself. "You're never satisfied, Chris."

It's true. Nothing's ever good enough for me. I always want more. Not just a little more, a whole lot more. I thought I'd be a rock star, a movie star, a sports star. A multi-millionaire. I thought I'd be fitter, healthier, more confident, a good friend, an awesome lover. I thought I'd be a success. But I'm nothing at all. And I hate it.

"You hate *everything*," continues Claire.

"You still don't get it, do you?" I seethe. "I hate *myself.* Do you understand? This isn't the life I want, Claire, so, yes, I hate everything about it. *Every-fucking-thing.*"

"Even me?" she murmurs.

Her words disarm me. Reluctantly, I look into her damp eyes. Countless emotions reflect back at me. They belong to the movie of us, but it's the version without the happy ending.

My gaze falls to the floor. "I just want to find something more than this," I mumble.

"Then leave," she says.

UPRIGHT - One who is courageous, compassionate, patient.
REVERSED - Fearful, despairing and full of self-doubt.

The Chapter About Claire

OF COURSE, I didn't leave Claire when she told me to, because I'm a man. And men like me don't actually want complete freedom, even if we say we do. We want freedom with a life-line; preferably one that leads back to a strong woman hanging on with fragile hope. We want the promise of casual sex, endless ego-stroking, and an understanding ear in our hour of need. What we *don't* want is a closed door. In other words, we want everything except commitment and responsibility.

So I stayed.

And life went back to normal.

As always, the icy stand-offs between Claire and me would thaw. Then the inevitable soul-searching would arrive, followed by the usual prescribed relationship cure-all of frenzied make-up sex. And amid the numbness and euphoria of that particular drug we would screw ourselves just that little bit more by believing that everything in our dysfunctional little world was fine.

But everything wasn't fine.

Eventually, after months of push and pull, Claire and I finally confronted the prospect of walking away and starting a new chapter. We discussed terminating everything. Everything that was the sum of us.

It wasn't like this at the beginning, of course.

Life used to be good.

Five years earlier, I had driven in from the bush (or the 'Outback' or the 'Wilderness' or whatever the hell tourism organizations like to label far-flung places governed by beer and dust) and I hit the brakes in Brisbane, a sleepy country city populated by irony-loving people who christened it Bris-Vegas. It was at this non-event location that I intended to morph from mine worker to movie star, because somehow, in my fantasy-fueled mind, that kind of implausibility made sense.

I was blue jeans, hard-faced, and rough around the edges. I owned an old four-wheel-drive, some owner-builder magazines, a pair of steel-capped work boots, and a music collection composed of equal parts country and heavy metal. Claire, in contrast, was shy, attractive, and soft of skin. She owned a bus pass, a wall of fantasy novels, a pair of *Doc Martens,* and two ears that belonged to the *Pixies*. A blind man wearing a welder's mask in a cave could see we had little in common besides a share-house advert and a desperate need to split the rent. So, like a shotgun wedding, a type of forced engagement was set.

Unexpectedly, what should have been an awkward housemate union proved to be heaven-sent. Claire was incorruptible, wicked smart and full of wit, like one of those free-spirited characters found in children's books—the adventurous heroine with 'girl next door' looks. She was a believer in truth, justice, and the power of good. For example, when charity-seekers knocked, Claire didn't hide like me… she stood.

In short, she was everything I wasn't—brave, bright, and benevolent. Which wasn't my type. Like most males, I was drawn to superficial stuff. I dreamed of finding a supermodel, a pop princess, or a movie star type. I needed a trophy addition for my insecure life.

Claire wasn't superficial.

She was real, level-headed and nice; the product of measured parents who had graduated from farm to university, yet still valued the simple life. I was the opposite. I was scattershot, pig-headed, and restless; the product of working-class parents who settled for a mining town life. Despite these differences, Claire and I connected through literature, art, and cinema. As a result, a dialogue started and the movie of us began to script itself.

At first, we teamed up as popcorn partners, planning our movie times around cheap deals and student concessions. Like film nerds, we walked in after the ads but sat through the end credits. We had a two-film-a-week addiction and when we were both too poor to satisfy that habit we shared hits of celluloid at home. This naturally evolved into us keeping company on the couch, sitting through news bulletins, cartoons, documentaries, *Seinfeld*, *Friends*, even *M.A.S.H.* reruns. We sat wide-eyed through elections, natural disasters and civil wars. And when we tired of that, we found solace in the intermission by sharing whatever was on our minds.

Claire was stimulating and fun. Each day was filled with accidentally-on-purpose touches, practical jokes, and lots of laughs. Month after month, we shared more and more, until one night, we gave so much of ourselves that we awkwardly became one. And in that instant, our spartan share-house morphed into a comfortable abode—one newly furnished with desperate hands, shared dreams, candlelit baths, and late-night condom runs.

Life was good. Almost perfect even.

Until it wasn't.

Eventually, after several years of see-sawing dependency, Claire and I grew to love and loathe each other, and ourselves. The shift was slow. Insecurities grew, uncertainties appeared, and finally our Hollywood romantic comedy turned into a convoluted arthouse melodrama with zero box-office appeal.

Playful montages of tickle torture gave way to cheap shots during pointless fights. Scenes of kitchen kisses evaporated into heated exchanges that simmered for days. Even light-hearted sex scenes were edited, cutting all the giggling, backseat, sweaty, outdoor, failed-tantric, and self-filmed moments of connection, and replacing them with occasional entanglements that left an overwhelming disconnection of self.

Praise was replaced with criticism, and fact became *friction*, until finally, our union became a dysfunctional wedding of circumstance with all the negatives of marriage and few of the benefits. We were trapped in a soap opera. A kitchen-sink drama.

So we broke up.

But barely weeks after separating, I began to miss Claire. By that time, I was house-sitting for my vacationing grandparents. I was lost, confused, and unable to express myself. As an escape, I began to write. The words came fast. The flow interrupted only by food, sleep, and the occasional visit from Claire.

At first, I welcomed her arrival reluctantly. I was desperate to see her but terrified to be drawn back into our recent past. But something had changed in Claire. She appeared more confident. Her laughter came easily, and all the insecurities and endless apologies had vanished. Somehow, she had been reborn or reinvented, right down to a new hairstyle that exposed a more relaxed brow. Despite the extreme trim suggesting a cut from her dependence on me, it—and everything else about her—had an intoxicating effect. She reminded me of the old Claire, the one I'd fallen in love with. And, suddenly, I wanted her back. It was clear to me that I needed affection and connection in my life. Maybe even more than everything I was blindly chasing—the fame, the fortune, the sex.

Tragically, the thing I had wanted most came along instead.

Success.

UPRIGHT - Success!! Let the sun shine upon you, golden one.
REVERSED - Remember Icarus? Flew too high. Got burned. Fell to earth.

The Chapter About Success

I SOLD A TELEVISION SHOW.

Or, more correctly, I sold the 'development rights' of a TV series I created to a commercial television network. It may not have been everyone's idea of success, but for me, it was the first step towards fame, fortune, and fornication; a hedonistic life filled with movie starlets, award shows, and private jets.

Of course, prior to this, I'd never actually done anything that suggested I could be a success as a TV writer, or any writer for that matter. Sure, I'd scrawled the usual self-indulgent rubbish that depressive-types spew out during adolescence—things like rock ballads, love poems, suicide letters. All of which were tragic and comical in their own right, but not exactly prime-time material. And yet, I wondered how hard could this TV writing caper be? According to the experts, all you had to do was find a story, mix in some drama, chuck in a few laughs, and pad it with stuff you know about.

So, with that in mind, I bashed out a television script set in a mining town. I threw in a once-headstrong woman who had slowly lost her identity, and let her butt heads with a brooding male who was unable to find purpose in the big bad world. It was the classic fish-out-of-water, enemies-to-lovers story. Once done, I hit 'print' and mailed the pages to a dozen television production companies in Sydney. Then

I sat back and waited for my genius to be recognized. I naively assumed that would happen overnight. Trusted sources said it would never happen. Thankfully, fate intervened, and my ramblings mistakenly landed on a TV executive's desk during an office relocation. One week later, opportunity knocked or, in this case, phoned.

I answered the call.

On the other end was Bryan, one of the creative minds behind Australia's largest free-to-air television networks. We got chatting. Bryan was friendly—narcissistic but self-deprecating, entertaining but earnest, Alpha male but…not. I liked him immediately, especially when he humbly praised my writing after listening to me arrogantly trash a dozen iconic Australian TV shows. Iconic shows, I would soon discover, that had one common thread: they'd all been created by Bryan.

Now, diplomacy and tact are not strong points of mine—nor common sense for that matter. So when Bryan called back a day later, I was terrified I'd blown my only shot at success. Thankfully, he threw a lifeline instead.

"We're working on a new series," Bryan said. "And I think your writing would be perfect. What we need is a country voice. Insight into the average straight male."

My confusion was immediate. Average *straight* male? Did that mean Bryan, the alpha male, was gay?

"Are you in a relationship?" he probed.

"Umm… newly single," I stammered.

"So would relocating to Sydney be a problem?"

"No problem at all," I replied.

"Excellent. Then let's fly you down to meet the creative team. Elliot's a sweetheart," said Bryan. "And Emma's gorgeous." Then he added these prophetic words: "You're going to love her."

UPRIGHT - A new hope to cling to. A guiding light in life.
REVERSED - A future of obstacles. Discouragement and other crap.

The Chapter About Emma

IT TURNED out Emma wasn't gorgeous.

Well, not in a supermodel way. She didn't have the tanned skin and toned torso that belonged to the *femmes* of fitness and fashion magazines. But she wasn't unattractive either. It's just that I had pictured someone tall, confident, and in a permanent state of undress. Instead, I was introduced to a short, shy woman who, upon meeting me, seemed equally unimpressed.

It was the first day of work. I'd barely slept, and my nerves were on edge as we gathered at Bryan's inner-city apartment for an informal meet and greet. I was anxious, scared, and felt out of my depth. My three co-workers had produced a thousand episodes of prime-time TV while I'd created a grand total of absolutely none. To compensate, I faked confidence and pretended I knew—well, everything. In contrast, Emma was tight-lipped. And when she did speak, it was measured, with the trace of a lisp. The impediment gave her an insecurity she couldn't disguise. Somewhat melodramatically, I imagined her being shunned in the school playground while longing to fit in, which made me want to console and protect her. As always, my assumption was wrong, because at the first hint of humor, the self-conscious spell broke, and Emma laughed like a loon. It was an uncontrollable, childlike guffaw that instantly swelled my heart. Before I knew it, I was staring at her with obsessive eyes, wondering if she was 'The One', which rarely makes for a good first impression.

"I'm IMPRESSED," says Emma as we wait, post-meeting, for Bryan in the foyer. "You actually wore a baseball cap on your first day of work!"

I shift uncomfortably and search her face for any trace of sarcasm. Thankfully, there is none, which is surprising since it suddenly dawns on me that wearing a baseball cap (and a t-shirt) on my first day working for a major television network is an *impressively* stupid thing to do.

To shield my embarrassment, I glance at the man standing alongside Emma, which doesn't help, because, in stark contrast to me, our co-writer, Elliot, is properly dressed for work—albeit as a middle-aged shop mannequin modeling corduroy trousers, wool sweater, and other menswear items that are favored by retired accountants.

"God, I'm busting to go to the bathroom," says Emma. "I've been holding on for an hour."

Elliot's brow furrows. "Why didn't you use Bryan's bathroom?"

Emma squirms. "I don't know. I just couldn't."

"Really?" asks Elliot, in a tone that translates as 'Don't be so neurotic, woman.'

Emma ignores him and directs her attention back to me. "I'm impressed you used his bathroom."

And there it is again...*impressive* little me.

This time, however, I know it isn't sarcasm. I know Emma is actually in awe because using Bryan's bathroom was, in fact, a difficult first step. It felt intrusive. Because Bryan is our boss, which would unnerve any employee on their first day of work. Plus, Bryan is outspoken, intellectually intimidating, and physically imposing.

Oh, and because Bryan is also gay.

Which is fine...

Because Elliot is gay too.

And since it's impossible to have a normal uncomplicated life within inner-city Sydney—or the entertainment industry—Bryan and Elliot can't just be gay workmates.

They also have to be ex-lovers.

Which is also fine…

Unless, of course, you're an anxious new staff member trying to work out what the hell is going on socially, professionally, and sexually between your boss, his ex-lover, and the female co-worker you suddenly want to screw.

Unsurprisingly, the whole anxiety-inducing scenario had me almost pissing myself with fear, which is why I desperately needed to use the bathroom. Of course, once I unzipped in Bryan's private space, it became obvious that my self-confidence wasn't the only thing that had shrunk. My dick had shriveled too.

I tried to pee, but couldn't. I had stage fright because I was completely out of my comfort zone. Bryan was taller, more muscular, and more successful than me, while Elliott was better dressed, better spoken, and better educated than me. As a result, I began to wonder if my *shortfalls* as a male weren't just professional; maybe they were physical and intellectual as well. Then I began to wonder if I was as *big* a man as Bryan. Or even Elliot. Or, more worryingly, if I was *big* enough for Emma.

When I tried to shake the thought, it was no use. I was supposed to be the straight country male, but I couldn't even *think* straight anymore. Eventually, I did the unthinkable—I sat down on the toilet and pissed….*like a girl*. The action confirmed one thing: I was a straight male who was less masculine than two gay men.

Back in the foyer, the recollection of that revelation is still playing through my mind as I stare at Emma. My bathroom insecurities return with a vengeance, and crazy thoughts begin to run through my head. I really want to impress this woman, just not with *little* things—like wearing a baseball cap or pissing with *gay* abandon.

Of course, none of this makes sense. Nor does me staring at Emma while visualizing *her* going for a pee in Bryan's bathroom, which, inexplicably, is what I do next. Inevitably, this leads to me thinking about Emma being nude from the waist down, and soon I'm aware that I have managed to imbue a degree of neurotic sexual tension in an otherwise boring conversation that was—well, at least from Emma's point of view—ostensibly about a hat.

To overcompensate, I muster up the manly straight-shooter from within, and get back to her original comment.

I'm impressed you used his bathroom, she had said.

"Nuthin' to it," I drawl. "When you gotta piss, you gotta piss."

I sound *hugely* impressive and very much like a real man.

Tellingly, it's the last time I will appear this way.

UPRIGHT - Illusion, mad genius. A crucible of brilliant plans.
REVERSED - Instability, confusion, distress. A real loose unit.

The Chapter About Distress

OF COURSE, my descent into infatuation wasn't instantaneous. Like Claire's emotional erosion, it was gradual.

At first, my new job felt like a dream: coffee, donuts, 10 a.m. starts, and endless laughter with quick-witted colleagues who were paid to make stuff up. Working in television was like one of those mythical jobs you heard rumors about—a tall tale that came from a friend of a friend who knew some lucky bastard who actually loved Mondays.

I was now that lucky bastard.

I had long lunches and early knock-offs. I had daily meetings where honest feedback wasn't just welcomed, but encouraged. I had workmates whose joke-telling had no equal. I had a chair alongside a dozen talented, lunatic writers who left me in awe. And I had a female love interest who was humorous and brilliant through it all.

Over the next few months, Emma and I connected. It started slow—small talks over office coffees—then deepened. We discussed movies and books. We listened to Bryan and Elliot's industry gossip during lunches, laughing in unison like celebrity-obsessed teens. We shared stories about friends and their foolish misadventures with love, life, booze, and drugs. After work, we'd talk on the phone. I'd call under the pretense of seeking writing advice, and she'd duly play along. The line between private and professional life began to blur. At least for me. We chatted about family, old loves, past regrets, future fears, and bit by bit, we exposed our vulnerabilities. We were both hurt, both lonely. Emma wanted family. I wanted her. One night, we went to dinner—and kissed. Once. But I was hooked. Infatuated. Obsessed. I knew I'd do anything for Emma, sacrifice any chance of fame, fortune, and success, if it meant I could be with her.

But she resisted my advances.

"Come on, one more dinner," I plead over the phone. "If this one sucks, I'll never ask again."

"Chris, I can't."

"Give me one good reason?"

"Stop being so persistent," she laughs.

"I will if you give me one good reason."

"I already did: Never get your honey where you get your money!"

She giggles and my heart soars.

"That's a terrible reason. Give me a better one. I'm serious."

"I know you're serious. So am I. I'm not going to mix work with pleasure. So suck it up and be an adult."

"What if I come over and strip you naked? That's pretty adult."

Emma groans in exasperation. "Really?! Is that your come-on line?"

I let out a self-conscious snort. "Trust me, you don't want to hear *my* come-on line."

"Try me," she goads.

"No way. I want you to actually *like* me."

"Do you use it on all the girls?"

"*All?* We're not talking scores of women here."

"Does it work?" she asks, a hint of intrigue in her voice.

"Depends on the woman. It's pretty raw."

"I'm sure I've heard worse," Emma says.

I hear the acoustics change as she enters a different room.

"I can promise you've heard better."

"Try me."

"Nope, not a chance."

"*Come on*," she begs. "Don't be a tease. Just say it. I'm not going to think any less of you than I already do."

We both laugh.

"It's just dirty talk." I pause and weigh up my chances. "Basically, I'd just tell you what I want to do to you."

"So what do you want to do to me, Chris?" she asks seductively.

Emma's prompt is all I need, so for the next minute, I entertain her with my sexual fantasy until it reaches its natural climax.

"The last bit is my come-on line."

"I want to fuck you right now," Emma whispers. Her breathless voice instantly arouses me.

"Give me five minutes," I say. "To get there, that is. The sex will be much quicker."

Emma laughs. "I guess I'm going to see how *big* a new talent you really are."

Her comment instantly throws me, and self-doubt immediately leaps into my mind. If Emma thinks I'm packing anything more than six inches she's going to be sorely mistaken. Well, maybe not sorely, but certainly mistaken.

"No, wait," she says suddenly. "You can't come over. We can't do this."

I interrupt as fast as I can. "Stop stressing. It's all good."

"No, it's not."

"Seriously, it is. It's fine. Just chill and have some fun."

There's no reply, and, with terror, I realize Emma's doing the unthinkable—she's collecting her *fucking* thoughts.

"You still there?"

"I'm sorry, Chris. I can't do this. This is my career."

"Nothing's going to go wrong," I say, trying to calm her.

"And what if it does? This is all I have. You have family to fall back on. I don't." She pauses. "I have a mortgage." She makes it sound like an incurable sexually transmitted disease.

"It'll be okay, I promise."

"No, it won't."

In a rare moment, I'm lost for words. And so is Emma.

"It's so unfair," she says eventually. "Because I really wanted a cute boyfriend."

I almost choke. Women have called me another word with the letters C, U and T. But it sure as hell ain't 'cute'.

"What if I come over and we talk about it?"

"No," she says firmly. "Please don't do that."

"We can get the topic out there—"

"Chris, you need to stop."

"—strip it naked—"

"Chris, I'm serious."

"—and explore it deeper."

"Chris!" she snaps. "I want you to stop. Now."

I stop.

But it's too late.

With or without sex, I'm completely screwed.

TRUE TO FORM, my life goes downhill over the next few months. Each of Emma's rejections shatters my self-confidence, and I begin to question whether her interest in me had been genuine or imagined.

In desperation, I make apologetic phone calls and send apologetic emails (not to mention flowers and love poems). I even make a random, unannounced appearance at her house to apologize in person. Unsurprisingly, this behavior distances Emma from me even more. In response, I make more phone calls and send more emails— to apologize for my previous phone calls and emails. After several months of this kind of manic attention, Emma has finally had enough.

She is now far from impressed.

To make matters worse, my professional life mirrors my personal one, which means no one at work is impressed with me either. My writing inspires no one, including me. Rock bottom finally exposes itself one morning when the network's aptly titled *Head of Drama* visits my office with an offer of coffee and small talk.

"So, how are things going, Chris?"

"Not good, Joe," I reply, ashen-faced and sleep-deprived. "I think I'm in way over my head."

Joe misses the subtext and glances at the TV scripts on my desk. "You'll be all right. Just stick with it."

I smile grimly. "Actually, I've just handed in my notice."

"Really? he says, genuinely surprised. "I'm sorry to hear that." A look of concern flashes across his face and for a brief moment I wonder if Joe's drama background extends to acting. "Is there anything I can do to help?"

Ironically, there is. I need a sounding board. I need to tell someone the same words I once hated hearing from Claire. I want to say that I can't understand why I'm so dependent on Emma. That I don't know who I am anymore. That the person sitting here isn't the real me. That I'm not this messed-up, clingy, emotional loser. That I'm actually cooler, stronger, and more confident than this. I need to say all of this to someone—even if that someone is a highly-paid executive from the country's biggest television network. Of course, I don't utter any of that insanity, instead, I blurt out this gem:

"To tell you the truth, Joe, the only reason I write is so I don't kill myself."

The comment leaves Joe stranded speechless, allowing an awkward silence to fill the room. It holds for what seems an eternity and looks set to continue that way, short of someone breaking it with forced throat-clearing or the sound of heavy footfalls beating a hasty hallway retreat.

Joe quickly obliges with both.

His premature departure leaves me feeling truly alone.

It's barely six months since Bryan's first congratulatory phone call. Since then I've gone from failure to success, and back again, in record time. That fact alone leaves me to conclude that I'm just one poorly composed love poem or rock ballad away from suicide. Thankfully, a ray of hope enters the office before I can start drafting a goodbye note.

"Good weekend?" I ask.

Emma mumbles a half-hearted reply as she strides to her desk.

"That interesting?" I say dryly.

Her response is caustic. "Did you want a diary entry?"

The jab rattles me so I turn to my computer and get back to the task of deleting penis enlargement spam emails from my inbox. Behind me, I hear Emma's desktop chime into life. The sound is followed by several forceful mouse clicks and a barrage of angry keyboard strokes.

Then silence.

"Megan and I had a tea-leaf reading," says Emma, brightly.

My heart warms to the peace offering and I swivel my chair to face her. "A tea-leaf reading?!"

"Yeah, you know, a fortune teller?" she says. "We went to a tea and tarot place in the city."

"She say you're going to be rich and famous?"

Emma gives me a look that speaks volumes about our respective priorities. "I didn't ask," she says. "But she did tell me something better."

I urge her to continue.

"She said I'm going to meet the love of my life by the end of the year."

I stare slack-jawed at Emma, blood draining from my face as I process her unwelcome news. I've only known this woman for six months, and yet I'm so inexplicably drawn to her that I can't bear to contemplate a future without her. Because I know we're meant to be together.

Unfortunately, Emma doesn't know that.

The realization makes me question my own worth and, suddenly, it becomes obvious to my fragile mind that Emma believes I'm not good enough for her—not successful enough, not rich enough, not smart enough.

I'm still staring at Emma like an imbecile when she says: "Apparently, it's going to happen on a beach. She could see a bikini, but she wasn't sure if I was the one wearing it."

"A bikini?" I state. "On a beach?" I feign an incredulous tone in an effort to regain some dignity. "Jesus, how much did you pay for that prediction?!"

"Twenty dollars!" says Emma, and we both laugh at the stupidity of it all.

"Well, I guess I know where you'll be spending Christmas holidays —sun-bathing on Bondi Beach."

Emma grins like a Cheshire Cat. "Nope, I'll be in Thailand, remember?"

I do remember. Her planned end-of-year vacation; a six-week adventure starting with a party-bus tour through Europe and ending with a New Year's beach resort stay in Thailand. Immediately, that last destination conjures visions of Emma drinking cocktails with some windswept and interesting backpacker who is charming her out of a skimpy bikini. The vision crushes my heart, and, suddenly, nothing else matters in my life except winning over Emma—not the TV show, not fame, not fortune, not anything. All I want is Emma. But I need something to convince her that we are destined to be together. I need to show her a sign from the universe. The most obvious thing I can think of is a matching bikini prophecy from a twenty-dollar psychic.

So I book an appointment at *Tea and Tarot*.

"This other woman...you *must not* hurt," says Celeste.

"I don't want to hurt anyone," I say, defensively. My voice sounds weak and unconvincing.

Celeste studies me for a long moment as if weighing the sincerity of my words against the truth of her cards. Her silent judgement makes me uneasy.

"Okay, let's go back to the beginning," she says, finally releasing me. "Let's go back to *Death*."

And she does, explaining that *Death* is actually rebirth and that *The Lovers* are, in my case, an obstacle to love, happiness, healing, creativity, and any other positive experience that makes life bearable. Then she reels off a number of details that nail everything about me, from my personal traits to ambitions, inhibitions, and expectations. It's all pretty disconcerting despite me not wanting to believe a word of it. After ten minutes, the fortune-teller notices my shellshocked expression.

"You have to remember that this is just in the cards," Celeste explains. "It's not a pre-determined future. Think of it as an early warning sign. A reminder to set things right. Like a cautionary tale."

I stare vacantly at the tarot cards. "Is there actually anything good on the horizon?"

Celeste points to the *Judgement* card.

"That's what this is about. Your past and present are bookended by conflict. The only way to move on is for you to resolve the source of that negativity by confronting it. How you do that is entirely up to you. Does that make sense?"

I nod my head.

But, of course, it doesn't make sense. Because I'm now so confused about my own life that nothing makes sense. No one wants to hear that their life is at a disastrous crossroads, especially someone whose life is at a disastrous crossroads. All I want to hear is that I will find true love on a Thai beach at the end of the year, thus confirming a shared destiny with Emma. Instead, I've been presented with two *Lovers* seeking *Death* and *Judgement* with sticks and swords. According to Celeste, this all adds up to a future of inner turmoil, low career outcomes, and unrequited love.

It must be the worst fucking fortune-telling ever. Plus it cost twenty bucks!

Deflated, I leave Celeste to her herbal tea and harrowing predictions, and resolve to take destiny into my own hands. Hatching a foolproof plan, I decide to quit my dream job, backpack for three months to make myself windswept and interesting, then surprise Emma on a beach in Thailand and make her bikini prophecy of love come true. It seems perfectly logical, entirely possible, and incredibly insane. One week later, all my senses take flight.

And so do I.

UPRIGHT - Travel. Taking control. The world awaits. Go, go, go!!
REVERSED - Distracted & stuck. Always avoiding the real journey.

Chapter One

RELATIONSHIPS ARE LIKE PLANE FLIGHTS.

Well, that's my theory.

In my mind, the perfect partnership is like flying first-class—a comfortable long-haul adventure that begins with an easy ascent to the heavens, soaring ever upward to clear skies that ensure smooth cruising in turbulence-free bliss.

Then there are the not-so-first-class trips.

These are the economy flights of love—the no-frills domestic connections that promise the world at check-in, but surprise passengers after takeoff with the realization that any caring personal service once considered complimentary now comes with a price, or not at all.

And finally, there are the unmitigated disasters.

These are the relationship flights of fancy that defy all logic to become airborne in the first place—the departures of mind that disappear off the radar of common sense. These tragic trips convince friends and loved ones that those on board are doomed to crash into an ocean of tears, leaving nothing but a tangled wreck of broken lives, sinking hope, and a raft of floating baggage to cling to. This is the flight I'm always on. Lately, though, I've started to suspect I'm not just a cursed passenger.

I think I might be the fucking pilot.

As if to confirm this suspicion, I board my plane in readiness to fly my stupid ass to Thailand.

The air hostess points me to my seat. I buckle up, then glance at the in-flight TV. On the screen is a picture of a world map with an arrow pointing to a stylized image of a chess piece. According to the monitor, the chess piece is five thousand miles northwest of our present location—somewhere in the Middle East—which, if I remember my high school geography correctly, is nowhere near Thailand.

True to form, my flight hasn't even left Australia and I'm already lost.

Minutes later, I realize the icon is a symbol for Mecca.

I'm flying with *Royal Brunei*, a Muslim airline, so I'm guessing the graphic is shown for directional prayer. Either that, or the airline's faith in their fuselage is so questionable that they encourage all passengers to call on Allah for a safe journey.

Right on cue, a pre-flight prayer flickers onto the screen.

"O Allah, You are ... the Protector for the family we leave behind... we seek refuge in You ... from the misfortune to befall our household."

The sobering plea does nothing to allay my fear of flying, so I pay close attention to every word of the safety presentation that follows. My worry is needless, of course, because the plane touches down safely in Bangkok eight uneventful hours later.

I grab my backpack from the carousel, then, gripped by travel virgin anxiety, brace myself for passport processing, expecting Thai customs officers to plant drugs in my backpack. They don't, so I settle for a little blue-ink entry stamp like every other tourist.

With dusk descending outside the terminal, I quickly locate an inner-city bus service, and awkwardly squeeze my ridiculously oversized backpack past two giggling English girls who look like high school graduates on a gap-year vacation. Sitting toward the rear of the bus are several older, solitary travelers. They peer pensively outside, looking melancholy and morose, or maybe just exhausted. Following their lead, I find a seat and silently study the foreign streetscape as well.

Suddenly, my chest tightens, and my breath constricts. Anxiety builds within, and, out of nowhere, reality hits me.

What the fuck am I doing?!

In a panic, I look to the door. I need to get off this bus. Now. I need to fly back home and call the TV network and get my job back. I need to fix my life before it's too late. Except it's already too late because I know there's no way to fix all the things I've ruined.

I take a deep breath and try to calm down.

Relax…

This was what I wanted, wasn't it? To reinvent. Start fresh. And move on. Like a nomad.

The word stops me cold.

Nomad.

A perpetual wanderer on an endless journey. A displaced soul.

In an instant, I'm transported back to a moment in my past, and I think of Claire. I wish she was here with me. Of course, if Claire was here, she'd look at me with little sympathy, shake her head and say something like 'Why do you always make such rash decisions?' And the truthful answer to that would be: I really don't know. Which highlights how different we are. For a start, Claire wouldn't quit her dream job on a whim because of a tea leaf reading, nor would she freak out on an overseas holiday. In fact, she'd love the thrill of going on an adventure into the great unknown. Plus, she's always been into that whole 'authentic' cultural immersion thing that backpackers go on about. Me, not so much, which, of course, was another source of contention back during our kitchen drama.

"Fuck backpacking," I say. "I want to be able to travel in comfort."

"That's so sanitized," counters Claire. She needles string through the spine of a handmade journal she's binding. "Don't you want a cultural experience?"

I scoff at the question. "You still see the same things. It's not like Angkor Wat has a perimeter of hemp-rope excluding everyone but backpackers."

"You're probably more of an organized tour person anyway." she taunts, knowing full well how much I hate organized…well, organized anything, actually.

"What are you talking about? I spent my childhood camping in the sticks. I'd hate an organized tour. But doing it your way would suck too."

My comment stings her.

"Sorry for having an opinion." She shoves her chair back and heads for the bedroom.

"Hang on a second," I snap. "I never said I didn't want to travel. I'm just saying I don't want to do it without money. But now you're pissed at me because I'm what…not 'cultural' enough?"

Claire stalls at the bedroom door and glares back at me. "Why are you getting angry?"

"Because you're walking away from me."

She shakes her head, exasperated. "I can't say anything without you overreacting."

"You're deliberately pressing my buttons. Just because I want to travel with money instead of doing it when I'm broke."

Claire turns her back on me. "Sure, do it your way." The bedroom door begins its vicious arc. "As usual," she says.

The door slams shut, and the driver stomps on the accelerator. The bus launches forward, heads down a service road, then merges onto the highway.

In the distance, Bangkok's skyline emerges. The modern metropolis looks like any other contemporary city, with tarmac arteries pumping millions of people into a topography of steel, glass, and concrete one-upmanship. It's only when we reach downtown that I notice this city is different from those in Australia. Here the urban architecture is adorned with exotic symbols of Buddhist faith, which suggests capitalism coexists with spiritualism. I mull over the clash of those ideas, right up until we hit a street that worships utter chaos.

The infamous Khao San Road.

Chapter Two

ACCORDING TO THE *LONELY PLANET*, Khao San Road is home to Bangkok's backpacker population. And judging by what I see outside the bus, I swear they breed the fuckers here too. Or half-breed.

The door opens and a wave of rank, humid air swamps the interior of the bus. I grab my backpack and step reluctantly into what looks like a street-market moonlighting as a nightclub run by techno-hippie drug dealers. Neon lights pulse down the entire length of the road, music pounds, and stalls hawk everything from pad thai to tattoos. Hundreds of travelers weave through the chaotic scene with gleeful faces. I glance at my fellow new arrivals to read their reaction. It's a pointless exercise since we're all playing a game called *Pretend You're Not Shitting Yourself*. It's a dumb game and not a single one of us is any good at it.

Thankfully, our surroundings are filled with familiar western faces. In fact, there are so many western travelers on Khao San Road that I am genuinely surprised when I finally spot some Thai locals. In turn, one spots me. Immediately, his face breaks into a wide smile, and fake friendship high-beams from his eyes. Paralyzed with politeness, I stand rooted to the spot as he advances. Fortunately, an auto-rickshaw arrives on cue and blocks the approaching man from view.

"Tuk-Tuk?" the driver asks.

I shake my head, and wave off his taxi trike offer. "No, thanks. Just got off the bus." Remembering the language barrier, I scissor two fingers past his eye-line, knowing full well that he'll recognize the universal charade as walking.

He doesn't.

"Tuk-tuk?" he repeats.

I shake my head harder. After an awkward beat, he takes the hint and drives off, which provides an opening for another...

"Tuk-tuk?" asks the newcomer.

I ready myself for round two, but my beaming buddy from before arrives in time to rescue me.

"Hey," he squawks, "you want sex show?" His wide grin is topped by a wispy, adolescent-like mustache. It twitches like a hairy caterpillar, drawing my eagle-eye as if it were prey. "Cheap, cheap," he chirps.

"What?"

"Sex show. Cheap, cheap."

I fend him off. "Nah, mate. I'm all good."

He smirks. "Ahh, Aussie, yes?! I show you good time, *maayyyte*. Cheap, cheap."

I glance at him. "Sorry, mate. Seriously, I'm not interested."

Undeterred, he shoves a brochure into my hand. "You look. Sexy girls. Very nice."

I scan the front of a flyer that is filled with images of nude females in sexually suggestive poses.

My new friend pats my shoulder. "You like?"

"Not right now, no." I hand the brochure back. "I have to find a room."

"You want room?!" He grabs my arm. "Come! Good room this way. Cheap, cheap."

It's obvious that this guy is a leech, so I shrug off his hold and bolt into the over-crowded street party, disappearing into a forest of dreadlocks. I scurry down the road, side-stepping tourists and restaurant tables—both of which overflow from the sidewalk and onto the road proper. I pass countless stalls selling food, clothing, jewelry, electronics, sunglasses, fried insects, and within minutes, I'm stressed out of my mind.

Desperate for guidance, I scan the heavens for a sign, ideally one that combines the words *budget* and *guesthouse*. Eventually, I spot such a sign above a dingy building. I stumble inside and book a vacant room sight unseen. A bored employee grabs a room key and beckons for me to follow. He shows me the shared bathroom amenities first. I peer into the cramped, damp enclosure and almost gag. A sign on the wall says, 'Don't flush toilet paper'. I immediately look for the toilet paper but, there is none —unless you count the fecal-smeared wads from previous depositors overflowing from a lidless trash can next to the toilet.

We reach the end of the hallway, and I'm shown my room. Unsurprisingly, it too is an uninviting shithole with decor straight out of Alcatraz. The bed is moldy, lumpy and hard, yet inexplicably soft in many places. Cracked, stained plaster clings to the walls, and torn segments of old linoleum are jig-sawed into something that vaguely resembles floor covering. It's everything I imagined budget backpacker accommodation to be: absolutely crap.

The view is memorable, though, especially if you appreciate middle-aged Thai women shouting the clichéd, 'Want good time, very cheap?' from the balcony opposite. I consider shutting the window on their hospitality, but there are no actual window shutters—just two pieces of cardboard that double as closures, both of which are on the floor.

Exhausted beyond belief, I collapse onto the stained mattress, stare at the cracked ceiling, and let Claire's idea of a 'wonderful cultural experience' overwhelm me.

Lucky for me, Bangkok is just a layover. Tomorrow, I fly to another Asian country—one famous for transforming even the dullest of humans into windswept and interesting adventurers. Which is why I've decided to travel there. Once that is done, I intend to return to Thailand a changed man—the kind of man Emma can't resist.

Of course, if a single day in a modern city like Bangkok can rattle my fragile little world, the obvious question must be this:

How the fuck will I survive three months in India?

Chapter Three

BEN IS adamant it's *legal* herb that he has smuggled into India, and who am I to argue? The old pothead certainly looks like someone who knows the vagaries of a country's marijuana legislation so it's hard to doubt him. Of course, what *could* be argued is whether Ben even knows he's in India.

I'm at Delhi's International Airport and, contrary to all expectations, the terminal is relatively quiet. I've only encountered a few hundred people since meeting Ben and his son, Josh, at the baggage carousel. That was thirty minutes ago, since then Josh and I have been waiting patiently for Ben to repack his Everest-like backpack.

My new friends are embarking on a father/son trek through the Himalayas. And like a novice mountaineer I've attached myself to them for safety, clinging to their rock-solid confidence because I'm terrified of falling into the abyss.

The one outside.

The one known as India.

"Seriously, it was legal herb, man!" Ben says, continuing the story about his run-in with security in Taipei.

"Like oregano and crap like that?" I ask.

Josh looks at me as if I'm an idiot. "Low-THC hemp," he says.

"They tossed all my stuff," Ben grumbles. "Like everywhere, man. Super aggressive. Such bad vibes, dude. You know what I mean, Chris…huh?"

My brow furrows in sympathy, but I'm unsure if Ben is stating fact, asking a rhetorical question, or just knitting his own version of the English language to mess with my head.

"They thought I was a smuggler, man," he continues. "Can you believe that?!"

Yes.

I can totally believe that.

Simply because Ben looks like a drug runner. His reaction time is vague and his mid-fifties face is unfocused. He has long hair, a greasy beard, and tattered clothes. I'm envious, of course, because at least Ben looks like a spiritual adventurer…or, at the very least, someone who truly lives in another dimension. As opposed to me, whose international travel wardrobe of board shorts and surf t-shirts makes me look like a walking billboard for a big-brand surf conglomerate.

I'm envious of Ben's son Josh too, who looks similar to his father—albeit half the age and with the addition of dreadlocks, backpacker swagger, and quite possibly even Khao San Road tattoos. This is Josh's third trip to India, for a total of eighteen months, which suggests he is either unbelievably cool or incredibly stupid.

Strangely, I'm finding it hard to get a read on Josh. I can't make out whether he is fake or real. Women would love him, that much is obvious. He's fashionably unwashed and oozes the kind of bohemian vibe that makes him appear aloof, carefree and charismatic. It's easy to believe he's a wise journeyman who has travelled many an enlightened path. Which is quite the accomplishment given that Josh is in his early twenties.

He looks to his dad. "You right, Ben?" he asks, hoping to speed up the process of us leaving the airport terminal and actually *arriving* in India.

"Uh huh, just get my socks on, yeah?"

For five minutes, I've watched Ben attempt to thread a pair of frayed shoelaces onto a disintegrating pair of ancient sneakers. The process is agonizingly unhurried—like watching jello set…in slow motion.

"So, which airline did you guys fly from the States to Taiwan?"

"China Air," says Josh.

"How was that?"

Ben shudders. "Whoa… Too long, man. *Waaay* too long."

"Ben's never been on a plane before," says Josh, thus partly explaining his father's herbal cure for flight anxiety.

"First time, man." The old stoner grins. "Been lost in Oregon for thirty years, and smoking pot for all of them."

"Guess you needed a vacation," Josh deadpans.

His unexpected show of humor causes us all to break into laughter.

"Well, thought I'd better take a look around, man," Ben says, swapping a mischievous smile with his kin. "Start a new journey, yeah?"

He raises his hand, and Josh obliges him with a forceful 'high-five'. Beards and dreadlocks bounce erratically as they connect, making the scene look like a *Nike* ad—for *Air Jesus* or something.

Of course, Ben isn't lost—his son is his compass. And Josh really does know his shit when it comes to India. Plus, the two men have a strong father/son bond. That easy bond twists something in me, and suddenly I recall life with my own dad. Like lots of boys, the relationship I had with my father was difficult to navigate. I grew up constantly thinking the towering masculine figure in my life was too hard, while knowing that he thought I was too soft. Growing up, I figured his harshness came from the fact that I wasn't his blood. I know better now. Truth is, my dad didn't hate me because he was an evil stepfather, he just wanted me to be *more* because, like most men, he had spent his whole life feeling *less*.

My evil stepfather theory also faded when I discovered that my biological father, and namesake, was even rougher. Unlike my new father, the old one physically hurt my mother. He even punched her in the gut when she was nine months pregnant. His reasoning was that I hadn't arrived at exactly forty weeks, which could only mean one thing—I wasn't his child.

This is the source of my DNA.

Of course, deep inside, I know I'm not him; I'm a better man. I'm not a violent drunk, nor someone who would ever repeat his whispered ultimatum of 'If you leave, I'll kill you both'. I've spent years trying to comprehend how this father of mine—this *man*—could hurt his partner and threaten to kill his own child. And yet, when it comes to parents, I was probably blessed. I mean, life could have been worse—I could have been related to Ben!

I don't really feel that way about Josh's dad, of course. I actually really like the man and I'm grateful to be in his presence. Both he and Josh befriended me when they saw my apprehension on landing. They have an easy mateship; one that's evidently been nurtured with love. I see it in their simplest of actions—a son helping to repack his dad's baggage, then offering to carry that burden on his own broad shoulders. I see a father placing a gentle hand on his little boy's back in a silent show of appreciation. Nothing masculine. Just affectionate. Loving. Protective.

Paternal.

Finally, with Ben packed and ready to go, the three of us are ready to, well… smoke the joint.

Chapter Four

DRAWING ON HIS INDIAN EXPERIENCE, Josh suggests we organize a pre-paid cab inside the airport terminal to avoid the notorious taxi touts who scam new arrivals outside the terminal.

We locate the designated 'pre-paid transport' booths near the exit, and pay one of the official taxi operators the agreed-upon fare to the city. The transaction is neither easy, nor swift; in fact, the harassment from rival 'official' booths is so intense that I begin to dread what unregulated taxi mayhem awaits beyond the door.

I find out soon enough.

As we edge towards the glass partition, a seething mob of predatory freelance taxi drivers swarm into view. The automatic doors slide open and scores of baying men immediately blanket us. Their raucous and unwelcome crush instantly puts me on high alert, and my fight-or-flight instinct kicks in. Not Josh, however, because he's lived this nightmare before. Barging through the onslaught like an angry bull, he deflects their advances with shoulder charges and repeated snorts of 'Fuck off'. In contrast, Ben and I timidly follow with wary steps, like anxious rainbow ponies.

Two minutes later, we find our designated pre-paid taxi van and clamber inside to safety. Dozens of inquisitive eyes peer at us through the windows as we buckle up, and I pray for a quick escape that fails to eventuate. After a full minute passes, we're still stationary. I catch the driver's gaze in the rearview mirror, and his eyes lock onto mine as if we are in an unspoken standoff.

"Baksheesh," he says, his tone all business.

Josh instantly replies with a firm "No!"

"*Baksheesh,*" repeats the driver, his tone hardening.

Josh shakes his head. "We already paid inside."

"Please," the driver pleads. "*Baksheesh!*"

"This is a *pre-paid* taxi," Josh reminds him.

"No pre-pay," shouts the driver. "You give *baksheesh.*"

Josh rises to the challenge. "Move it now," he bellows. "Or I'll go inside and report you."

The driver considers this threat in silence.

I turn to Josh, bewildered and uneasy. "What's going on?"

"He wants a tip. If we don't pay he'll drop us in the middle of nowhere."

"Please, sirs," the driver interrupts. "Very poor. Very big family. Many, many children."

I glance at the man's reflection, searching for any hint of dishonesty that might discourage my instinct to be diplomatic and compassionate.

I look back to Josh. "How much does he actually want?"

"That's not the point," he says, reluctantly peeling a twenty-rupee note off a wad of cash. "They pull this shit every time."

He offers the money to the driver, who stares at it as if personally insulted.

"Very poor family, sir. One hundred rupees. Very, very poor."

Josh unfurls some extra cash. "Fifty rupees," he counters. "That's it. No more."

I mentally tally the cost. Fifty rupees is roughly equivalent to the price of a can of Coke back home.

The driver snatches the notes from Josh and stuffs them into his shirt pocket. Argument now over, the man casually puts the van into gear and drives us into Delhi's peak hour traffic.

For the blissfully uninitiated, like myself, India's road rules are a complete mystery. Nothing I see makes sense. Eight lanes of vehicles cram onto a four-lane highway. Dozens of motorcycles—some carrying entire families, all without helmets, except for the actual 'driver'—zig-zag across the blacktop. Around them are scores of auto-rickshaws, cars, buses, trucks, and, of course, cows. All going wherever the hell they please.

Ben and I exchange shocked looks.

"Whoa...man," he stammers, mesmerized by the vision outside. "Dudes, I can't believe this place. This is just... *man*... this is just... this is *blowing* me away, Joshy."

"Fucking Delhi," says Josh flatly, with a seen-it-all-before resignation.

"Did you see those cows?" Ben asks, wide-eyed. "They've got broken legs, man. Dude, that is so cruel. Why not put them out of their misery?"

"They're sacred," Josh explains. "Hindus don't kill cows."

"Brahman cattle," I say with authority, remembering a different time and place. "They breed them by the millions back home."

"What for?" asks Ben without thought.

I notice the driver eyeing me in the rearview mirror.

"Steak," I say quietly.

I divert my gaze back to the view outside. At the edge of the highway, on dusty patches of earth, males of all ages are engaged in the same impromptu bat-and-ball sport that featured heavily in my youth—the game of cricket. The scene reminds me of a carefree time playing with friends, our bare feet shod with dirt as we fielded balls that held zero interest for the muscular Brahman beasts that roamed the harsh Northern Australian scrub that lay beyond the barbed-wire fence. I smile at the memory and begin to relax. I can do this. I can survive three months here. I can survive India.

Unfortunately, my newfound confidence is short-lived.

Chapter Five

OH, *fuck*...

As our taxi jerks to a halt in the Main Bazaar of Old Delhi, I am broadsided by a rare moment of clarity: I'm going to die in India. I'm going to have a heart attack or a brain aneurysm. My blood pressure is already rising and my chest feels tight.

Outside the taxi, thousands of people choke the narrow dirt street. Dilapidated multi-story buildings loom over them, their cracked concrete walls supporting dozens of dust-caked awnings, faded shop signs, and crumbling balconies. Everything seems to be held together by nothing more than a million knotted electricity cables and a shit ton of good luck. Nothing is uniform. Paints of every hue have been slathered on walls, doorways, and advertisement boards. It's as if a million rogue kindergarteners, armed with rainbow crayons, had been unleashed on the streetscape. The wild inconsistency of my surroundings disorients me so badly that it's impossible to get my bearings. Where are the sharp 7-Eleven signs from Bangkok? Where are the monolithic, golden arches of McDonald's from back home? All I see is confusion, chaos, disorder, and impending disaster.

I steel myself and take a glance at Ben, desperately hoping to find composure on his face, but the old hop-head is wired, his eyes darting frantically like a skittish cat, tracking every twitch of movement beyond the taxi window.

"Huh, whoa… I've never seen *anything* like this, man," he mumbles, awestruck. "This is… this is *insane*, man."

A flicker of masochistic delight illuminates Josh's face as he hefts his backpack onto his shoulders. "Welcome to India, boys!" he says, with a wry, knowing grin.

Welcome to Paharganj, to be precise—Old Delhi's notorious budget backpacker haven. According to Josh, accommodation can be had for five bucks a night in this neighborhood, which explains why the tight-fisted prick brought us here.

The three of us climb free of the van. Immediately, the perfume of Paharganj assaults my nostrils with an aromatic *potpourri* of diesel fumes, human waste, and rotting refuse. It's another less-than-subtle sensory reminder of the joys of 'cultural immersion'.

"Follow me," orders Josh, already plunging into the throng.

I don't need to be told twice, so like an obsessed lover, I blindly stumble after him through a pulsing obstacle course of wandering cows, scrawny dogs, and sweaty human bodies. I glance back to gauge Ben's progress and am rewarded with the sight of him gingerly tip-toeing through a minefield of fresh cow shit with all the grace of a drunk ballerina attempting to pirouette on a broken leg.

We dance past a gauntlet of hole-in-the-wall shops overflowing with vibrant saris, cheap shoes, colored bangles, pungent spices, and the cloying scent of incense. Our march of madness is interrupted only by a barrage of shop sellers, travel touts, rickshaw drivers, and any other opportunistic soul vying for our attention…and money. It's beyond exhausting, and within minutes, I'm taut of body, mentally overloaded, and feeling more alive than I've ever felt in my life!

Five minutes later, guru Josh shepherds us into the foyer of his chosen sanctuary, where we finally find some inner peace. After a short exchange with a pair of mouthy, middle-aged male receptionists, we go our separate ways and inspect the accommodation on offer.

Upstairs, a guesthouse employee shows me a single room that is beyond horrific. The walls are unpainted, and the crumbling render is adorned with graffiti—names, poems, declarations of love, and obscure, spiritual quotations seemingly scribbled during moments of midnight madness. Filled with apprehension, I peer into the ensuite. The toilet has no seat, the shower has no shower head, and dozens of tiles are missing from the filthy recess. It's as if the task of interior design was outsourced to a trigger-happy urban assault force procured from the nearest war zone.

The room does, however, have one attraction—the price tag. It costs five dollars a night, just as Josh promised. Plus, its aggressively weathered patina could convince any insecure, wide-eyed backpacker that they are, in fact, a rugged, windswept and interesting, world adventurer.

I trudge back to the foyer to surrender my five bucks. Ben and Josh are already at the reception counter, waiting for the two Indian clerks to sign in a Japanese backpacker. On show is 'Indian Bureaucracy in Action'. It's a performance that requires two people to read a single passport, write a single name in a ledger, and hand over a single room key. And, apparently, these two people need a lifetime to do it.

"You know what 'Japan' stands for?" one clerk asks, eyeing the Asian traveler's passport.

The bewildered backpacker shrugs his shoulders in confusion.

The clerk spells it out: "J-A-P-A-N. You know what this stands for?"

The Japanese dude remains oblivious.

"Jumping And Pumping All Night," says the clerk, bursting into self-congratulatory hysterics.

His buddy chimes in, goading the hapless traveller. "That is you, yes? *Japan* man…looking for sexy time, yes?"

The backpacker is all at sea, drowning in a cultural wash of Indian English and bizarre sexual innuendo.

Eventually, the clerks still amusing themselves, relinquish a room key, and the visibly relieved Japanese kid hot-foots it to safety.

Josh and Ben step forward and take his place. They offer up their passports and the clerks study the embossed eagle insignias.

"Ah, USA. United States… of… America," one of the men dramatically intones. "Do you know what U.S.A really stands for?"

"I'm sure you're going to enlighten me," Josh says cynically.

The clerk beams. "Unloved Self Abusers!"

Again both Indian men laugh at the joke. The exhausted Josh and Ben, however, stay mute.

"You hear this joke before?" one clerk asks.

Josh shakes his head, seemingly unamused.

"Oh, you are a serious backpacker?" the clerk continues. "Or tired, maybe? Not much laughing in you."

Josh forces a strained smile and waits stoney-faced for his name to be laboriously transcribed into the reservation book. With the task finally complete, the clerk slides the passport back to Josh.

"My friend," the man says, his voice subdued and sincere, "I am just joking. In India we like smiling talk. Everyone is happy in India. See?" He flashes a wide grin to demonstrate. "Please, Mr America, be happy…and enjoy my country."

Josh manages to coax a weak smile. He takes his room key, then he retreats from the counter, leaving me exposed to scrutiny. I present my passport, bracing for the inevitable mockery.

"Ah… Australia?"

"Yeah," I say with a smile. Big smile. Much smiling to be happy in India.

The two men look delighted. "*Achha, achha*…very good. Australia very good cricket players. Steve Waugh, Adam Gilchrist, Shane Warne. Very, *very* good."

My smile grows.

The uttered names may not mean anything to Ben and Josh, but to me they are heaven sent, and soon the two clerks and I are discussing India's true national religion—cricket.

"That game is even worse than baseball," scoffs Josh.

"Baseball?!" barks one of the Indians with derision. "*Silly* American game." He looks to me for confirmation, but I'm not in the habit of trash-talking friends. Well, not in front of them.

I interject in an effort save Josh. "I actually have something you guys might be interested in."

I unzip a compartment on my backpack, and after a rudimentary search, retrieve an object. It's a twenty-cent coin minted with an image of the world's greatest cricket player on one side. I toss it across the reception counter to one of the clerks, who snatches it mid-air.

He studies the coin intensely. "Who is this?" he asks. "Bradman?!"

"Yeah, *The Don*."

"Sir Donald Bradman?!" gasps the other clerk in surprise.

"Yep, special edition."

"From Australia?"

I nod as the two men take it in turns to trace the coin's raised relief with their fingertips.

"Very good batting average," says one with a reverence reserved for a god.

"Very, very good," parrots the other.

"99.94," I add. "Near perfect batting average." I can practically feel the waves of boredom radiating from my American friends. "Bradman was the Babe Ruth of cricket," I explain to Ben and Josh.

Barely a breath later, I notice Bradman vanish into the shirt pocket of one of the clerks.

"Thank you very much," he says. "For you, my friend special discount for your room."

"You have more of these coins?" his offsider enquires with hungry eyes.

"No," I lie. "That's the only one."

In truth, I have over a dozen more. But I didn't cart them to India to barter for a fifty rupee discount on a shitty room in Paharganj. I brought the coins for a specific purpose—to repay a personal debt. Because, unlike the great Don Bradman, the legacy of my past is far from perfect.

Chapter Six

BY DAWN, I'm convinced—even at five dollars a night—that my discounted room is a rip-off. The toilet doesn't flush, the shower runs cold, the air-conditioner doesn't work, and the grotty mattress is a commune for bedbugs.

Reluctantly, I drag my exhausted, sleep-deprived body downstairs and step outside. Thankfully, Old Delhi's streets, still half asleep, are oddly calm and inviting. Any fears of hardship and peril fade and I begin to see the promise of fun and adventure. Slinging my daypack over my shoulder, I set off to explore the surroundings. At first, filth and neglect dominate my vision, but soon my perspective shifts to an optimistic childlike curiosity until, surprisingly, I form the opinion that Old Delhi might actually be an interesting place to visit.

That optimism evaporates an hour later when the city awakens. Peak hour swells, and a flood of cars, bikes, and rickshaws swamp the streets, drowning me in honking horns, construction noise, and the footfalls of a million souls seemingly oblivious to the concept of personal space. The barrage is inescapable. Even casual chats with strangers are a challenge, as the line between sincerity and manipulation blurs. Each intrusion saps me, and my patience frays.

It is in this state of frustration that I'm intercepted by yet another in a string of eager conversationalists I've encountered during my morning walk.

"Excuse me, sir, where are you going?"

I turn to find a guy of similar age to me. I note the Armani jeans, Ralph Lauren polo, and a thick gold chain partially hidden by a deliberately popped collar.

"Just walking around," I reply.

"Walking where?" he asks.

"To the Red Fort."

"Walking to the Red Fort?!" he exclaims in dismay. "Why is it foreigners always *walking*? In India, this is only for the very poor."

"You see more on foot," I say in my defense.

He weighs this up, a flicker of comprehension in his eyes. "Ah, okay, no problem."

I offer the universal 'smile and nod', hoping it will conclude our chat.

It doesn't.

"How long have you been in India, my friend?"

"One week." The lie is an attempt to mask my virgin traveller status.

"And you have travelled where in India?"

"Just Delhi so far."

He regards me with open suspicion. "Just Delhi? In one week? And still you have not seen the Red Fort?" He pauses, letting my fabrication hang in the air. "My friend," he says, a shift in tone, "what is your good name?"

This peculiar question has become such a common occurrence during my morning walk that I'm beginning to wonder if all Indians are christened with 'bad' names as well.

"Chris," I say.

"I am Surinda," he declares, extending a hand.

We shake, and time seems to stretch to eternity before he releases the hold.

"So, Chris," he continues, "what do you think of my country?"

"It...vibrant." I hunt my brain for another nuanced descriptor. "And unique."

"More *vibrant* and *unique* than your country?"

I note the playful challenge in his eyes.

"It's *different* from my country."

"You are Australian, yes?"

I nod.

"Very good cricket team," Surinda acknowledges with a genuine smile. Then with perfect timing, he adds: "Almost as good as India."

The humorous jab makes me laugh out loud.

"You are traveling with a wife?"

"No, I'm not married," I reply.

Surinda gives me an incredulous look. "You are how old? Forty?"

"Almost thirty," I correct.

"Almost thirty and still not married?!" The implausibility baffles him. "Just girlfriend, yes?"

"No girlfriend either," I mumble. "Just single."

"Just single *good time* man!" He gives my shoulder a brotherly slap. "I think sex is very easy for you, yes? Western women love fucking." The statement is spoken as fact.

I play along. "I'm sure you attract more women than I do."

"Yes, *many* women. Lots of fucking for me." He pauses for a moment, deep in thought. "Tell me, Chris, where are you going after Delhi?"

"Somewhere cooler. And quieter," I say vaguely. "Probably north."

"Manali, perhaps? Very popular destination for tourists. Or Kashmir—very beautiful, like paradise. If you want, my friend, I can get you the best price on a deluxe air-conditioned coach to Kashmir."

A slow smile spreads across my face thanks to the sudden show of Surinda's hustle - he's a commission tout for a travel company.

"Isn't there a war in Kashmir?" I ask.

"No, not war," he says emphatically. "Just…misunderstandings. Kashmir is very safe. Lots of tourist houseboats on the lake. Trust me. Chris, my friend, if you want, I will give you best price." He thrusts a hand into the back pocket of his jeans and retrieves a travel brochure. "Here, for you," he says, pressing it into my hand. "This is my business."

I wave the offer away. "I don't want to go to Kashmir."

Surinda shrugs, unfazed. "Sure, no problem. I can do best deal to anywhere, Chris. Come—" He grabs my shoulder, attempting to steer me. "It is too hot in this fucking street. Too much shit and smell. Not like Kashmir. Please, come with me."

I gently, but deliberately, shake off his grasp. "No, thanks. I want to check out the Red Fort."

Surinda pauses, seemingly hurt by my rejection. "Okay, okay," he relents, pivoting smoothly. "Come to my office for a chai and I will find you a rickshaw to Red Fort. Much better than walking."

"I'd rather walk."

Surinda considers that absurdity for a moment, then moves on. "Tell me, Chris, what is your job?"

"I write television," I say, with a degree of self-importance.

"This is good money, yes? You must be very rich."

"I wish. I barely have enough money for this trip."

Which is true. Because, unlike Emma who can afford to travel all over Europe before heading to Thailand, I stupidly quit my well-paid job before I was debt-free and financially secure. As a result, I need to make five thousand dollars last three months.

"But still, you are richer than most people in my country, I think."

His uncomfortable truth pricks me. Compared to many here, I probably do seem like a millionaire.

Surinda presses on. "Do you know Bollywood?"

"Yeah, of course."

"Then you must visit Mumbai, my friend. They make many movies there. Always looking for Westerners like you. I can get you the best price bus ticket from Delhi to Mumbai."

"Can you throw in a sexy Bollywood actress as part of the deal?" I ask, indulging in the banter.

Surinda plays along. "Yeah, yeah, lots of Bollywood stars, man! All for you."

"You'll probably bus me to some porno film set," I joke.

Surinda smiles. "You know 'blue movies', yes? Indian men love watching these movies."

"More than cricket?" I ask, cheekily.

The travel tout erupts in laughter. "Chris, in India, there are just two loves for men: sex and cricket!" He emphatically declares this truth as he grabs my shoulder. "Come. Chris, I want to show you some DVDs."

I stand my ground. "Thanks for the offer, mate," I say, finally drawing the line. "But we're wasting time." I gesture towards a pair of passing tourists. "Business opportunities are passing you by."

Surinda's eyes narrow, and every trace of warmth, feigned or otherwise, vanishes. "You think talking to me is wasting time?"

"I meant for you," I say, backtracking to save face. "Not for me."

His gaze turns icy, then he clears his throat and spits a thick wad of phlegm onto the dirt between us.

"You walk to Red Fort now," he commands in a tone stripped of all pretense and pleasantry.

Before I can respond, Surinda spins on his heel and unleashes a rapid-fire burst of Hindi that I don't understand. No translator is necessary, however, because the venom in his voice speaks volumes. I know exactly what has been said.

Surinda has just christened me.

With a *bad* name.

Chapter Seven

SURINDA WAS RIGHT, I should have taken a rickshaw.

I've been lost in Old Delhi's backstreets for hours. Every road and alleyway looks identical. There are no signposts, maps, or street names—just masses of people filing through labyrinthian laneways. Unexpected sights shock me at every turn. Disfigured beggars sit alongside stray cows, so-called untouchable humans sweep streets, and shoeless children traverse gutters of waste for recyclables. Sickly mothers are sprawled on roadsides with grubby kids clinging to their hips. Elderly people hug the earth, asleep, and seemingly near death. There are food carts, shop staff, and thousands of people going about their daily routines in a life I can't comprehend.

In desperation, I swallow my pride and approach several street vendors for directions. I ask a seller of leather goods, a cigarette *wallah*, and even a barber. None understand me, and after our interactions, all I've gained is a new wallet, a haircut, and a packet of smokes. I look more suave, sophisticated, and worldly. But I'm still lost.

Thankfully, Delhi has landmarks. Big ones. So even the vaguest backpacker will eventually bump into something of significance, like, say, a giant fortress.

It is this very vision that looms large as I finally shuffle down the famed market street of *Chandni Chowk*. The sight of the imposing

400-year-old Red Fort fills me with relief, and even the army of touts and snake charmers near the entrance fails to dampen my spirits. I approach the tourist attraction—ignoring pleas to purchase hats, sunglasses, balloons, water pistols, and, incomprehensibly, fake beards—and join a long entry line that winds its way toward the fortress gate.

I take my place in the queue and, like every other tourist around me, count the minutes as the midday sun fries my skin. The heat is so sweltering that I even hear Indian tourists complain about it. I also hear something else—Australian accents. The familiar tones come from a couple two spaces ahead. The woman turns, and I catch her eye, eager to initiate conversation.

"Bit warm, hey?" I say.

The woman sighs audibly. "Is it ever. Worse than back home."

I sidestep the Indian couple between us in an effort to continue our discourse.

"You guys been in India long?"

"A week." She takes a swig of water from a plastic bottle, then passes it to her partner, who acknowledges me with a nod. "Lloyd's dad is here on business, so we tagged along."

"You backpacking?" Lloyd asks.

"Yeah."

"How's that been?"

"Bit of a culture shock."

Lloyd takes another sip and nods. "Place is crazy, isn't it?!"

His comment sparks a brief discussion about the 'crazy' things we've seen. The exchange ends as we reach the gate, and after a casual farewell, we go our separate ways into the fort.

It's a thousand degrees hotter inside the walled compound, and I begin to bleed rivers of sweat. The heat and humidity is so taxing that it's a challenge to hold interest in anything. With few places to hide from the midday sun, I stride quickly over the numerous paved pathways, stopping briefly at each impressive example of ancient Mughal architecture that rises from the hundred acres of manicured lawn. Like a dutiful tourist, I snap photos of sandstone turrets, columns, domes, ponds, and take a moment to appreciate every pretty pavilion, balcony, and archway on show. Collectively, the experience is both captivating…and unbelievably fucking boring as well, and soon, every architectural detail merges with every historical plaque until every agonizing second feels like an eternity in hell.

It's not just me who feels this way.

Every Indian tourist around me seems just as bored, because the only thing attracting their full attention are pockets of shade. I follow their lead and search for an isolated haven of my own. I spot the perfect place, but it's already occupied by two people who are drenching their heads with bottled water.

"Not looking forward to the walk back to my hostel," I say as I near Mel and Lloyd.

Mel wrings her wet locks with her hands. "Do you want a lift? We've got a car and driver out front."

The offer sounds amazing, but I decline, not wanting to put them out.

"Mate, it's no drama," says Lloyd, soaking his *Newcastle Knights* footy cap. "We have to kill a few hours before we fly out tonight."

"You're welcome to do a drive-by tour with us." adds Mel.

I decline again.

"You sure?" she asks with a grin. "The car's air-conditioned."

SWEET RELIEF WASHES over me as I climb into the *Ambassador's* back seat. The refrigerated cabin is perfect, especially for Mel's proposed Delhi drive-by tour—a tour that requires us to motor past a bullet list of attractions without ever having to stop the car or interact with humans. Given the heat and the city's twenty-million inhabitants, it's a brilliant plan.

Our driver edges the vehicle into the bustling traffic, chauffeuring us to our first stop: the scene of Gandhi's assassination. Silently, we drift past a crowd of political pilgrims who are paying their respects. We learn nothing, see nothing, but check it off our list nonetheless. Next is India Gate, then Raj Ghat, then Parliament House.

We never leave the car, which is perfect—until it isn't.

As the drive continues, our sense of cultural aversion begins to niggle me. It feels shallow and privileged. I keep my moral discomfort to myself, however, because Mel and Lloyd are easy company. Both are good intentioned, laid-back and fun. Their travel yarns are told with just the perfect mix of awe, horror, and self-deprecation. Unlike me, my countrymen are vacationing with no higher purpose. They have no social angst, ego, or burning need for self-discovery. They're simply here to enjoy themselves and see something different. That's not to say they haven't been *touched* by India. They have. But 'spiritual' travelers they are not. Mel and Lloyd are strictly mainstream. Which is probably what Claire thought of me when I said I didn't want to go backpacking.

Truth is, I'm not like Mel and Lloyd—or Claire. I'm lost somewhere in between.

Finally, a tourist attraction we can't drive by appears. Its distinctive arches rise like a stylized phoenix above Delhi's central business district of Connaught Place. Lloyd instructs the driver to pull over, and we spill onto the pavement and quickly find shade under a colonnade filled with fast food chains, department stores, and fashion boutiques. It's a middle-class India I never knew existed. The media stereotype I've been fed is one of disease, disaster, and deprivation…with an occasional cricket match thrown in.

Minutes later, a smoked-glass frontage adorned with two golden arches triggers a smile. The logo is the antithesis of spiritual travel, but for shell-shocked western tourists, McDonald's familiar surrounds and ice-cold air-conditioning ensure it is an absolute must-see attraction. Possibly even a place of worship.

As we approach the shop front, a legless leper drags himself to the door and blocks our path. His desperate begging makes me instantly uncomfortable, and I wonder if there is a shittier example of human callousness than stepping over this man to buy fast-food. That thought weighs heavily on my mind… until Lloyd opens the door and a blast of refrigerated air evaporates my guilt. Without missing a beat, the three of us sidestep the leper and enter McDonald's.

Once inside, the injustices of the world are quickly forgotten. The restaurant's well-known design reassures and sedates me—the lighting, the menu boards, the laminate tables, as well as the million little logos that subconsciously scream 'happiness in sameness'. If I closed my eyes

I could be anywhere in the world: London, Paris, New York, Sydney. Anywhere less challenging than India. Anywhere less challenging than what lies directly outside the door. Or inside my head.

Lloyd and I approach the serving counter and stare at the menu board like health retreat escapees. Both of us order a *Maharaja Mac* (*sans* sacred beef) and half a dozen other artery-clogging treats. Mel orders whatever the hell it is that satiates the appetite of a twenty-something female—apparently, a burger the size of a hockey puck, a handful of skeletal fries, and a thimble of juice. Once done, the three of us find a table and compare the food to what's on offer back home.

There are high hopes our choices are delicious given that Indian cuisine is renowned for its flavor. Unfortunately, it's the usual McDonald's fusion of bland meat, local spices, and an after-taste from the unknown, which, to be fair to McDonald's, is consistent with the cuisine they serve everywhere. Lloyd and I are used to eating beef, so we donate our half-finished burgers to the nearest bin. As we do, I inconveniently remember the beggar outside. Suddenly, I'm overwhelmed by a familiar sensation of guilt and remorse. In an instant, my world slips from under me. My spirits plunge, and I feel the urge to run away and be alone. I sneak a glance at Mel and Lloyd and wonder who these people are. Or why I'm with them. They look like every other middle-class suburban couple—normal, happy, oblivious.

And I can't bear it.

Maybe Claire was right. Maybe this type of travel is too sanitized and unchallenging.

Like McDonald's.

Maybe the real recipe to a better life is found in experiences that can't be simplified or duplicated or franchised.

With my sunny disposition long gone, an awkward air sits over our table. The conversation becomes stilted, and my voice turns monotone. Lost for words, we leave Macca's. I sidestep the beggar once more, then follow Mel and Lloyd down the shaded colonnade. I feel more lost than when I left for the Red Fort. I'm confused about relationships, travel, life…and India. With mixed emotions, I say goodbye to my compatriots, who seem eager to leave thanks to my sudden sadness. Unfortunately, I can offer no apologies or insights into my mood, so we shake hands and part with few words.

As my fellow Aussies walk away, I am hit by an epiphany that reveals where I went wrong: I should never have bought that *Maharaja Mac*.

I should have ordered a *Happy Meal* instead.

Chapter Eight

A PROTECTIVE HAND falls on my shoulder.

"Chris! Oh, wow, dude, you're all right, huh? I've been worried about you, man."

It's mid-evening, and Ben and Josh are leaving the hostel's rooftop restaurant.

"I'm all good," I say, wondering just how lost I must look if a self-confessed, directionless stoner is concerned for my wellbeing. "It's a crazy place, though."

Ben nods fervently in agreement. "It is, man. It is. Out of this world. Dude, did you see the wet market? Man, that was like stepping back in time. They butcher live goats right in front of you. Live goats, Chris. They slit their throats."

Josh saunters over after paying for their meal. "So what do you think of Delhi?"

"It's fucking hot."

"It's a fucking hellhole, that's what it is. Go north as soon as you can—Shimla, Manali, McLeod Ganj. Way more chilled."

I notice he doesn't mention Kashmir. After a few more minutes of travel advice, our conversation wanes. Eventually, we shake hands, wish each other well on our respective journeys, then Ben and Josh walk out of my life.

But not really.

Because the restaurant is full of Ben and Josh clones.

Dozens of budget travelers are seated around old timber tables, yellow candle-light flickering on beer bottles and stoner grins. Their sweaty bodies, clothed in baggy fisherman's pants, faded earth-toned tank tops, or tie-dyed shirts, sit in an atmosphere already tainted with the scent of cheap beer, fried spices, and clove cigarettes. It's the kind of place that attracts an alternative spiritual adventurer. Bras seem optional for women, facial hair mandatory for men. Jimi Hendrix would be a saint here. Bob Marley a god. A barber, the devil.

Ben is right, India is like stepping back in time, specifically, Woodstock circa 1969.

I'm miles away from my comfort zone among these people. I wish I could be chilled out and effortlessly cool like them, but I can't be, because I'd look like the one thing I truly hate—a hypocritical fake. Of course, in reality, all this is just a *scene*. And I know it's not *my* scene… simply because I have no idea what or where my scene actually is.

I scan the joint for a vacant table. There is none, so I grab a bottle of Coke and search for a lone diner who won't mind having their meal spoiled by an awkward, mildly depressed Australian male. Finally, I spot two potential targets. The first, a western male around my age, who is engrossed in his *Lonely Planet* guidebook. Dressed in cargo shorts and a t-shirt, he looks exactly like me. So I immediately dismiss him and turn to contestant number two, a lone, olive-skinned female, who is reading a book. Draped in a red Bohemian maxi dress, she looks like the soft-focus star of a TV commercial promoting tourism in Tuscany or an organic coconut oil shampoo. I steal a glance at her long brunette hair, bare shoulders, and the bra-less contours of her breasts. Two beer bottles are within her grasp, one is empty, while the other competes for kiss-time with a roll-your-own cigarette that begs for resuscitation from a nearby ashtray. Everything about this woman—her solitude, book, beers, and smoke —screams 'Stay away', so I listen to my gut instinct…then promptly ignore it.

"Excuse me, do you mind if I sit?"

The woman looks up from her book and assesses me with a steely gaze. "Sure, if you want," she says in an accent I can't place.

I thank her, then pull out a chair. "Nice to finally relax. Delhi's pretty full on."

She gives me a bored smile, as if wondering whether to engage. "How long have you been in India?"

"Just over twenty-four hours," I reply, stretching one measly day into the more impressive double-digit hours.

"You get used to it," she says.

"Have you been here long?"

"Six weeks." She forces another weak smile. "Your accent… you are from where, America?"

"Australia."

A hint of skepticism appears on her face. "You don't sound Australian. Too easy to understand."

"I'm trying to talk slower over here. No one would understand me if I spoke the way I do back home. Where are you from?"

"Israel."

"Lots of Israelis here," I say. "In Thailand too."

She plucks her cigarette from the ashtray. "That's because it's cheap." She takes a drag. "People finish military service, then come to these countries to have fun."

"Kinda like Australians in Bali."

"You do military service too?"

"No, I mean the cheap fun."

"I don't know about Bali. I can't visit."

I tilt my head, slightly confused. "Why's that?"

"Jews are not welcome in Indonesia. This is the same for most Muslim countries."

"Really?"

"Of course," she says, looking at me like I'm a moron. "Australians can go anywhere?"

"Pretty much. Kiwis hate us, though."

"Kiwis?"

"New Zealanders."

An alarmed look appears on her face. "Because of war?"

"No, because of sport."

"Oh, ok. Football, yes?"

"Rugby, actually. And cricket."

"Cricket?!" She slaps the book on the table, and suddenly sits upright, her face finally animated. "Oh, my god, please, tell me, what is this cricket? I see it everywhere here—kids playing, men playing. It is like a religion."

I laugh at her reaction. "The English brought it to India. It's popular back home too, but nothing like here. Trust me, cricket in India is on a whole different level."

"And *you* play this game?"

I nod. "Used to. I was hoping to play some games here. I brought some coins over that have a famous Australian cricket player on them to give to kids."

She leans in, intrigued. "Who told you to do this?"

"I read it in a magazine article. It said to bring something from your own country to show local children."

The woman looks me directly in the eye. "That is a very nice thing to do."

I know. I'm excellent like that. We should have sex now. Preferably in your room, especially if it has a working air-conditioner. And shower. And toilet.

I say all that in my head, but in real life I introduce myself instead. Tahlia does likewise, and we continue our chat about cricket for an extra minute.

"You look out of place," she finally says, glancing at my white *Rip Curl* t-shirt. "Like a surfer."

I watch as she rolls another smoke. Her tongue seductively wets the edge of the cigarette paper, convincing me that she could sell smokes to people with cancer.

"I probably should try and blend in more."

Tahlia shrugs. "Wear what you want." She lights her cigarette, exhales a thin cloud of smoke towards the ceiling. "It's all just costumes. Masks. Not real skin."

She closes her tobacco pouch and offers it to me. I haven't smoked for years but it seems to be a backpacker norm in India. It's probably healthier than breathing the air, so I take the tobacco and set to work.

"Why did you come to India?" Tahlia asks.

"Cheap travel, like you guys. I wanted to do Thailand for three months, but knew my money wouldn't last. How about you?"

Tahlia takes a sip of her beer, then with a look of indifference says: "My husband was killed in a plane crash."

Her shocking admission stuns me. I freeze, unsure of what to say or where to look. Suddenly, the expression on her face makes sense. It's not indifference, it's grief and the numbness of loss.

"He was doing his national service," she adds flatly.

"I'm sorry. I don't know how you even begin to deal with that."

Tahlia raises her bottle and smiles bravely. "Beer and cigarettes."

"How long are you here for?"

She shrugs. "I don't agree with everything in my country, so maybe forever." She takes another mouthful of beer. "My parents want me to finish my law degree. But I don't want to be in Israel. That's why I came here."

"To a country full of Israelis?" I say lightly.

Tahlia laughs at the irony. "I know! I hate these people. They are everywhere. All I want is to be immersed in India. With all the distractions." Her face softens. "And so much life."

As her words trail off, a waitress arrives to take my order. The interruption prompts Tahlia to gather up her belongings.

"I will leave you to order your meal," she says. "It was nice to meet you."

She smiles, but it's a tired deceit that masks a deeper sadness.

As she walks away, I get the feeling that India is a magnet for directionless foreigners with wounded souls.

Alarmingly, some of whom are more lost than me.

Chapter Nine

MY LACK of direction in life can be explained by a single trait: I have the navigational skills of a lemming; a life radar that directs me toward random acts of stupidity, all of which are my own doing.

It's four in the morning, and I'm lost in Old Delhi's backstreets. Again. Which is not good. Plus, I've just submerged a running shoe in cow shit. Also not good, since I'm supposed to be boarding a train in an hour. Of course, the chance of that happening is slim, given that I have absolutely no idea where the train station actually is.

I was hoping that the persistent rickshaw drivers who hound tourists during daylight hours might deliver me to my destination. Unfortunately, rickshaw drivers do what most people do before dawn —they sleep. Dozens of them. All lying prone, with their dirt-encrusted feet extended over handlebars, or curled in fetal positions on rear passenger seats. Unbelievably, this is luxurious accommodation when compared to the roadside resting places occupied by Delhi's homeless, dispossessed, or destitute. These silhouettes sleep on *any* surface, alone or huddled against tiny kin. It's the kind of dark vision of a dirt-poor life that should awaken those who are more fortunate (people like me, for instance).

Old Delhi is an entirely different city in the darkness. Unlike daylight's chaos, the post-midnight hours bring an eerie silence.

Stillness takes over, and once-busy streets lie empty, save for fearless Delhi dogs who greet passing shadows with vampire smiles. Instinctively, I quicken my pace, marching with purpose lest the mutts realize I'm easy game. Or completely lost. And I am lost. In more ways than one. Because last night I ventured off the map of common sense and did something truly stupid.

I contacted Claire.

I'm guessing this kind of stupidity would rank quite highly on a top ten list of 'Ways to Completely Screw Your Heartbroken Ex-lover'. Possibly just behind, quite literally, screwing your heartbroken ex-lover, which, as it happens, I did the night before I flew out of Australia. Of course, Claire's no fool, so I had to beg and lie to persuade her to sleep with me. Eventually, she caved in. Unfortunately, for every upside, there is also a downside. As a result, my actions sent Claire a mixed message, and now I know she is probably digging up a past that I wanted to keep buried.

And yet, I sent her an email last night.

I only did that because Tahlia's story made me fear losing someone dear. After she left, I felt a deep sense of grief that made me miss Claire, which is confusing, given that I'm in love with Emma. I think my problem is that I have too much love inside me…but not enough care. Thus last night's mixed message.

> To: Claire
> Subject: Delhi Dog
>
> I think I left two malaria tablets on the floor. Hopefully, the cat didn't eat them!
>
> See ya

With a clarity reserved for all morning-afters, I can now see that sending that email was a mistake, because receiving *any* correspondence from a past love can trigger complicated emotions. I am concerned about the welfare of the cat, but, in hindsight, I should have kept my distance.

Everything is easy in hindsight.

Even finding a train.

I open my guidebook beneath a street light and quickly identify where I lost track. It seems I made the usual error: I trusted my gut instinct. According to the map, all I had to do was step outside my guesthouse, turn right and walk in a straight line for five minutes until I bumped into a big steel train. I chose a different path. The wrong one, unsurprisingly.

At 5 a.m., I stumble into New Delhi Railway Station. The place buzzes with life. Scores of people crowd the platforms, from corpulent figures in fitted garments to the bedraggled poor, clothed in soiled hand-me-downs. Everywhere I look, I see a mix of social class, skin color, and age, all united by one common goal—to escape Delhi.

Sidestepping the hundreds of waiting passengers, I find a vacant square of concrete on the platform. I drop my backpack and anxiously recheck my ticket for the departure time, then note the name of the train.

The Himalayan Queen.

The moniker alone conjures up visions of romantic rail travel. I imagine cedar-paneled walls, crisp martinis, and billowing steam that vaporizes into the cool mountain air. However, when the train finally arrives, all that vaporizes is my romantic vision. *The Himalayan Queen* is neither elegant nor opulent. It's just a diesel locomotive pulling a dozen passenger carriages.

The engine shunts to a stop, and within seconds, almost every human on the platform rushes the cattle-class wagons. Thankfully, I've booked a first-class ticket, so I slowly make my way towards the coach that has the word 'air-conditioned' emblazoned on its hide. Inside, I find my seat among well-off Indian vacationers. I'm the only foreign passenger in the carriage. I'm also the filthiest and worst dressed. Plus, I have two different colored shoes—one brilliant white, the other a cow-shit hue.

Feeling self-conscious, I turn to the window and silently contemplate the adventure that lies ahead. I hope to see spectacular scenery, quaint villages, and amazing people.

Nothing prepares me for what I do witness.

Chapter Ten

I SEE ASSHOLES.

As the sun rises, my window frames the sight of countless bare backsides squatting alongside the track to take a morning crap.

Prior to this moment, I'd never considered the lack of toilet facilities for India's poor. I figured Delhi's sprawl of tarp-roofed, dirt-floor slums wouldn't have sewers, but this public display of morning ablution has caught me by surprise.

I stare transfixed at the squatters dotting the landscape, but eventually tire of the crappy view and turn my attention to the surrounding farmland. The level landscape numbs my mind until we arrive at Kalka; the halfway point of our trip, and the start of our ascent into the Indian Himalayas. The steep climb requires a narrow-gauge train, so I exit *The Himalayan Queen* and board a locomotive aptly named *The Toy Train*. It's an aged, half-sized rail motor with a hint of 1950s Disneyland conveyance about it, painted in faded pastels and stains of neglect. The train has seen better days, but there's no doubt it was originally built to give the impression of journeying to a better world. A happier, calmer one. Possibly even free of assholes.

I clamber onboard. Self-conscious about my sweaty clothes and smelly shoe, I avoid every Indian and claim a seat opposite two other perspiring backpackers. Like me, both wear cargo pants, t-shirts and caps. We exchange greetings and instantly become a gang of Average Joes just shooting the breeze.

"Were you guys on the Delhi train?" I ask.

"Yeah, second-class," says one of the men, unimpressed.

Kevin's an attorney, so it's hard to feel sympathy for him. But I almost do. The American has an instantly likable smile. The kind of smile that should have been wiped off his face after a second-class Indian train trip. But Kevin just spent eighteen months working in Africa, so maybe this kind of travel is normal for him.

"Was that as fun as it looked?" I tease.

His Italian mate, Tommy, pipes up. "It was shit," he groans. "Wooden seats, bars on windows. Everyone spitting and farting. Disgusting."

Apparently these guys met on the train. I'm guessing they must have been forced to sit together, otherwise, why the hell would anyone befriend a lawyer?

"Did you board at Delhi or Chandigarh?" asks Kevin.

"Delhi. But I was in first-class." I smile broadly. "So I had to put up with air-conditioning, soft seats, and hot Chai."

Tommy's eyes twitch. "How much was your ticket?"

"Umm, four bucks, I think."

The Italian is stunned. "Four dollars?!"

"Yeah, I think so."

I watch Tommy calculate the physical and emotional cost of his financial saving, but his progress is interrupted by the arrival of the ticket master.

I present my stub for approval. It's checked and returned without drama. The boys present theirs next.

"This is wrong carriage," the man says sternly. "Second-class only."

Tommy's face tightens. "What about these seats?" he pleads. "They're empty."

"Not possible," says the official. "First-class only this carriage."

"But no one has booked them."

The man points emphatically at Tommy's ticket. "This is second-class ticket."

"Can we upgrade?" Kevin interrupts, fishing for a loophole. "We can pay extra."

"I am sorry, is not possible."

Tommy throws his hands up in exasperation. "But there's no one sitting here!"

The ticket-master jabs at the ticket. "*Second-class* only."

"So we can't sit here even if it's vacant?" Kevin asks.

"For *first-class* only, sir," confirms the ticket Nazi.

"And we can't upgrade from second to first?"

"Not possible."

Kevin's Kenyan experience kicks in. "Can we buy a *new* first-class ticket instead?"

The ticket master bobbles his head. It looks like a denial, but it's not, it's an Indian nod.

"Yes, this is possible."

Kevin sighs in relief. "How much is that?"

"One hundred and fifty rupees, please," says the man brightly.

The two travelers dive into their wallets and quickly hand over the equivalent of four American dollars.

Once settled, the *Toy Train* begins its six-hour journey towards Shimla. My *Lonely Planet* guidebook claims we will cross eight hundred bridges en route, and pass through one hundred tunnels. All at walking pace. It seems torturous but after the oppressive lowland heat, the prospect of reaching cooler mountain air is worth any sacrifice.

As we climb, the temperature begins to fall, as do the stresses of Delhi. Eventually, a postcard panorama of lush green valleys appears. The vista triggers a collective mood shift within the carriage. Passengers become relaxed and animated, and, suddenly, it feels like we're all on vacation. I love this kind of travel. I love the dramatic shift in mood via scenery. The rhythmic *clickity-clack* of narrow-gauge wheels. The journey into the unknown.

I open the window and the scent of pine and eucalyptus clears my mind. The fresh arboreal air carries me back to a hinterland day trip with Claire, when we tried to escape a brutal Brisbane heatwave. Our destination was an isolated mountain creek that was cold enough to freeze the balls off a snowman. Upon arrival, we jumped in buck naked, then scrambled out seconds later. Our skin was pink, our lips glacial blue, and our bodies shivered like tuning forks. Needing warmth, we dressed, then high-tailed it to an old timber fire tower, whose stairs beckoned us closer to the sun. With each step, we rose like mercury until we looked over an endless valley stretching to the coast. Vertigo hit me unexpectedly, and I clung to the rickety handrails like an anxious boa constrictor, while Claire leaned over the side, carefree and happy. She turned, giddy with endorphins, and gave me a look that suggested we should have sex right then and there. Out of character, I took a rain cheque, too scared to join her on the edge.

My world goes dark on that thought, as the train enters yet another tunnel. Musky air fills the carriage and, for a minute, in the pitch blackness, I'm left alone with my memory of Claire.

Suddenly, I see the silhouette of a child and I wonder if it's in my mind?

The child comes between me and Claire and perches himself on the seat in front. His pre-teen features are gradually illuminated by the approaching light at the end of the tunnel. I offer a friendly smile, which he refuses to return. Then I offer a 'Namaste', which is met with a silent stare. The moment is awkward and I get a sense of being assessed, even judged, by the kid. At a loss, I look out the window and watch the train's carriages snake in a sweeping arc around the face of the mountain. I lean out, raise my camera, and click off two frames. I go for a third, but my view is obscured by the arrival of the kid's head. I take the picture anyway and give him another smile. He glares at me, stony-faced, and I fantasize about tossing him from the train if it ever moves faster than a maimed turtle on valium.

It doesn't.

And an hour later, the kid and I arrive safely in Shimla, *The Queen of Hills*.

Chapter Eleven

SUNRISE IN SHIMLA is a stark contrast to dawn in Delhi—blue sky and crisp mountain chill, instead of grey smog and sticky lowland heat.

I close the door on the previous night's lodging and join Tommy and Kevin outside the guesthouse. Eager for breakfast, we follow one of the many terraced paths that line the town's steep inclines, until we reach a picturesque public square that is out-of-bounds to all but foot traffic. From this vantage point, it's easy to understand why Shimla is known as 'The Queen of Hills' and 'The Land of Gods'. Dominating the square is a neo-Gothic church that looks over a mountain vista fit for royalty and gods.

The town was good enough for the British colonials back in the 1800s as well. In fact, it was such a favored destination that India's entire government was relocated from Delhi to Shimla each summer. And it's easy to see why. Besides pretty panoramas, Shimla is blessed with a serene calm, and the kind of mild climate that's perfect for sipping tea…while plotting how to *civilize* a nation with sandwiches and sidearms. Nowadays, however, the town is largely a honeymoon destination, or a getaway for people wanting to taste a slice of Europe in India.

The boys and I scope out several cafes and restaurants, until we find one that looks promising. A waiter ushers us to a table and we peruse the menu. Food is a huge part of the Indian experience for most travelers. But not so much for me. I know nothing about the local cuisine. Meals of subtle saffron or spicy masala are simply mild or hot curries to my palate. I don't even know what Indian vegan dishes are made of. Plants, I guess.

In my defense, I grew up in an era where breakfast was cornflakes, lunch was Vegemite sandwiches, and dinners were meat and three veg. In the 1970s, cosmopolitan food in Australia was a pizza or spaghetti. In the 80s and 90s, it was Asian stir-fry or a kebab. Indian food was less prevalent. Obviously, Tommy and Kevin's upbringing was as culturally insular as mine, because they've avoided virtually all local food since their arrival, and have chosen to exist on a diet of potato chips and Coca Cola.

Our collective ignorance is on show as we attempt to translate the offerings on the restaurant menu—even though it's written in English. It's as if the three of us are *dish*-lexic. Our incomprehension is further magnified by our waiter's lack of English, and breakfast turns into a lucky dip grab bag.

As we eat, suggestions for the day's itinerary are bandied between us. Kevin and Tommy decide to visit a monkey temple, while I opt for the grander-sounding Chadwick Falls. We split up post-meal, and I begin my sightseeing trip with an overpriced taxi ride down a dirt mountain road. The driver drops me at a signpost pointing to a forest track. I walk the final stretch, arriving at a sight of wonder that leaves me gob-smacked.

Because the Chadwick Falls are absolutely shit.

I can piss harder than this. Plus, there's garbage everywhere—plastic bags, broken glass, chip wrappers. I spot other foreign additions also. Perched on granite boulders nearby, are two backpackers. Both are scribbling pensive thoughts in travel journals, no doubt something memorable like 'Falls are absolutely shit. Should've gone to the monkey temple'. The studious sightseers acknowledge my arrival with a raised eye, then return to their erudite musings. I figure they must have swung in from some concrete jungle, because no one but a city-dweller would think this poor example of natural wonderment was worth anything more than a cursory glance, let alone a diary entry.

Of course, on the flip side, it's quiet here, which, in itself, is a rare and sought-after attraction in India. In an attempt to assimilate with the travelers, I sit my backside atop the nearest granite rock and extract my own unused journal. Despite my aversion to diary writing, I've actually brought two travel journals to India. Both are handmade with expensive Japanese paper, thick card stock, sturdy cotton binding, and a collage of vivid *Indo-Asian* images inked with quotations. Neither book was a conscious purchase, they were gifts—made by Claire and presented to me the day I flew out of Australia.

I gently run a palm across the cover of one journal, the ridged paper's perfect imperfections feeling like braille beneath my fingertips. The pulp's highs and lows mapping the terrain as if it were my life with Claire. I read the familiar quotes on the cover. The first, attributed to Khalil Gibran, says "The deeper that sorrow carves into your being, the more joy you can contain." The second remark from Oscar Wilde states that "We are all in the gutter, but some of us are looking at the stars."

Claire inscribed these insights in an attempt to prompt me to travel towards the light, to move on rather than dwell on. Frankly, such wisdom is lost on blokes like me. Nevertheless, I open the journal and wait for writing inspiration to hit me with its usual force of a down feather. When it fails to arrive, I default to my usual procrastination and daydreaming. Eventually, I pencil in three words:

CHRIS LOVES EMMA.

Then I play a childish game I recall from fifth-grade where letters are crossed and numbers added to calculate 'true love'. According to my math, the three-word statement is just 52% true. Which is exactly why I gave up believing in this crap back in fifth-grade.

I add some surnames just in case.

The bumped up 'love total' isn't much better, and short of adding a street address, town of birth, and name of first pet, I can't see the percentage rising anytime soon.

Out of curiosity, I substitute Emma's full name with Claire's. Unexpectedly, my heartbeat quickens as I calculate the answer. Apparently, me loving Claire is 85% true. Which I know is 100% false. Well, minus those days when I multiply my guilt with the addition of some alcohol and a few divided thoughts.

I close the book on the sum of both relationships and stare at the falls. As if on cue, the backpackers shut their journals as well. Then, in unison, and as if late for a bus, they quickly disappear up the bush track that leads back to the road. Their hasty departure confounds me for a full ten minutes until I realize they are, in fact, late for a bus.

And so am I.

I race after them but when I reach the road, I discover I've already missed the bus. Unfortunately, it's one of the very few that plies the mountain route, so I begin the long walk back to Shimla. After twenty minutes, I stop at a busted concrete block that moonlights as a bus stop, and contemplate whether I should continue my hike, or wait for the next service. Before I can fully calculate the benefits of either choice, a group of children emerges from a nearby cluster of dilapidated buildings. Fresh from school, the sociable tykes waste no time testing their beginner English skills on me, with varying degrees of success.

Despite my innate selfishness, I have an extremely high tolerance for kids, simply because children aren't hypocritical assholes like grown-ups. They're raw, but honest. Their priorities simple. Instead of fixating on money and success, they live for tickles and wrestles. I need that kind of outlook in life, which is why I wish I was a dad.

Figuring the crowd of little Indians can't grow much larger, I decide to do the unthinkable and extract the *Lonely Planet* guidebook. From experience, I know that even an *unopened* copy of the book can attract a crowd of 'helpful' locals within seconds. Thankfully, the kids aren't as brazen. Instead, they stand back as I skim through the book's pages. The photographs capture their attention and several curious bodies edge closer, and lean against me, then, as if we were best friends, their arms drape over my shoulders and legs. The gentle touch catches me off guard and, suddenly, I'm fighting back tears. My reaction, though unexpected, isn't foreign, because, during the last year, I've noticed I have gained a rare superpower—one that enables me to find sadness in every single moment of joy.

Within seconds, I regain my composure and return to flipping pages under the scrutiny of expectant eyeballs. The kids are spellbound by the images as we go on a pictorial journey through India.

"This is where?" a kid asks, pointing at a golden-walled fortress.

"Jaisalmer," I tell him. "In Rajasthan."

"What country?"

"Here."

The child looks at me, confused.

"India," I say, pointing to the ground. "Your country, dude."

More questions follow but the language divide means I provide few satisfying answers.

We reach the end of the guidebook and the conversation stalls. I feel awkward and unsure. To cover my discomfort I pick up a small rock and toss it at a plastic bottle on the other side of the road. It misses but the action prompts half a dozen boys to join in. Before long, we are all lobbing stones at bottles, trees, cans…other kids. Pelting rocks is a universal language for little boys. It's competitive, fun, plus it annoys girls.

Finally, a bus arrives. Unfortunately, it's heading *down* the mountain, while my journey is *up* the mountain. My school friends, however, clamber aboard. Once seated, they push their arms through the windows and wave madly at me. I return the gesture.

As the bus departs, I wonder what the future holds for its little passengers, and what adventures will be written in *their* journals, and whether those stories will be epic like India's history—full of pride, honor and resilience.

All the stuff I know nothing about.

Chapter Twelve

BORED OF WAITING, I continue my hike up the sparsely populated hillside. The quiet monotony of walking is welcome, until it leads me to the last place I need to visit, which is inside my head. As a result, I soon find myself reflecting on things like fatherhood and fun, and the general lack of purpose in my life. Before I know it, I'm venturing down another path—the one that leads to depression. It's an unwelcome detour but I've traveled this route often, so the signposts are easy to read.

The level ground in my mind suddenly gives way to treacherous terrain, marked by extreme ups and downs. Self-loathing and insecurity wrong foot me. I become unbalanced and erratic, lost and disoriented. My mood veers wildly from gregarious and friendly to unapproachable and cold. I overthink, then underperform, as my interest slips away and my motivation stalls. Simple steps seem like unscalable cliffs, minor barriers become impassable mountains, and eventually, every manic high erodes to a flatline of neurotic lows, leaving me wanting to reach just one destination—the end of the road.

But I never make it that far, because I'm too scared to take my own life. So I self-destruct in a different way, not with drugs or alcohol—I poison myself from within. I grow angry and harvest hate. I alienate friends, sabotage relationships, walk out on jobs, and then I run away and restart the same journey. Again. And again.

I always thought fame, fortune, and success would bring me direction, but I'm starting to think I'm stuck in my darkness because I lack purpose and connection.

As if on cue, two kids brandishing a cricket bat and ball sprint past me. My arrival on their home turf sparks excited chatter.

"Hello, what is your name?" asks one, addressing me from a safe distance ahead.

"Chris. What's yours?"

He shouts a name I fail to grasp.

His buddy asks: "From which country?"

"Australia."

My answer causes the boys to recite the usual roll-call of famous Australian cricket players. Satisfied with our brief exchange, the kids hightail it to a stretch of road a hundred yards ahead, and soon, the surrounding forest is absorbing the dull *thwack* of bat on ball. I hang back, sizing up their cricket skills. The pair can't be more than ten years old, yet they're both impressively coordinated. Especially the little fella who's batting. Instead of just flaying wildly, he selects his shots, smashing the ball into the roadside overgrowth for easy runs.

Suddenly, the mountainside comes to life, and I begin to notice previously unseen details with childlike eyes. Each bump and rut in the road surface becomes a prospective target for ball deviation. Even the steep terrain bordering the pitch becomes strategically important. Whack the ball onto the high side of the hill, and runs will come freely as the incline hampers retrieval. Deflect it downhill into the impenetrable undergrowth, and the game will most likely cease altogether—lost ball.

Where did this childhood world go? And all its vivid details? I used to see everything in high definition as a kid. But somewhere along the way to adulthood, I got distracted by some hazy big picture.

The ball flashes past the batsman and rolls to a stop beside my feet. The kids watch expectantly. Instinctively, I scoop it up. But it's not really a ball; it's a wad of rags hand-stitched in a tight knot. I cock my wrist and whip the bundle of cloth in a low arc back to the bowler. The boy snatches it out of the air and grins. His smile instantly banishes my depression, so I halt my hiking and wait for him to send down a few more deliveries.

Before long, the ball tracks wide of the batter and flutters through to me along the ground. Once again, I send it back without a word.

I'm reluctant to delay my long-term goal of reaching the top of the mountain, but I really, *really* want to play cricket right now. Perhaps it's because of the hope that flashes in the kids' eyes—the hope that a grown-up will join in the fun. It seems ridiculously simple to make their wish come true, so I remove my daypack and stand it upright on the ground directly behind the batsman. Both boys beam knowingly, because not only have I provided an important piece of cricket furniture, I've officially proclaimed my intentions.

It's game on.

Chapter Thirteen

I SNATCH the rag ball then address the kids. "How about Australia versus India?"

The boys nod vigorously.

"Who's batting first?" I ask.

"India!" They both yell.

I give the lads a hard stare. "You sure? I'm pretty fast with the ball."

The kid with the bat swings aggressively, indicating that any ball I deliver will be knocked out of the park.

"Okay, dude, you asked for it." I say, determined to send down some serious rag ball heat. "You ready?"

The kid nods excitedly.

I charge in like a beast, then in a fluid sequence, my hands rise, my back arches, and my arm windmills with aggressive intent. The resultant action slings my wrist toward the target with speed. But at the point of release, I roll the ball out the back of my palm, lobbing it harmlessly down the pitch. It's a light-weight delivery tailor-made for a beginner batsman.

The beginner batsman promptly smashes the ball, and we all watch it sail into oblivion.

"Tendulkar *blasts* the Aussie pace attack out of the ground," I say, launching into some backyard commentary. I bound after the ball, clambering up the forested incline. "It's a massive hit from the Little Master. Ten rows into the Gavaskar Stand. The crowd is on its feet, taunting the big Australian." I glance back and am greeted with two smiling faces. "Okay, no more easy stuff." I return to the road. "You ready again?"

The batter nods.

I steam in and send the next ball down faster. It too is dispatched. I give chase again, vaulting across a mud-filled table-drain and into the scrub. Breathless, I pluck the ball free from some prickly undergrowth.

"Faster," shouts the batter.

I happily oblige, increasing the speed of successive deliveries until I am rocketing the rag ball down the pitch as fast as I can. Time and again, it finds a new trajectory into the mud or scrub. Time and again, I fetch it. It's the most fun I've had in years, so for the next thirty minutes, play continues without a break.

Finally, a bus arrives, and we pause the game. Unfortunately, it's heading down the hill, so I'm obliged to stay. The vehicle halts on our pitch, and students of various ages spill from its doors. The passengers eyeball me with confused expressions. I hear staccato phrases of Hindi, no doubt questioning why some bloke dressed in a surf shirt and board shorts is playing cricket on their remote hillside.

The bus pulls away and the game resumes with an Indian batting line-up that has suddenly quadrupled in size. Adults and kids alike are eager to face my rag ball wrath, while a handful of college kids gather to spectate from the roadside. Within seconds, an internal dispute erupts over the Indian team's batting order. The squabble is settled by an adult wresting the bat from his smaller teammate. The youngster protests and earns a sharp backhand around the ear for his trouble. I watch as he retreats to the roadside with wounded pride and tears in his eyes. My blood boils at the sight and violent thoughts simmer inside me.

"Hey, ease up, mate," I say, striding towards the offending adult. "Just take it in turns, okay?"

Consumed with rage, I storm back to my mark, determined to embarrass the man. Around me, the crowd watch on expectantly for the contest they know will come. Delivery options run through my head. I'm keen to teach him a lesson so I decide to target his body.

Turning on the spot, I sprint in and let fly with all my strength. The ball rockets down the pitch, bounces once then tracks towards his body. The guy takes a wild swing, but the fastball flashes past his bat… then gently bunts into his shin with the force of a marshmallow fist. I may as well have floated down a fart for all the physical damage the rag ball has caused. Despite this, the spectators cheer my effort, simply because bat has been beaten by ball.

From then on, we try to outdo one another until, finally, my nemesis signals enough. He relinquishes the bat to a pre-teen, and the game becomes a blur of batters, laughter, and good-humored sledging. Before long, I'm smeared from head to toe with dirt and mud. I point out my filthy appearance to the college lads standing at the edge of the road.

"Look at me," I wail lightheartedly. "I'm absolutely filthy."

"Only an Australian would play with such blind commitment," says a bemused onlooker. "Just like an Indian."

His comment triggers laughter from everyone, and, despite my home being a world away, the distance between us all suddenly feels non-existent.

I'm among kin here. I can feel it. These are my brothers.

The sound of another approaching bus disrupts our game. As we clear the road, it dawns on me that this bus is going *uphill*, which means I need to get on it. I quickly take photos of the Indian batters then hastily shake many hands.

The bus stops.

I wave a final farewell, climb aboard, and slide into the nearest vacant window seat. I am outrageously happy. Outside, my two original cricket buddies rush towards the bus. They raise their hands to the open window, and I extend mine outside.

"Coming back tomorrow?"

The question comes from my original batting foe as he latches onto my palm.

I shake my head. "No."

"Next day?" asks the other boy, eyes full of hope.

I shake my head. "I have to catch another bus."

Disappointment lines their faces and I immediately wish I could raise their spirits somehow. Then I remember the Don Bradman coins…the ones that are back in my hotel room. The missed opportunity devastates me, because this moment is exactly why I brought them to India.

"Catching bus where?" the Little Master asks.

"Manali."

His fingers tighten around mine. "Why?"

"Because I have to," I say lamely.

"Stay here," he pleads.

I smile apologetically. "I can't. I need to keep moving."

The kid remains silent, accepting the story of my life.

Finally, the bus lurches forward, my hand pulls free, and our connection is broken.

Chapter Fourteen

IF THERE IS one truism I've seen and heard repeatedly in India, it is this: *Everything is possible.* Keen to balance your entire family on an aging Honda scooter down the highway? *Yes, is possible.* Feel like driving through central Delhi with three goats squeezed into your auto-rickshaw? *Yes, is possible.* Fancy clinging to the roof of a public bus, perched atop your luggage with no restraints?

"Yes, is possible. My friend, in India, everything is possible."

Even the impossible is possible. For example, consider a perpetually lost man finally finding direction. That's what happened to me yesterday with the cricket game. I had an awakening. Of sorts. I felt happy. Truly happy. Curiously, it had nothing to do with attaining the vacuous things I've been chasing in recent years. It came from living in the moment and having fun.

That was my awakening: *Live in the moment and have fun.*

Not exactly a momentous epiphany, I know. Certainly not the kind of enlightenment that passes as a deep spiritual awakening. But it's a start.

With that in mind, I've decided to part company with Kevin and Tommy and take a different journey. Instead of heading to the popular Himalayan resort town of Manali, I'm making a pilgrimage to the Buddhist enclave of McLeod Ganj—home of the Dalai Lama.

Unfortunately, my trip to McLeod Ganj will be rougher than I hoped, due to the fact that every air-conditioned tourist coach leaving Shimla is booked solid. As a result, I've had to settle for a seat on a non-air-conditioned public bus to Mandi, a small town located midway.

I question my new travel plan as soon as the bus pulls into the station. Its battered, dented exterior hints at death-wish driving and multiple near disasters. Within seconds of boarding, I understand why tourists avoid India's public buses. Besides having panels that look as if they were repaired by blind blacksmiths with anger management issues, the vehicle is dusty, hot, noisy, and incredibly fucking slow.

Ten minutes after we leave, I want to get off.

This feeling intensifies the further we go, as our bus scrapes against the sides of other approaching buses. Gripped by fear of a crash, I peer beyond the unguarded edge of the notoriously dangerous mountain road, and spot the twisted wreckage of vehicles scattered at the base of the steep gorge. Thankfully, it's only 100 miles to Mandi.

But there's a catch.

Our public bus *terminates* at Mandi, but it *stops* every few miles for hailing passengers, which, apparently, stretches the trip to six hours.

Accepting my fate, I stare at the mountain landscape as we snake up dozens of twists and turns. Despite the pretty scenery, our journey soon gets ugly. The constant sway of the bus slowly agitates my stomach and I feel the effects of motion sickness. As a precaution, I swallow two travel sickness pills. My stomach eventually settles…just as the stomach of another passenger empties.

The contents of the woman's gut sprays the seat in front of her, and a bilious odor taints the cabin air. In horror, I watch her vomit pool on the floor, then spider out in foul tributaries. My tummy churns as the wretched rivers creep across the cabin, threatening the feet of passengers. Trying not to gag, I turn my nose towards the open window, and hope the bus will stop so someone can douse the floor with water.

But the bus doesn't stop.

In protest, the woman keeps heaving, and soon a din of complaint rises from many travelers. Finally, the bus driver veers to the shoulder of the road, and a stampede of grossed-out passengers, including myself, rush to the exit seeking fresh air. The sickly woman follows with her husband. He leads her to a grassy spot where a handful of inquisitive male passengers gather to watch her hurl with abandon. Concerned with the woman's wellbeing, I pull out my motion sickness capsules and show them to her husband.

"For travel sickness," I say.

The husband doesn't understand, so I rub my stomach and repeat the words.

He grabs the pills warily, then talks to the men around us in Hindi. Clearly displeased by their replies, he thrusts the pack back at me. Confused by his response, I take the pills and retreat from his wild eyes.

Suddenly, a hand touches my arm.

"Excuse me?"

I turn and see a conservatively dressed male who could pass as a stereotypical nerd.

He points to the pills. "Can I see those, please?"

"Yeah, no worries." I give him the packet.

"I'm a medical student," he explains, as several men close in on our conversation.

"They're a natural remedy for motion sickness," I say.

"Ahh, *natural* remedy." He turns the foil packet over, obviously searching for the ingredients. "Herbs, yes?"

"Yeah, natural herbs."

He glances at me, while the other men fixate on the blister pack. "What kind of natural herbs?"

I ditched the cardboard box they came in ages ago, so his guess is as good as mine.

"Chamomile and ginger, I think."

He gives me a skeptical look. "And this works?"

"Does for me," I say, lightly challenging his cynical tone.

"Perhaps a placebo effect, yes?"

I shrug. "Maybe."

He considers this for a moment, then approaches the sick woman's husband. Words are exchanged briefly before the man aggressively waves the trainee doctor away. My new friend backs away and passes the pills back to me.

"This man says he does not want his wife taking drugs."

"Oh, okay. I understand."

But I don't understand. Because getting high on herbal motion sickness pills is about as likely as tripping on incense or lavender *potpourri*.

I pop one of the soft gelatin capsules into my mouth and chew on it just to make a point. The crowd of onlookers watches on with interest, presumably waiting for me to fall into a chamomile-induced coma or suffer some fatal olfactory overdose. Neither happens, so it isn't long before another curious passenger asks to see the blister pack.

"Feel free to try them," I say, handing it over. "I have more in my backpack."

The med student translates my words for those gathered around us, then turns to me and introduces himself. We shake hands, then with pleasantries over, Vijay asks:

"Where are you from, Chris?"

"Australia."

"Oh, great cricket players." He names several sporting millionaires.

"Lots of legends in your team too." I mention three Indian superstars, triggering multiple nods of agreement from those who are eavesdropping. "Good batsmen," I say. "Very very good."

Over the past few days, I've caught myself slipping into the rhythmic speech some locals use. I have no idea why. Short of it being proof that I'm possibly a culturally insensitive dick, I guess.

Despite its frequency, the cricket talk isn't entirely unwelcome. It's inclusive, provides an easy ice breaker, and always brings out the best in people. Maintaining that spirit, I pull out one of the Don Bradman coins that I now carry at all times in my money belt, instead of my backpack.

Without a word of explanation, I pass the coin to Vijay. The curious crowd huddles close, their eyes focused on the loose change. Vijay says something in Hindi, and I hear the words 'Australia' and 'Bradman'. Several men look up and reassess me. They glance at my creased cargo pants, and dirty white runners, leaving me to wonder if they think I'm a famous Australian cricketer who's down on his luck. Or worse, a New Zealand cricket player.

Vijay holds the coin up. "Chris, in rupees how much is this?"

"Probably about ten rupees."

He gives this some thought, then asks: "Can I keep it?"

I silently curse myself for once again showing the coins to adults, but agree to relinquish it to Vijay.

Overjoyed and appreciative, he pulls a small notebook from his pocket and flips it open to a blank page, then he hands it, and a pen to me.

"Please sign," he instructs.

"Sign?"

"Yes, autograph, please."

I laugh but it soon becomes apparent that Vijay is actually serious, so I dutifully scrawl my name with a flourish like a minor celebrity. Half a dozen heads crane in to study my penmanship, and suddenly I am obliged to vigorously shake half a dozen hands.

The scene couldn't be more surreal.

There are head bobbles, smiles, and earnest looks as the men pass the twenty-cent coin between themselves. Behind me, a stunning valley vista frames a vomiting woman, who is flanked by an angry husband, and a handful of curious onlookers. Several of whom are chewing herbal travel sickness pills.

I look at the smiling Vijay, who is clutching my worthless signature.

"I will be remembering this day forever," he says gleefully.

As will I, Vijay. As will I.

Chapter Fifteen

I OPEN my hotel window and welcome a new day in Mandi. As I stare at the bland streetscape in front of me, *Lonely Planet's* five-word description immediately springs to mind: 'Mandi is no tourist town,' it states.

No shit.

At first glance, the market town looks drab and unattractive, which may explain why most travelers bypass it. Of course, *Lonely Planet* does Mandi no favors, suggesting just two tourist attractions of interest —some temples and a sunken shopping complex.

I opt for the nearest sightseeing opportunity, and soon find myself standing at the edge of a football stadium-sized excavation in the earth. A nearby sign identifies the crater as *Indira Marketplace*. Intrigued, I lean over a low concrete wall and see a sprawling multi-level subterranean shopping complex built into the wall of the cavernous abyss. It's as if someone constructed a square version of Rome's Colosseum and dropped it in a massive hole.

The four sides of the marketplace wrap around a manicured central park that features curved pathways, conical shrubs, trees with mushroom-top canopies, and a cartoonish clock tower. The view is anything but dull. In fact, it's quirky as hell, and makes me wonder if the architect was stoned, mentally unstable, or just a really big fan of Dr. Seuss.

I locate a set of stairs in the oddball mall and descend to a lower level, reaching an underground walkway lined with dozens of busy storefronts that overlook the park. With no purpose other than to kill time, I stroll the entire length of the market, stopping here and there. I buy a coffee. I buy some breakfast. I buy a pack of gum. Then, in keeping with the theme of my Dr. Seuss-like surroundings, I stop at a shop that stocks locks. Then one that hocks socks. I buy a small lock. I buy some thick socks. I buy this and that as the garden clock ticks and tocks.

After an hour, I'm bored senseless, so I bolt for the nearest exit with the intention of spending the remainder of the day in bed. But as I climb the stairwell, I am surrounded, midway, by a group of young men, who fire the usual questions at me: name, nationality, job. In perfect English, the college kids then query me about Australian immigration prospects, and career avenues for doctors and engineers. I give them optimistic answers, which are based less on fact and more on ignorance, guesswork, and well-meaning lies. These offerings of faint hope are rewarded with backslapping and an invitation to join their gang—in this case, the Mandi District Under-19 Cricket Team—for an afternoon training session. I rack my brain for an out so I can watch TV in my room, but, of course, Mandi is no fucking tourist town, so I'm stuck without a solid excuse.

THE GANG'S CHARISMATIC LEADER, Pushap, leads me onto a local sports field dotted with two dozen competent cricket players and a dozen incontinent cows. Our arrival coincides with the gruff barking of a coach, who orders players into line for inspection.

"I'll introduce you to the coach first," Pushap says, glancing warily at his trainer.

We approach the humorless man and Pushap chats to him in Hindi. After a brief exchange, the coach confronts me.

"You play competitive cricket?" he asks, showing no interest in a handshake or proper greeting.

"Not for years."

"Other sports? Football, tennis?"

"Mixed tennis a long time ago."

"Basketball?"

I shuffle self-consciously.

"Hockey? Baseball?" He's grasping at straws.

"To be honest, I haven't played any sport for about a decade."

He raises an eyebrow. "But you came to Mandi to play cricket?"

"No, I came for a vacation."

Disbelief twists his face. "In Mandi?!"

I shake my head. "I'm on my way to McLeod Ganj."

Finally, the puzzle pieces fall into place, and his lips curl into a smug smile.

"*Achha achha…* To see the Dalai Lama, huh?" His tone drips with sarcasm.

I start to answer, but he abruptly abandons our conversation and turns to the team.

"Warm up," he bellows, before directing his attention back to me. "If you want to join, please line up."

I do as I'm told and soon find myself in a routine of stretching exercises and training drills designed to test both coordination and patience. The torture ends after ten minutes, and senior players are ordered to the training pitch. The coach tosses me a cricket ball and tells me to send down a few fastballs to his best batter. I expertly mark my run-up in front of the other players, then proceed to embarrass myself by spraying several erratic deliveries in every direction, except at the actual batter.

The coach calls me over and motions for the ball. His face is grim and serious.

"I think, perhaps, you are trying too hard."

I nod and reluctantly hand him the cricket ball.

"Please wait over there," he orders, pointing to the sideline, "with the juniors."

Humiliated, I slink across the field to a sideline flanked by a dozen pre-teen boys. I sit among the kids and watch the on-field proceedings with no further involvement. It's an agonizing wait, and by the time the training session ends, I'm itching to escape back to my hotel room.

Sensing my disinterest, Pushap and his friends invite me to the clubhouse, where they buy me a Coke and a packet of chips, but refuse my attempts to reimburse them.

"You were coached for how long, Chris?" Pushap asks, as we sit in chairs alongside the other players.

I sip my cola. "Coached?"

"In cricket."

I laugh. "None! Can't you tell?"

"So this is just natural talent you have?"

I laugh again. "Mate, I couldn't even make the second-grade team in my town."

"But this must be a very large town, correct?"

"Only three thousand people."

"And how many people in Australia?" he asks.

"About twenty-five million."

"So Delhi has more people than your whole country?" He shakes his head in disbelief. "Tell me, how is it possible that Australia can produce so many good cricketers when India has fifty times more people?"

"Probably just a cultural thing. We're pretty full-on about sport."

"Yes, but I think the same can be said of my country too."

"I guess. But it feels different here," I say. "Not as aggressive."

I mull over the primal rivalries that drive Australian males—the everyday showdowns where blokes calculate where they rank against each other: who's a better fighter, who's scored the most chicks, who's got the biggest biceps, dick, paycheck, beer intake. It's a game that makes the average guy feel small and useless compared to the other over-confident, but secretly insecure, men around him. I don't see many of those kinds of aggressive, winner-takes-all fuckheads in India.

"There's a different vibe here," I continue. "You guys place more importance on education."

"Australians don't value education?"

"We do. But not like you guys. No one would admit to doing well at school in Australia. That'd be like signing your own playground death warrant."

"This is really true?"

I nod in confirmation.

"Because being intelligent means you are weak, yes?"

"Soft," I say, trying to stifle a Coke burp. "Well, that's how it was when I was growing up."

"That's interesting," says Pushap.

"Just different cultures, mate. Look at the way you guys interact. Men actually hug each other and hold hands." I note the instant change on Pushap's face and quickly add: "Which is awesome. Seriously. But we don't really do that in Australia."

"Because this is gay, right? Especially the hand-holding, yes?"

"Kinda, but… I dunno. Look, most blokes back home don't even hold hands with their wives, let alone men."

"And women like this because the men are manly?"

"You're asking the wrong man, because I wouldn't have a clue what women like."

"I think that is true for all men," Pushap says with a smile.

"I reckon you're right."

I rip open the packet of masala chips and offer them to Pushap… since he paid for them. He claws out a handful, and we both chew on the topic of our conversation in silence for a moment.

"The hand-holding here is just between best friends," Pushap explains. "It's not love."

"You don't do that with females, though?"

"No. India is very conservative about this."

"So how do you guys actually meet women?"

"Friends, parties, dating sites. Some people use *matrimonials*."

My ears prick up at the mention of the last word. I've read these personal ads in the newspapers. Some are hugely entertaining, but they give the impression that a small percentage of Indian males shouldn't be left unsupervised with sharp objects, computer keyboards, or females. The best ads, by far, are the ones that make no sense but speak volumes. For example:

> **Looking for qualified bride:** This is information given by brother, Arish. By nature he is so decent, shy, and jolly by nature. My brother really want to help every time to needy people. Every

person who sees him once really memorize that person. My family wants a suitable nature, good-looking, homely, non-working girl. Wheatish complexion. My father is sub-inspector, mother is simple housewife. Sister has done web-design course. One uncle, he is bank officer. He lives in Bihar with his family. Our family is God fearing, dipped with religious feelings. If suitable person or girl read this please contact me.

"Some people pay for sex," Pushap continues. "Do you have this in Australia?"

"Prostitution? Yeah, of course."

"This is legal?"

"Mostly. We're kinda laid-back about that stuff. The only thing we take seriously is sport."

Pushap laughs with unrestrained delight. "So in Australia, sport is more of a priority than sex?!"

"Maybe that explains our cricketing success," I say with a smirk.

"And our population," adds the grinning Indian.

Chapter Sixteen

AFTER TRADING contact details with Pushap, I stroll back to town alone. Mandi's mountainous terrain dims the afternoon to a purple dusk by the time I reach the main drag. Dinner is on my mind, so I find a table in a restaurant on the lower level of the marketplace. My meal is expensive but delicious. *Really* delicious. Possibly even worth writing home about…if you were bored enough. I am, so I venture off in search of an Internet cafe.

Outside, thick clouds have rolled in, bringing damp air and turning the night sky pitch black. The temperature has dropped, and a chill penetrates my thin surf shirt. My poor choice of cool-climate attire hasn't gone unnoticed by others. In Shimla, an Italian backpacker approached me in the street and asked if I was Australian. No greeting, just 'Excuse me, are you Australian?'

"Yeah," I replied, suspiciously. "How did you know?"

He glanced at my board shorts and t-shirt, then laughed. "Who else would wear surf clothing in the Himalayas?"

What makes that fact truly absurd is that I don't even know how to surf.

I find an Internet cafe and the owner points me towards a vacant computer. An adolescent male tries to shield a screen of porn as I approach. I sit down and log on.

I have mail.

To: Chris
Subject: Update from home

Hi Chris,
Hope your adventure is going well. A quick update from home—the show has had amazing reviews. It scored the highest rating of any TV drama debut ever!! So it looks like we have ourselves a hit. The network has green-lit a second series for next year so stay in touch because there will be episodes for you to write.

Lots of love, Elliot
PS: Emma is in Europe. Apparently, she got lucky!

I skim past the stuff about the show's popularity and the resurrection of my TV writing career, and zero in on the only line that matters.

Emma is in Europe. Apparently, she got lucky!

The words punch me in the gut and I instantly revert to my old obsessive self. Petty jealousy consumes me, and I feel the darkness from outside creep in, casting shadows on my thoughts. I want to curl up and cry.

Then the frustration arrives. Followed by anger.

Six months!

Six fucking months!!

Correction: six *non*-fucking months.

That's how long Emma refused to sleep with me. But she sleeps with someone else the very first week of her European vacation.

How could I be so stupid? She was never interested in me; she was just letting me down gently. That's why she didn't instigate anything—not the phone calls, the dinner, the kiss, or the make-out session in her car. None of it. The relentless pursuit was all me. Me spilling my guts, opening my heart, and telling her the secrets I couldn't tell anyone else. Me making myself vulnerable, soft, insipid, and weak as piss.

I feel like such a soft-cock.

Why wasn't I good enough, Emma?

Why?

I read the offending line again. I know why. I've always known why.

I was broken…and she never understood.

I raise my hands to my face and knead my forehead in frustration. My heart aches. I feel cheated. Cheated on. Betrayed. And yet…. something else bugs me. Is it karma? A double standard? Because despite embarking on this trip of 'true love' for Emma… I packed a dozen condoms, specifically, for other unplanned encounters.

So much for true love.

This thought then leads to another…

What about the night with Claire before I left Australia? Or the other women I hooked up with in Sydney while I was professing my undying love to Emma via phone calls, emails, and my big fucking mouth? Why did I do that? Did I just want sex? Or was I clinging to every single woman I met?

"I'm in love with someone at work."

That's what I callously told Claire over the phone during my first month in Sydney. My admission was met with silence. There were miles between us. And yet, I heard the unspoken question:

"Why wasn't I good enough, Chris?"

"Why?"

Because you were broken, Claire…and I never understood.

I close the internet browser. There will be no writing home. Too many thoughts in my head, but no words.

I pay for my five minutes of personal hell and walk out into the anonymity of the night. The welcome gloom swallows me as I shuffle, downcast and depressed, along the street. My progress goes unchecked until I am ambushed, beneath a streetlight, by a father walking with his small child. Armed with ice creams, they hold me up.

"Hello," the father says, extending his hand.

I shake it. "Hi."

The man angles his head towards the timid toddler and says a few words. The boy cautiously raises a hand, and I gently grasp it. When I let go, I see the doting dad smiling proudly. Nothing is said. Novelty moment over, the man lowers a trusted hand to his son, then simply turns and leads the youngster away.

From behind, the thick mountain fog and dim streetlight haze give them an ethereal, almost saintly glow. They look like the subjects of a sentimental Father's Day card—man and boy, pure and perfect. With a heavy heart, I watch them vanish into the night.

A fading memory of what could have been.

Like ghosts from a future lost.

UPRIGHT - Listen to your intuition, you know it's right.

REVERSED - Then again... isn't ignorance supposed to be bliss?

Chapter Seventeen

"THE THIRD POISON IS IGNORANCE," Dolma says.

I nod, acknowledging the middle-aged Tibetan woman sitting opposite.

"This is when we choose to only see *our* version of the truth," she continues. "We get clouded by delusions and refuse to accept reality."

Dolma's spiritual sermon is being delivered, rather appropriately, high above the common people. In this case, outside a quiet tea shack atop a mountain in Rewalsar—a holy town revered by Buddhists, Hindus, and Sikhs alike. To reach this spiritual summit, one follows an arduous path with many defined steps (possibly even a thousand of the bastards). These stairs lead pilgrims from a small lake in the village up to where I now sit. Once at this elevated level, those strong of mind and body are rewarded with a clear perspective and a fresh outlook on life.

Obviously, I don't belong up here.

"Each of these poisons blocks true happiness," Dolma continues. "And each poison leads us to sadness and depression."

Dolma is a theology lecturer at a university…and in her spare time too, apparently.

Unfortunately, the only thing I successfully passed during my multiple failed stints at university was time, which means that I'm struggling to absorb Dolma's impromptu lesson. But I think I get the gist of it.

To summarize: I've learned that Buddhists believe all human suffering arises from just three poisons—greed, hatred, and ignorance.

In point form, it translates as something like this:

a) Bad shit happens when we lust after things we *think* will make us happy.

b) Bad shit happens when we deliberately avoid experiences that make us unhappy.

c) Bad shit happens when we fail to understand the true source of happiness (hint: it comes from within).

A valid theory, but like all lectures, I'm distracted after five minutes.

It's not that I don't see the value of Dolma's teachings. I do. It's just that I'm already familiar with the content. Everyone is. After all, it's the central theme of countless fairy tales, children's stories, self-help books, and, well…lectures on happiness.

Dolma's gaze narrows on me, teacher-like. "This is what Monk Norbu specializes in," she says. "He uses tantric healing mantras to help remove the poisons from people's lives."

Two other men are with me sharing Dolma's tea, biscuits, and unpalatable truths; one is her slightly built husband, the other is an imposing granite-faced Buddhist monk. This is her brother, Norbu.

I cast an eye over the big maroon-robed unit, still unsure what to make of him. Norbu is over six-feet tall, and has the facial expression of an aggrieved member of the Yakuza. He sure as hell doesn't look like someone who dispels unhappiness with tantric healing mantras. In fact, he looks like someone who administers unhappiness with his bare hands. A happiness hitman, so to speak.

When I first saw Norbu, an hour ago, I assumed he was some rough-head local masquerading as a monk in an effort to scam gullible tourists. But I was wrong. It turns out Norbu has a full-time gig traveling the world as a chant master and mandala artist for the Dalai Lama. It also turns out that he presides over private prayer ceremonies on the top of isolated mountains. I know this for a fact because I rudely interrupted one when Dolma caught me eavesdropping near a huge boulder that was draped in Tibetan prayer flags.

"Can I help you?" she had asked pointedly.

I sheepishly stepped out from behind the rock. "Sorry, I thought you guys were a tour group."

"We're not." Her tone was sharp. "This is a private ceremony." After an awkward moment, she found her Buddhist compassion and softened. "But you're welcome to join us."

So I did. And after a short round of introductions, I watched in silence as they continued their prayer ceremony, which concluded when Norbu motioned me forward, and quietly chanted an unnervingly long prayer.

"Monk Norbu has said a *Metta* prayer for you," Dolma explained. "This is a special prayer for peace and happiness."

Good call, Norbu.

It was a kind gesture, and much needed, since I'm feeling neither happy nor at peace today—largely because Emma screwed some random guy in Europe. This unwanted development has thrown me off course in several other ways. Firstly, I struggled to maintain good-humor on the cramped bus trip to Rewalsar due to a sleepless night… because Emma screwed some random guy in Europe. Then, my walk up the mountain was compromised because I forgot to eat breakfast or bring drinking water. Now, as a rule, I wouldn't normally forget a detail like eating and drinking…but Emma screwed some random guy in Europe.

I know it's dumb to let Emma consume me like this, but I'm hardly the only lost soul wandering Rewalsar. In fact, the village attracts tens of thousands of deluded pilgrims each year, most of whom are here to pay their respects to a man known as the 'second Buddha'.

According to local legend, this tantric guru holed up in a nearby cave with the King of Mandi's daughter. And it was in this cave that the Buddhist master helped the princess reach enlightenment by filling her void with his, umm… special tantric healing scroll. Of course, when the king cottoned onto this carnal caper, he went bat-shit crazy, and immediately condemned the guru and his daughter to a fiery death.

And that's the end of the story.

Actually, it's not. Because like all good spiritual myths a miracle needs to occur. In this case, the deadly fire that had engulfed the two lovers miraculously extinguished itself. And when the smoke cleared, it revealed a pristine lake. And floating atop that pristine lake was a beautiful lotus flower. And standing unharmed atop that beautiful lotus flower was the beautiful princess and her guru.

Unsurprisingly, the sight of all of this pristine beauty rendered the entire awestruck populace of Rewalsar speechless. Because not only had they witnessed a miracle…the lucky fuckers now had lakeside realty.

As for the king, well, he was so overwhelmed by the unexpected outcome that he gave the couple his blessing and offered them his kingdom. And everyone lived happily ever after.

Or something like that.

Thing is, I don't really know the finer details. What I can say with certainty, however, is that this love story is a big deal in Rewalsar. So much so that numerous statues of the 'second Buddha' and the princess have been erected in town. All of which serve as bait to lure lost souls hoping to *find* themselves at the top of a mountain. Oddly enough, this is exactly what happened to me. As I was scaling the hillside stairs, I had a major epiphany—I seem to be having a few of these lately—and it was this:

Emma can fuck whoever she damn well pleases.

This was immediately followed by another equally forceful emotional response. Which was this:

Emma can also go fuck herself.

I know that's a nasty thought—probably sparked by one, or possibly all three, of Dolma's poisons. But it's how I truly feel. So, from this moment forth, I'm done with the obsession. Done with unrequited love. Done with the heartache. And, finally, I'm done with Emma.

I look behind my companions, beyond their tea and biscuits, and stare at the steep *decline* that awaits me. I know I have to go back to the start—literally and metaphorically. First, down the seemingly endless stairs that cascade from mountain top to miracle lake. And, secondly, back to a time before Emma.

Neither task holds any joy.

"How are you getting back?" Dolma asks, on cue.

I point to the stairs behind her. "Same way I came up."

A look of disbelief appears on her face. "You can't walk down there. It's too far. You can ride in the car with us."

"I already have a bus ticket," I say.

Dolma leans forward and touches my hand like a mother. "I insist."

Without any further prompting, I accept her offer, and we make our way back to Mandi in their van. Surrounded by good company, the miles disappear with ease. There's barely even enough time to wear out my welcome, and even if there was, I wouldn't get a chance to say much because Dolma force-feeds me muffins, cake, and spiritual allegories.

Before I know it, we are parked outside my hotel. As I say my farewell, I sense a lightness inside me—an inner peace. Maybe Norbu's prayer has worked. All I have to do now is rid myself of Dolma's three poisons—let go of the desire, the hate, and the delusions.

And let go of Emma.

The second I crack open my hotel room door, my newfound clarity clouds over. Who am I kidding? I can't let go—of anything. I cling to everything. It's just who I am.

Unlike my Buddhist friends, I don't know how to flush out life's poisons. All I know is that I have to continue my journey toward a better future, preferably with Emma, because I can't bear to revisit my sad past with Claire.

To do that, I need to keep moving.

And follow my heart.

UPRIGHT - Spiritually wise. Listen to those who have gone before you, idiot.
REVERSED - What the hell, do your own thing. You know better. Maybe.

Chapter Eighteen

"YOU THIEVING MOTHERFUCKER!!" screams a psychotic backpacker. "You stole my fucking money!"

The accused, a mole-like bus conductor, raises a hand in feeble defense. "Sir, I promise, no thieving. I gave you the correct change."

"You did not," bellows the backpacker. "You scammed me. You fucking Indians are all the same."

It's mid-afternoon, and I've just boarded a bus in Dharamsala, a town that is home to the Dalai Lama and the geographic and political center—at least in India—of all things Tibet and Buddhism. Things like self-governance, compassion, selflessness, and understanding. All of which are apparently foreign concepts to the pair of idiots up front.

Primed for a brawl, the burly traveler shrugs off his backpack. A woven patch of the Dutch flag stitched on its hide catches my eye.

"Now give me my fucking money," he spits.

"Please, sir," squeals the conductor in fear. "You *must* be taking your seat now."

The big Dutchman inches his menacing short-cropped head towards the nervous little Indian. "You stole forty rupees and you fucking know it."

Around me, a score of passengers stare transfixed, anticipating a trade of fists. Our excitement proves premature, however, and a handful of cash appears in the ticket seller's grasp instead. The livid Dutchman snatches the notes and counts the total. Satisfied, he gathers up his pack and retreats to his seat in silence.

And with that, my journey towards a happier future resumes.

Today's leg of that trip will end a few miles up the road at a new-age nirvana known as McLeod Ganj. The hill-top hamlet is, judging by the looks of the passengers on board, a haven for holistic hippies and budding Buddhists. From my point of view, these travelers look like the kind of world citizens who have recently traded the soulless materialism of modern life for a more self-aware, back-to-basics lifestyle. One that packs snugly into, say, an expensive state-of-the-art backpack made by some socially and environmentally progressive multinational adventure company. Possibly even handmade—by underpaid workers in, well… China, for instance. The very same China that scared the Dalai Lama and half the population of McLeod Ganj out of Tibet in the first place.

Mine's a cynical worldview, I know.

Thankfully, this cynicism dissipates as we near town. The easy chat, ready laughter, and sense of camaraderie that permeates the cabin wins me over, and, unexpectedly, I find myself enjoying the company of my eclectic travel companions, many of whom come from all corners of the globe.

The bus finally reaches the ridge and pulls into a town square pock-marked with potholes. We all disembark and take in our surroundings. Several shops and eateries encroach upon us, but not much else. There are the usual cattle and canine inhabitants loitering beneath multicolored signage, but very few people. And any local resident who does pass by looks distinctly Tibetan rather than Indian.

Using landmarks around me, I try to pinpoint my location on a vague map in the *Lonely Planet*. As usual, I'm unsuccessful in my attempts at finding any sense of direction.

This is the toughest part of backpacking for me—the group arrival at a new destination and the subsequent disorientation, confusion, and alienation. I could just ask for help or advice but, as a male, those two words are missing from my vocabulary. Fortunately for me, there is one person nearby who isn't afraid of cold contact. Unfortunately for me, that person is a psychotic Dutchman.

"You looking for a guesthouse?"

"Yeah," I reply. "I'm trying to work out which road we're on."

He stands alongside me and I reluctantly angle the guidebook towards him.

"Lonely Planet is fucking shit, man. Better to find your own place."

I nod, then stupidly stare at my book, wondering whether to keep reading until this lunatic leaves or simply follow his unsolicited advice. The Dutchman doesn't budge, so I close the book and introduce myself.

Contrary to what I witnessed earlier on the bus, Marten actually seems normal. What is disturbing, however, is that he looks unnervingly like me with his cargo pants, t-shirt, and intense frown. There are lots of people like me in India. And they're either extremely intense or very ordinary.

After a brief rant about the duplicity of Indian bus conductors, Indian shop sellers, Indian police officers, and Indian people in general, Marten shuts his mouth, and we head off in search of a suitable home. By the time we near the end of our chosen rutted road, Marten has dismissed every single guesthouse as being too dirty, too damp, or too expensive. Finally, an establishment with the right balance of slum, sanitation, and savings appears. We enter and are shown a room. The Dutchman does a reconnaissance of it with military-like scrutiny, checking light switches, pillow softness, and mattress rebound before vanishing into the bathroom.

"We have very good rooms," says the clerk over the background noise of Marten's shower test and toilet flush. "Very cheap. And if you are wanting anything else you can call for me. Personally." He gives me a knowing smile. "Maybe for good times, yes?"

I grin back until it clicks in my thick skull what he is hinting at. The clerk thinks Marten and I are lovers. Possibly looking for a threesome. I'm about to correct the clerk's misunderstanding when Marten strolls back and plants himself next to me. Right next to me. Our shoulders brushing.

"There's no fucking hot water," Marten grunts.

"Cold water only, sir," confirms the hotelier.

"How much for this room?" the Dutchman asks.

"One hundred and seventy rupees."

Marten ruminates on the figure for a second, glances at the bed, then at me. "I think we should take it, man."

My eyes widen.

We...?!

He notes my discomfort. "You okay with sharing?" He gives me an apologetic smile. "It's the only way I can afford it."

I nod unenthusiastically but remain speechless.

Marten places a hand on my shoulder. "Thanks, man."

Returning to the reception, we each pass ninety rupees to the clerk.

"I am sorry, I have no change," the man says. "Tomorrow ten-rupee change, no problem. No problem at all."

Wrong.

Big problem.

I notice Marten's face redden.

Big, big fucking problem.

"YOU ARE SCAMMING US!" screams the Dutchman. "This is a fucking hotel. You must have ten fucking rupees in change."

Fear flashes on the clerk's face. "No, please, there is no change."

Marten looks to me. "See, man? You can't trust these assholes. They all lie."

"Sir, I am telling the truth. Money is in safe. See—" The clerk opens his cash drawer for inspection. "Please, look. Drawer is empty."

Marten peers into the empty compartment. Satisfied, he leans back. "Tomorrow," he says pointing a finger at the man. "Tomorrow you give me ten fucking rupees. No scamming, okay?"

The clerk nods a silent promise, and without further discussion, Marten strides off, leaving me with little option but to follow him back to the room.

Our room. Our single room. With the double bed. That we are sharing.

"We can find a better place tomorrow," says Marten, opening the door. "Maybe even cheaper." He turns and looks me in the eye. "What's your daily budget?"

"Depends."

"I can spend five hundred rupees a day," Marten says.

"For a room?"

"For everything. Room, food, and transport."

I do the conversion. Ten US dollars a day is unheard of.

"How the hell can you survive on that?" I ask.

"No choice, man. These fucking Indians stole all my money."

"Stole it?"

His forehead creases in anger. "Yeah, first day I got here. Gem scam."

Every guidebook warns travelers about India's infamous gem scams. As a result, only the ignorant or greedy fall for them.

"How much did you lose?"

"I don't want to say, man."

"That bad?"

"Yeah," he says solemnly. After a moment, he looks at me and says: "Five thousand US dollars."

I stare at him in disbelief. "Are you fucking serious?!"

Marten gives me a look to indicate that he is, indeed, very fucking serious.

"Indians are smart, man. World-class scammers. They know how to mess with your emotions."

He's right, they do, but it's hard to believe anyone could be stupid enough to hand over thousands of dollars to a stranger.

"I don't want to talk about it," Marten continues. "It makes me want to kill someone."

The conversation ends as Marten flops onto the double bed with my *Lonely Planet* guidebook in his hands. Marten is a 'lock it up tight' kind of guy, so I leave him to his 'time-out' and walk to the nearest window.

The view from my high vantage point extends across the rooftops of scores of brightly-colored buildings. A bell tolls, and I trace its knell to a nearby school. Raucous youngsters spill from its classrooms and into a waiting parent body that ushers them through the gate, and up a long chase of concrete steps that pass directly below my guesthouse window. As they near, several tiny faces turn upwards and wave at me. I return the gesture, triggering the kind of beaming smiles that melt a parent's heart. Repeated shouts of 'hello' immediately follow. I reply in kind, and soon a seemingly endless echo of 'hellos' crosses the narrow gulf between us.

"School kids?" asks Marten.

"Yeah, heaps of them."

I turn from the window and grab my backpack, unzip the lower compartment and retrieve a bag and a plastic hand pump.

Marten gives me a puzzled look.

"Balloons," I explain. "For balloon animals."

My roommate bounds to his feet like an excited child. "Where did you get them?"

"Brought them with me from home."

"To sell?"

"Nah, just thought kids would like them. I tried twisting a few for practice before I left, but I'm absolutely shit at it."

Marten spots the 'How to tie balloon animals' instruction booklet. "Can I look at this?"

"Yeah, go for it."

I grab a skinny balloon, breathe life into it with the pump, and knot the two-foot-long sausage. Then I fold and twist it multiple times until I'm left holding something that resembles, well, a string of shorter sausages, rather than the instruction booklet's promised outcome…which is a dog. I lean out the window and float the mangled mutt down to a passing mother and her child. The woman catches the sausage dog, smiles broadly and gifts it to her son. The child, who is ecstatic with a gift that has literally fallen from the sky, holds the balloon aloft and yells out to his friends.

My heart swells. Inflates even.

Immediately, a dozen kids charge toward the boy and squeal frantically at me. Spurred on by their reactions, I quickly create another poor excuse for an animal. This time it passes as a mutant giraffe or, for those children wishing to study human anatomy, a distended intestine. I drop the deformed creature into the rabid horde below. Several kids maul it upon arrival, and an inevitable *pop* follows.

The kids scream for a replacement, so I grab another balloon and set to work. In quick succession, I make another giraffe, another dog. One after another, they go out the window. Behind me, I hear Marten describing the scene in Dutch for the benefit of a video recording.

I turn towards his camera and grin like an idiot. "I'm going downstairs."

I race outside, skirt the base of the guesthouse, and find the waiting mob. The kids instantly spot the balloons in my hand and quickly jostle me against the wall.

"Who wants a dog?" I yell, sounding like one of those effervescent hosts of children's TV.

Half a dozen hands paw the air. Some of which belong to the mothers. I blow up balloon after balloon to satisfy demand. Clawing hands rob me of the inflated lengths before I can even twist them into any shape, and in no time, I burn through my entire supply of balloons. I look around at my handiwork. Not a single balloon looks like an actual animal…besides a snake. Nonetheless, my dwarfed disciples are delighted, which inflates my ego. Their feverish worship makes me feel larger than life.

I'm like a God to them.

More popular than Jesus.

More loved than the Dalai Lama.

Chapter Nineteen

I MUST BE A NARCISSIST.

Because I think the world revolves around me.

I'm not Robinson Crusoe on that front. Millions of people think they're more important than your average Mr. or Mrs. Ordinary. The one crucial difference with me, however, is that I've spent my entire life thinking I wasn't just *more* important than everyone else; I also believed I was destined for greatness. And I based this idiocy on one simple belief: I thought I was *special*.

In fact, I was certain I occupied a rung on the evolutionary ladder above the rest of humanity. It was on this lofty pedestal of self-righteousness that I looked down on followers of religion, figures of authority, and, of course, the average brainwashed worker. From this vantage point, I cast judgment because I was convinced I was a superior being. A leader. A wise man. Possibly even a modern-day prophet and savior. Like a slightly jaded version of Jesus, or a mildly agitated reincarnation of the Dalai Lama.

At times I even believed I could be a superhero…if I did a little gym work and martial arts training. Not as a full-time gig. Christ, I'm not *that* crazy. I figured I could just do it part-time, you know, like during peak-idiocy hours on a Friday and Saturday night. Times when I could save people from violence by using, well…more violence, I guess. As a result, I envisioned that I would become famous and attract a cool moniker from the press and an adoring public. Something that branded me with that reaffirming word 'man'—like Super*man*, Spider*man*, Bat*man*. Or, in my case, Mad*man*.

Whatever the case, I knew I was destined for bigger things in life because I knew I was unique. I knew I was a *chosen* one.

Well, it turns out McLeod Ganj is full of self-obsessed fruitcakes like me.

As I walk the town's main street, my attention is drawn to a number of these self-involved yet well-meaning freaks. Some are shy souls searching for a cause that needs them, while others are overconfident vagabonds who seek to cure the world's ills with either socialism, spiritualism, and spliffs. Or all three.

As is often the case in India, these people believe such higher-plane insights can only be attained by those who are truly enlightened. In other words, by those who have experienced the *real* India. (Which I'm now convinced is a fantasy land located behind a demarcation line that excludes *all* of the country's mainstream tourist attractions…but *none* of its cool cafes, German bakeries, or yoga retreats.)

In reality, McLeod Ganj isn't a full-strength Indian experience either—it's 'India Lite'. Which is a watered-down, Buddhist brew that is like Kool-Aid for backpackers. Despite my cynicism, I do actually like the town. Unlike India's usual chaos of noise and crowds, McLeod Ganj wraps newcomers in a postcard-perfect Himalayan view, complete with prominent snow-lined peaks. It's also truly eclectic; a place of relaxation for Indian tourists, a home for devoted Buddhists, and a hideout for wannabe hippie empaths (most of whom are intoxicated Israelis or newly graduated gap-year kids who are on a journey to consciousness, enlightenment, or wherever it is that a community of depressives go to reaffirm their collective uniqueness—besides art college and drama school).

There are countless signs of personal growth here too.

On every noticeboard, well-designed flyers and handwritten notes promote yoga retreats, cooking lessons, massage courses, healing ceremonies, and meditation workshops. There's even life guidance in the form of horoscope, numerology, and tarot readings. Staring at these boards is like perusing an alternative McDonald's menu. This menu advertises a mega-combo deal of cherry-picked, spiritual fast-fixes guaranteed to satiate the eternally and internally starved Westerner: a quick Eastern snack of spirituality to be consumed in the name of betterment. Not a better *world*, of course…just a better *self*.

To a new arrival like me, this kind of 'mainstreaming of the alternative' makes the town seem like earth's epicenter of self-improvement. In fact, if you judged the town by the number of self-growth ads on the noticeboards or self-help titles in the bookshops, you could be forgiven for thinking that McLeod Ganj was inhabited by the most useless, emotionally incapacitated humans on the planet. The fact that I've found my way here isn't lost on me.

Thankfully, it's these very souls who give the village much of its charm. Far from being despised, their alternative worldview and eccentricity are embraced by the town's locals. Consequently, nothing here resembles normal life as I know it. Out on the streets, old Buddhist nuns twirl prayer wheels, young monks rock brand-name sneakers, and Tibetan vendors peddle crafts so colorful they'd make Bob Marley look monochrome in comparison. It's an odd human tapestry that results in a rainbow cake of spiritualism, social justice, and souvenir sales—all of which are sought, shouted, or sold via prayer, political activism, or profiteering, from a not-so *free* Tibet.

Truth is, I didn't come to McLeod Ganj to interact with any of these people or find self-awakening via the teachings of Buddhism. If I'm honest with myself, I have to admit that I only came for one reason—to see the Dalai Lama.

Not 'see' him as in 'seek a private audience'. I mean, just glimpse him in the flesh, so that I can go back home and name drop like an insufferable prick to anyone who cares to listen. And by 'anyone' I mean Emma.

But that's not all.

There's one other reason why I'm here. And this drills deep to the heart of my messiah complex. There's actually a part of me that is convinced that the Dalai Lama will sense my presence here. That he'll acknowledge my unique identity with a wink and a knowing smile, thus confirming that I'm not a lost cause. I'm just a misunderstood soul who is one rung below that of deity. Much like him.

Obviously, I'm aware that this kind of thought process suggests I might not be your everyday garden-variety narcissist. I might be a full-blown lunatic too.

Like Marten.

Who, thankfully, has since moved on.

After collecting the ten rupees he was owed, the big Dutchman hot-footed it to the next Indian destination that is sure to ruin his day.

"This town sucks," he spat emphatically as we checked out of our room. "Too many fucking tourists."

After Marten bailed out, I checked into the nearest guesthouse with a view over the valley. I'm paying double what Marten and I spent, but having relaxed French, American, and British neighbors is worth every rupee.

My new neighbors are so relaxed and welcoming that I'm starting to wonder if McLeod Ganj is populated with the kind of like-minded souls who, despite their self-obsession, have moved beyond society's fixation with fame, career, or wealth, and are determined to change themselves and the world for the better. Compared to these people, I'm neither special, nor the least bit windswept and interesting. In fact, I'm just another boring, run-of-the-mill middle-class guy.

A tragic Mr. Ordinary.

Chapter Twenty

TOVA GLANCES at the two almond croissants on my plate and smiles. She has perfect teeth, perfect hair, and a perfect face.

"You have an unhealthy obsession," the Israeli beauty teases.

I redirect my smitten gaze from her perfect assets to my pastries.

"Just a sweet tooth," I say.

"And a big appetite," she adds.

My cheeks flush at her unintended sexual innuendo, prompting me to scan to the bakery for a distraction. It's not a hard task because Tova isn't the only appetizing thing here. There are lots of attractive women—slender-hipped yogis, lithe massage students, and half a dozen meditative Mediterraneans. Even Tova's best friend, Ruth, sitting beside her, could turn a six-inch eclair into a foot-long baguette with nothing more than a sultry glance.

The three of us met several days ago when we were forced to share a table at the busy bakery. Since then, we've had three breakfast dates together, which is enough to learn Tova's life story: a career in financial law, two years national service in the military, American accent from a New York grad school, world traveler, and, most importantly, single.

I have no idea what Ruth's story is. I've been too distracted.

"So, Chris," Tova says, leaning forward on her elbows, "have you decided when you're leaving?"

"No idea. Why's that?" I lift the croissant to my mouth.

She looks to her friend conspiratorially, then says: "Ruth and I have a proposition for you."

Her words cause me to draw a sharp breath mid-bite, and I inhale a portion of powdered sugar off the top of the pastry. The dust hits my windpipe, and, involuntarily, I take a deep gasp for air. The action immediately forces more sugar into my lungs, and an uncontrollable coughing fit follows. Within seconds, tears flood my eyes, making me feel as masculine as a Disney princess.

Tova and Ruth, along with the breakfast clientele around us, watch as I battle to subdue the savage attack of silken sugar on my respiratory system. Ruth offers her orange juice, I grab it but my convulsions slosh the contents onto the table. Finally, after what feels like a lifetime, I recover enough to breathe like a human, albeit one that sounds like Darth Vader with emphysema.

Tova eyes me with concern. "You okay?"

I point an accusatory finger at the evil pastry. "Powdered sugar," I rasp.

Thankfully, the girls make no further comment and the moment passes as if it were a trivial experience. But it's not, of course. It's a monstrously humiliating experience and any hope I have of impressing Tova vanishes. The feeling is all too familiar, and immediately I am transported back to a different time and place. Back to a dining experience in Sydney.

Back to a humiliating first date.

EMMA IS SITTING opposite me in her favorite Asian restaurant. She has perfect teeth, perfect hair, and a perfect face. She's so perfect that I'm filled with more first date nerves than usual.

"I'll be eating like this every day at the end of the year," says the star of my romantic fantasy.

"Restaurant meals?" I ask.

"Thai food," she clarifies. "I just booked a vacation to Phuket. Nine months and counting."

I go for the lame joke. "Are you pregnant with anticipation?"

"Well, it wouldn't be with anything else," she says, playing along. "Unless it was an immaculate conception."

The admission about her sex life triggers an awkward silence and I wonder how to fill it.

"In a bit of a drought then?"

Emma laughs. "I'm stuck in a desert!"

Once again, I find myself temporarily short of words. So, instead of talking, I moisten Emma up, by filling her glass with water. Of course, this simple act doesn't go to plan. In fact, it goes terribly not to plan. As I pick up the carafe of water, my hand begins to shake with an anxious intensity that makes me look like a Parkinson's patient with hypothermia.

"Elliot said you went to America last year," I say in an effort to distract her gaze from the agitating water.

Emma nods. "I had six weeks in New York."

I half-fill her glass then move to my own.

"Why New York?"

She picks her glass up and takes a sip. "I did a screenwriting workshop."

"For six weeks?" I ask.

"No. I did other stuff." A sly grin flashes on her face. "But I claimed everything on my tax return as professional development."

For the first time it dawns on me that Emma is actually a proper grown-up—one living a life of tax deductions, career development, and international travel. Which is a far cry from my recent life of unemployment benefits, tight-ass Tuesday pizza deals, and train ticket evasion. The realization of my inadequacy makes me more anxious, and leaves my throat drier than Emma's sex life. To counteract it, I reach for my brimming glass of water. My ever-increasing first date nerves makes the contents ripple violently, so I ground it rather than risk any attention-grabbing spill.

"How about you?" Emma asks. "Traveled anywhere recently?"

"No, it's been a weird couple of years."

Her eyebrows rise in anticipation. "Sounds intriguing. Weird in what way?"

"Just the usual relationship dramas," I say, dismissing the topic. "I did a trip around Australia when I was younger." I neglect to tell her I was in a car with my parents…and that I was fifteen.

"That's on my bucket list," she says. "After I do my overseas travel. I want to save the Australian stuff for old age. Well, *older* age," she says with a giggle.

Emma is three years older than me, but a hundred years more mature.

I frown at that thought and then, in a show of courage, try my water again. This time the glass makes it halfway to my mouth before waves break its sides. In frustration, I thrust my lips toward the rim and begin slurping at the contents like a rabid Rottweiler. Emma, unsurprisingly, watches on in alarm.

Unfortunately, this embarrassing act is just an entrée compared to the main course of utter disaster that is to come.

This feast of humiliation begins when the waitress arrives.

I order a stir-fry, but due to being consumed with so much anxiety, I fail to notice what Emma orders. I also fail to observe normal dining etiquette when my meal arrives before hers. Instead of waiting for all the dishes to appear, I simply slide the large serving of chicken and cashew stir-fry in front of me, and begin shoveling it into my stupid face. When Emma's meal arrives, I stop, but only because I notice my grave error—not only am I eating alone, I'm eating directly from a communal platter that was meant to be *shared* with my dining companion. The gravity of my mistake truly registers once I see what Emma has ordered.

"Oh, shit!" I say, unable to look away from her food. "I'm so sorry. I didn't even think."

"It's fine," she says. "This is what I wanted to eat."

I visibly cringe. "Please don't say that."

"Seriously, it's all right." She smiles cheekily. "I wanted to start a detox."

Mortified, I raise both my hands to my face. "Holy shit, this is so embarrassing."

"I'm serious," she repeats. "It's fine."

I'm unable to let it go, so for the next fifteen minutes we eat our separate meals in an awkward and surreal silence; a silence that is broken only by the soft clang of cutlery, and the audible crunch of

Emma gnawing her way through her oversized platter…of steamed broccoli. Nothing else. Just broccoli. Piled high on a platter.

For *two*.

The scene is hilarious, in an 'Oh, god, please kill me this instant' kind of way.

Of course, even an end to that humiliating moment isn't enough to cap off the disastrous first date. Nope, that tragic moment arrives shortly after dessert when our stilted conversation turns to family.

"So what do your parents do?" I ask, wiping my mouth with a napkin.

"I don't have any," Emma says without emotion.

I laugh at her dry comedic delivery. "Are they that bad that you have to disown them?"

"No," she clarifies. "They're both dead."

The earth shifts, and suddenly my legs begin to shake in tandem with my hands. Ignoring the sensation, I look Emma directly in the eye.

"I'm so sorry. I actually thought you were joking."

"I wasn't," she says unhelpfully.

I stare at the table in shame and wrack my brain for a solution to end my agony. I settle on the most obvious, which is to pray for a stray asteroid to breach the atmosphere, smash through the restaurant's roof, and punch my stupid head deep into Earth's molten core. Of course, I'm not that lucky, so I try to shovel myself out of the shit using the very thing that buried me in it—my big mouth.

"How long ago did they—?"

"Mum passed away two years ago," she says, pre-empting me. "And Dad died when I was sixteen."

"Oh, okay… I'm so—"

"It's all right" she adds. "They were both quite old when they adopted me."

The word explodes in my head.

ADOPTED.

What the fuck…?!!

My mind tries to process the tragedy of her life: broccoli, dead parents, adoption…a date with me. Then I wonder what's taking that asteroid so long.

"Do you have any siblings?" I calmly ask.

"A brother," she says, opening up a possible exit. "But I don't really want to talk about it."

Stupidly, I ask why.

"Seriously, Chris, I'd rather not talk about it. We're estranged. So, let's leave it at that, okay?"

I apologize once again, then in silence, I absent-mindedly shift the soy sauce bottle to the center of the table. As I do, I notice that my hand is no longer shaking.

"I'm just worried about you, that's all." My voice is calm and mature.

Emma's eyes soften. "I know. But I'm fine. I can take care of myself."

"But what about—"

"But what about *you*?" she interrupts, brightly. "Are you enjoying the job?"

"Yeah, it's all good. Not really where I want to be long-term, though."

"Where do you want to be?" she asks.

"Making movies."

"Why can't you do both?" Emma asks. "Earn money from TV, then do film stuff on the side."

"Is that why you did the workshop in New York?"

She shrugs. "I'd like to write a film one day. But I'm not going to give up my day job for it."

I nod, but she sees I'm not convinced.

"Not everyone falls into the industry like you, Chris. I worked for years as a receptionist in the production office before they even let me submit a treatment. Would I like to write something more challenging? Sure, but that isn't going to pay my mortgage."

I study her with new eyes. Unkind ones that see her as a sellout.

"So you just write for money?"

"Of course. That's what you do in soapies. We're hacks. There's no time for navel-gazing. But that doesn't mean you can't flex your creative muscle on occasion."

Her transactional view on creativity doesn't sit well with me. It's too, I dunno, rational.

"So what would you do if you had ten million bucks?"

"For a job?" she asks. "Or do you mean where would I go on vacation?"

"No, I mean what would you pursue? Like what do you want in life?"

She thinks for a moment. "No amount of money can buy what I want."

"Which is?"

I stare at her, naively hoping that her answer is 'life partner' or 'true love'.

Emma's eyes meet mine. "I want my mother back," she says.

Her heartfelt admission instantly buries my selfishness and I want to apologize ten million times over. Unlike her, I've lost nothing in life, not a single friend or family member. Each waking day has been focused solely on me—my goals, my ambitions, my frustrations, my needs.

My *self*.

"I miss her every single day of my life," Emma adds.

A silent beat passes, then Emma suddenly stifles a snorting laugh. I give her a quizzical look.

"What's so funny?"

A wistful smile pulls at the edges of her mouth. "I was just remembering her response after I told her that I wasn't going to write for *Neighbours* anymore."

The recollection of the soap opera and her mother brightens her eyes, making her seem vulnerable and beautiful at the same time.

"What did she say?"

"She said, 'Thank god, now I can stop watching it.'"

We both laugh at the anecdote, and for moment life feels good.

"So, tell me about your juicy relationship drama," Emma asks, breaking the spell. "What's *that* about?"

Unlike earlier, I now welcome the change of topic, and within minutes, we are trading gossip about friends, family, and aborted past relationships. Emma's recollections are somewhat guarded. She's classy, restrained, and mature. I, however, launch into a recent relationship tale that starts lightly in the first act, builds complexity in the second, and ends with an emotional outburst in the third that climaxes with me crying uncontrollably in front of the entire restaurant. The room goes silent, and every patron turns their attention to our table. I look across at Emma. Her hands are shaking but her face is paralyzed with fear.

'Tis truly a moment of great fuckedness.

"So what do you think?" Tova asks.

I stare at her blankly. "About what?" My eyes are still moist from choking on the sugar.

"About the meditation course?" She points to a small green flyer she has proffered while my mind was elsewhere.

I focus on the paper. Her *proposition*.

Presented in Comic Sans font is a short paragraph outlining the details of a ten-day meditation retreat that forbids talking, eye contact, and sign language. Bullet points outline a daily schedule of silent torture sessions—beginning at 6 a.m. with yoga meditation, then moving onto normal meditation, eating meditation, and creative meditation.

According to the flyer, this exciting routine is spiced up with a one-hour midday siesta. Once rested, the thrills begin anew, as the entire morning routine is repeated right up until evening, when the night is ushered in with a dose of 'Yogic Sleep'.

Frankly, I've never even heard of yogic sleep, but I'm sure I'd be absolutely crap at it, given that I can't even master normal sleep.

"It's in the blue building near the school," Tova says. "You should come with us."

My gaze strays from the flyer to her eyes, lingering longer than necessary.

Tova smiles dreamily before continuing. "Imagine the peace and quiet," she says. "No reading, no music, no talking. Just ten days of silence, alone with your thoughts."

My brain tells me it sounds like hell, but my libido disagrees.

"Sounds heavenly," I say.

Chapter Twenty-One

I FOLLOW Tova and Ruth down a dirt path that leads to a lonely building with faded blue paint and rough stucco walls. The no-frills retreat has the kind of spartan appearance and amenities that are tailor-made for hardcore yoga and meditation students—or, given our present location, mistreated political prisoners. It's no luxury spa resort, that's for sure, and the prospect of paying two hundred dollars to be locked inside it for ten days almost makes me leave before we arrive.

I note expressions of faint trepidation on the girls' faces too. But, unlike me, there's also a hint of giddy excitement in their eyes. No doubt, they're more flexible—in both body and mind—than I am, because the mere thought of sitting cross-legged for more than a minute cripples me.

As we near the building, the retreat's resident guru, dressed in muscle shirt and shorts, welcomes us. He introduces himself as 'Luke' in an almost inaudible husky whisper, then welcomes us into a cracked concrete courtyard.

Sensing a potential rival for Tova's attention, I immediately size-up my competition. Luke's American, about my age, and radiates the kind of natural confidence that comes from one who has mastered a transcendental pursuit. In this case, yoga…and, knowing my luck, mountaineering, big wave surfing, tantric sex, guitar playing, Latin dancing, and the almost mystical ability to roll the perfect joint. He's also tall, handsome, and muscular.

Naturally, I hate the prick.

Luke hands each of us several information sheets. I read over the printed pages that outline the terms of our voluntary imprisonment—there's advice, warnings, and a personal liability waiver.

"Once you've filled out the paperwork, I'll show you to your dormitories." His tone is calm but firm. "And from that moment on, you'll maintain silence for the duration of your stay."

He sizes up the three of us before finally settling on Tova's figure. Jealousy stirs within me, and I wonder if the retreat's 'no contact' rule applies to instructors or just students.

Luke turns and catches me staring at him.

"This experience isn't for everyone," he continues, "It is rewarding but it's not without challenges. So read the information carefully before you sign."

Suitably spooked by his intensity and the daunting list of rules, I return to studying the document. I notice that, in addition to the vow of silence and no contact rule, there are bans on snacks, drugs, alcohol, reading, writing, music, and generally partaking in anything that might be construed as pleasure, including masturbation and sex.

Eventually, I reach the signature section.

I stall at the moment of truth and look up from the dotted line. Luke's eye-line shifts from Tova's ass to my face, his neck muscles flexing as he angles his handsome head toward me. There are so many reasons why I don't like this guy—the toned biceps, the tanned skin, the piercing blue eyes, and the not-so insubstantial bulge distorting his yoga pants. All of which Tova will inevitably become acquainted with over time.

"I don't think I'm ready for this," I finally say.

Luke looks at me grimly. "It's important to be ready," he says.

"Well, I don't think I am," I admit.

Luke gives me a knowing smile. "Can I impart some wisdom to you?"

Oh, yes, please do, you patronizing asshole, I think to myself.

"You won't find inner peace here." The San Diego Sage draws out the words for full guru effect. "You need to have that within you."

"I'll give it a miss then," I say, wondering which self-help book his platitude was lifted from. "Because inner peace is the last thing I have inside me at the moment."

He takes the unsigned forms from me. "That's probably a wise decision."

Tova tunes in. "You're not staying?" Her tone is flat—with disappointment, I hope.

I shake my head. "I can't do ten days of silence."

"You sure?"

"Positive. But I'll see you guys after you finish."

I wait for her to try to change my mind. But she doesn't.

After an awkward beat, I say goodbye, then self-consciously abandon them. The weight of my decision settles as soon as I leave the courtyard, and any anxiety turns to relief. I take a deep breath, grateful for my escape. As usual, quitting feels like victory instead of failure.

I ruminate on this telling fact for several minutes, until I stroll past a building that houses a not-for-profit organization devoted to educating political prisoners. Out front, a sandwich board proclaims their mission as 'Healing and rehabilitating those who have endured mental and physical torture in Tibet'. Beneath that, a handwritten addition says 'Conversational English volunteers needed—no experience necessary'. I pause, struck by the contrast between the meditation retreat's solitary silence and this call for connection. I let that sit with me for a moment, simplifying the message in my head.

Communication as therapy.

Instead of quiet.

Any fool welcome.

Crossing the threshold of my usual indecision, I enter the building. Inside, an eclectic bunch of travelers are engaged in friendly discussion. Some dressed in jeans, others in yoga or cargo pants. The atmosphere radiates an emotional warmth that is unmistakably community-minded, not exactly church-like, but definitely charitable.

A man with kind eyes and a gentle smile approaches me from the fringe of the group, and offers an outstretched hand. I shake it and immediately note that his grip strength invites camaraderie instead of competition. Feeling at ease, I enquire about the volunteer program advertised on the sign.

"It's a relaxed affair," Tim says. "No class or curriculum. We just pair volunteers with a nun or a monk who wants to improve their English. You can chat with someone tonight if you're interested?"

The invite catches me off-guard. Unable to conjure a worthy excuse or quick get away, I agree to help the cause.

Tim smiles warmly. "Let me see who's available." He walks to a nearby counter and scans a daily planner. "Trinley is free at 6 p.m. She lives in the women's residence just across the road. She has a really interesting story." He ferrets through a folder of thick envelopes, extracts one and passes it to me. "Here's a letter she wrote about her experiences in Tibet."

I tentatively open the envelope and find six photocopied pages of handwriting inside. The front and back of each folded page are filled with words that tell the nun's story.

"You can keep that," says Tim. "We use them as conversation starters because it's easier to talk about topics that are familiar to them."

I nod pleasantly while wondering how to extricate myself from this particular obligation. It's just one night, I tell myself. Not ten days. So, instead of quitting before I've begun, I decide to do something useful without personal reward. For once.

Three hours later, I find myself sharing a bed with a nun.

Chapter Twenty-Two

NUN TRINLEY GIVES me a shy smile as she readjusts her backside on the mattress.

"I read your biography."

A puzzled expression appears on the young woman's face.

"Your letter," I clarify, "about your experiences in Tibet."

She nods politely but says nothing. An awkward beat passes, with me sitting on one bed and the Buddhist nun on the single mattress opposite. Unsure of where to look, I shift my gaze from Trinley's shaved head to the slender neck and honey-toned arms that protrude from her maroon silk vest.

"You must have been very happy when you got to McLeod Ganj?"

"Yes." She nods once more. "So happy."

My closed question elicits no further response, so another drawn-out silence follows. Beyond the bedroom door, I hear the sound of several nuns giggling in the hallway; their laughter, I imagine, sparked by titillating gossip about the man in Trinley's bedroom.

"Where did you go after you escaped Tibet?" I ask, hoping this *open* question will coax a longer answer.

"Nepal," she says. "Delhi after. Then McLeod Ganj."

The brevity of her reply confirms that I'm the world's worst conversationalist. Trinley senses my discomfort.

"Sorry. My English very bad."

I shake my head in protest. "No, I should be saying sorry to you. I'm terrible at this. What if we talk about Drapchi? Is that okay?"

The mention of the notorious prison causes no visible stir, and her consent arrives with a nod. Just to be certain, I wait for the eyes in her cherubic, rose-cheeked face to meet mine. But when they do, I see two orbs that, despite their gentle appearance, appear lifeless, making me wonder how many ghosts haunt Trinley's mind

"Can you tell me what happened after the demonstration?"

Unruffled, Trinley meets the challenge, and for the next ten minutes, every mispronunciation and mangled sentence brings to life a traumatic past that makes mine look like one of entitled luxury. Her words come slowly at first, then gain strength as she recounts. I hear about the pro-independence demonstration Trinley organized with friends in Lhasa, her sudden arrest, and subsequent incarceration. All at the age of just seventeen. The tale of horror continues with her 're-education'—through hard labor and torture, through beatings for moving her lips during prayer, and through sexual assaults with electric cattle prods.

I've read it all before in her letter, but this is different. This is a first-person account of pain that Trinley can't erase from her face, despite how valiantly she tries.

To mentally survive the hardship of prison, Trinley and her friends did *years* of silent meditation, while I couldn't face the prospect of ten days, even in relative comfort.

After four years in detention, Trinley fled Tibet. Then, like thousands of persecuted Tibetans before her, she embarked on a fifteen-day trek through Nepal's snow-lined mountains to avoid recapture. Once safe in India, the refugees were invited to McLeod Ganj for an audience with the Dalai Lama.

"Were you excited to meet him?"

Trinley beams at the recollection. "So happy. I cry and cry."

"And your friends...did they come too?"

"Some, yes." She leans forward and pats the mattress I'm sitting on. "Best friend sleep here."

"The one who was in prison with you?"

"Yes, yes. You can meet." Trinley moves to the door and summons her friend.

Seconds later, a tall, thin nun appears, and I am introduced to Lobsang. The girls sit together on Trinley's bed, and, with two against one, our roles are reversed. Suddenly, it is me who is required to answer probing questions about my life and all things Australian—kangaroos, koalas, beaches, even *Crocodile Dundee*.

It's conversational English in full flight.

After an hour, the constant rephrasing and deciphering has mentally exhausted all of us, so we call it a night. We share a moment taking photos and exchanging contact details, then I farewell the women, feeling high from the interaction.

Outside, the chill evening air numbs my face. The streets are silent, but there's traffic in my head. I zip up my *Gore-Tex* jacket and begin the walk home, my mind racing through the pitch black, trying to chase down the source of Trinley's resilience. Does her courage and strength come from faith, friendship, or self? Maybe all of the above? It's certainly not from desire, wealth, or power. That realization impacts me more than it ever has. Of course, come daybreak, I'll be back to fixating on my own needs. But right now, I'm content with less wanting, less searching, and less *me*.

Tonight I'm happy to abstain like a monk.

And end the day with thoughts of nun.

Chapter Twenty-Three

"I NEED TO GET LAID."

The Englishman looks at me in sympathy as he raises a joint in the darkness. "You and me both, mate," he replies. "We need to visit that sex ashram and fuck our way to enlightenment." He takes one final toke then flicks the butt into the night.

"Is that the Orange People place?" I ask.

"Osho," he says, slowly exhaling a thick plume of smoke. "They're down south somewhere."

It's been ten days since I arrived in McLeod Ganj. During that time, I've seen a few monasteries, gone for a hike, and interacted with a handful of humans when necessary, but mostly I've been aimlessly drifting about. There's been no yoga, no meditation, no massage courses, no volunteering, and, most troubling of all, no sex.

"Maybe I should check it out," I say, lining strands of tobacco onto a cigarette paper.

James holds out a baseball-sized sphere of hashish and I peck at the sticky resin. I place it on the loose tobacco, then try to roll it into something smokable. It's a task that is virtually impossible since I'm slightly stoned, moderately drunk, and extremely cold.

This last fact is because James and I are freezing our asses off at an open-air trance party located on the side of a rocky mountain…in the

Lower Indian Himalayas…at midnight. There are just seven other people with us, including the Israeli DJ, his spaced-out girlfriend, and two random guys who are trying to charge backpackers five bucks to enjoy what is, in all honesty, a terrible evening of entertainment. Tellingly, this is the second trance party I've attended. Run by the same people. At the same location. Both have been equally shit. Mind you, it is better than sitting in my room and playing with my dick. But only marginally better.

"What are you doing tomorrow?" James asks.

I light the smoke. "No plans."

"Party at mine if you're up for it?" he says, downing his Johnny Walker. "I got loads of Valium and Special K if you're into that."

I acknowledge the invite, but don't commit. I won't be taking Valium or ketamine with James. I barely even know the guy. We only met this evening, on the forty-five minute walk from McLeod Ganj to Bhagsu Falls. James is a nice bloke but he has a few unhealthy vices. His goal isn't to find enlightenment in India, it's to smoke as much hash as he can before jetting off to Thailand for some sex tourism.

In some ways, I envy the young Liverpudlian because he knows who he is and what he wants. He's wearing sandals, a football jersey, and has a beer gut that strains the waistband of his shorts, but he couldn't care less. Whereas myself, and every other walking paradox in McLeod Ganj, is less certain of who we are. We're in India physically, but mentally we're lost. We crave simplicity and escape from consumerism, yet we seek out cafes and concerts. We believe in free health and education, but we rebel against the systems that pay for them. We yearn for socialism or communism, but we denounce censorship and borders. And most of all, we want the world to be one big happy global community, as long as it adheres to *our* concept of order.

Christ, I'm a joyless prick sometimes.

I take a big toke of the joint then pass it to James. As he grabs it, a woman's voice interrupts my thoughts.

"Is that a joint?"

"Yeah, help yourself," says James, offering the smoke.

The woman grabs the cigarette and takes a draw. I watch the expansion of her lungs push her breasts against a taut white top. She hands the joint back to James, then introduces herself with an accent that sounds British but also antipodean. The three of us exchange pleasantries for a few minutes before the usual topic comes up.

"How long have you guys been here?" Lisa asks.

"About two hours," I reply.

"I mean in India."

"Flew into Delhi two days ago," says James.

Lisa looks expectantly at me.

"Four weeks. You?"

"This is my first week. I came overland through Afghanistan and Pakistan."

Her courage impresses me.

"By yourself?"

"Yeah."

"Wow, you're game."

Lisa shrugs. "Africa is tougher." She grabs the joint off James again, takes another hit then hands it back. "One of you has to come dance with me."

James looks at the rock-filled paddock that is populated with two neon lights, one dim DJ, and zero ravers. "Fuck that," he laughs. "I'm not dancing out there."

"And I *can't* dance," I say sincerely, knowing full well that I possess the natural rhythm of a tormented stick insect.

Lisa grabs my arm. "Come on," she insists. "No one's watching. Just move to the beat."

I relent, letting her pull me from the granite boulder to a grassed area near the sound system. The hypnotic beat assaults my body as I feebly attempt to mimic her dance moves, and soon our limbs and torsos are pulsing like zombies trapped against an electric fence.

I hate every fucking second of it.

There isn't enough Valium in the world to dull the embarrassment I'm currently experiencing, so after a few agonizing minutes, I draw Lisa into an embrace, attempting to end the indignity. She throws her arms around my neck, and we stare into each other's dilated pupils as our hips pump to the beat. The movement awakens my numb loins and I lean in, risking a kiss. Lisa readily engages—until she becomes aware of a rigid intruder pressing against her midriff. She pulls away and studies my face for several silent seconds. Nothing is said about my erection. Eventually, she reaches forward and gently turns up the collar of my grey wind-stopper.

"You need a different jacket," she says. "This one makes you look like a dork."

My pride shrinks in an instant.

"I'm gonna get another drink."

I pull away and leave Lisa to dance by herself and stumble back to reclaim my spot on the boulder alongside James.

"Looks like you're in there, mate," he says.

I glance back at Lisa. She's dancing in the paddock by herself. Like a dork.

"I dunno. Pretty weird chick."

I take a shot of whiskey then roll myself a normal cigarette. Lisa returns after my first drag and helps herself to the whiskey bottle.

"I'm *so so* cold," she says, taking a swig.

In a show of chivalry, I take my dorky jacket off and hold it open for her.

"Here, wear this."

Lisa wriggles into the coat, suddenly unconcerned about fashion aesthetics. I zip her up and she gives me a kiss. I catch James in my peripheral vision, staring into space. His pensive profile is accompanied by a soundtrack of trance beats that don't match the imagery. The music increases in tempo, prompting Lisa to scale a large rock behind us. She starts to dance on top of it, body gyrating sexually as she looks down at me.

"Come up and dance," she implores.

Even with a semi-functional brain, I know it's a dumb idea, but my awakened libido intervenes. Ignoring reason and common sense, I scramble drunkenly up the boulder. The surface is uneven and slick with night dew. I take two steps, then, suddenly, I lose my footing and topple into darkness. Naively, I expect a soft landing in the grass, but instead my hip smashes into a jutting edge of granite mid-fall. A lifetime of hurt whips through my body like a pain orgasm as I hit the earth. Despite the numbness from hash and whiskey, the agony is off the chart. I want to throw up and cry at the same time. Clutching my side, I stagger back to James.

"You all right, mate? You look ill."

"I just fell off a rock," I say through clenched teeth.

He shakes his head. "You fucking bell-end. Hurt yourself, yeah?"

"I feel like passing out," I say, almost hyperventilating.

"Have some more hash. It'll dull the pain."

I try to quell my gag reflex as Lisa reappears beside me.

"Jesus, are you okay? You landed hard."

"Doesn't feel good. I think I'm gonna head home."

"Do you want me to come with you?"

I weigh up her offer while sucking in deep breaths to combat the pain.

"Jimbo, you okay if we bail on you?"

James gives me the thumbs up. "All good, mate. Talk tomorrow, yeah?"

Abandoning him, Lisa and I scramble down a dark track that traverses the base of the waterfall. We stumble over loose rocks and erosion ruts until we hit the dirt road that leads back to McLeod Ganj.

The slow and painful walk allows me to calm down and gives Lisa a chance to chat. Her talk is intelligent, witty, and self-assured, which, of course, makes me want to sleep with her.

That possibility won't take place in Lisa's room, however, because when we reach her guesthouse she discovers the main entrance is locked. A sign posted on the heavy timber door proclaims a midnight curfew. I check my watch. It's long after midnight. Lisa bashes on the wooden panel to rouse the manager, but her knocks go unanswered. Perplexed, she turns to me, short of ideas. It's neither the time nor place to be without shelter—it's late and cold—so I offer the only solution I can think of.

"You can stay with me if you want," I say warmly.

UPRIGHT – Love, union, alligned values. Me + U = forever.

REVERSED – Disharmony, imbalance, intensity. "It's complicated."

Chapter Twenty-Four

LISA LIFTS the Dalai Lama's *Art of Happiness* from the small tower of books on my bedside table, and reads the blurb on the back cover. Once done, she returns the Buddhist bestseller, and spots the next book in the stack.

"Ever had a reading?" she asks, raising a tome titled *How to Read the Tarot*.

My cheeks flush with embarrassment. "Once," I mutter.

"Here?"

"No, in Sydney."

The revelation takes her by surprise. "When were you in Sydney?"

"I was living there until a couple of months ago."

"Me too," she says. "Where were you working?"

I drop the name of the television network to impress her.

"Production crew?"

"Creative staff," I quickly correct. "I was a scriptwriter."

She gives me a skeptical look. "For which show?"

"Nothing you'd know. First episode only went to air last week. Where were you working?"

"At an investment bank. Doing mergers and acquisitions." She puts down the tarot guide and raises the next book in my collection. "Really?!"

I smile thinly in defense but can think of no justifiable excuse for having a copy of *Men are from Mars, Women are from Venus* in my possession. I'm guessing I have it because I lost something vital to me a year ago.

My masculinity.

I have no idea how or when this happened. All I know is that I woke up one morning and discovered I had been castrated. My manliness removed, along with my love for televised sport, cheap pizza, and daily masturbation, and replaced with an insatiable craving for sentimental movies, side salads, and self-help books.

"Any good?" she adds.

I shrug. "It's ok, I guess. I'm only a few chapters in."

Lisa puts the relationship bible back on the pile. "Mind if I use your loo?"

"Go for it."

Expecting her departure to be a prelude to something more intimate, I quickly strip to my boxers and crawl under the bed covers. After five minutes of waiting, my anticipation sours as a sheepish Lisa reappears.

"I think I might have a stomach bug."

The toilet topic would be too much information anywhere else in the world, but in India it's a regular part of backpacker conversation.

Desperate for warmth, she burrows under the covers, her back toward me. The bed creaks as I weigh my next move. It's a prime time to 'spoon' her and offer my body as a heat source, but I play it cool. On the mountain, we were two strangers body against body, lips locked, but here, in this room, we have distinct personalities and known pasts—specifically, me as an unemployed TV writer with a dubious collection of self-help books, and Lisa as an aggressive corporate raider with diarrhea.

"It's so cold," Lisa says, shivering visibly. "We're going to freeze."

"I might have a solution for that." I rub her back with my palm in an attempt to rekindle her internal fire.

Lisa shakes me off. "Your hands are like ice." She lets out a frustrated sigh. "I think I'll try my guesthouse again."

"I'm trying to warm you up."

"Please don't."

I comply, withdrawing my hands as we lie in silence. Finally, I break the quiet and ask her how long she intends to stay in McLeod Ganj.

"Three days," she replies. "Then I'm going to Delhi to catch a train to Jaisalmer. After that I fly to Nepal."

I tell her my plan to visit Amritsar, a town bordering Pakistan.

"I came through there via Lahore," she says.

"Worth checking out?"

"Not so much the city. But the flag ceremony at the border is fantastic. If you can stand the crowds."

Her review puts doubt in my mind, and I wonder about an alternative destination.

"You should come to Rajasthan with me," Lisa says.

This is the first time—excluding my bed share with Marten—that I've thought about the pros and cons of being shackled to another traveler. The upside, of course, is that I'd quite happily share a bed with Lisa, as opposed to Marten. The downside is that there's something equally reckless about her that unsettles me. It's clear, after talking to her for the last hour, that little fazes Lisa. This is a woman who did a road trip in America with a biker gang, train-tripped across Russia during winter, then ran the gauntlet of several Middle Eastern countries, alone. She's a force of nature, determined and unstoppable.

Despite some commonalities—present location and prior residence —our underlying DNA is vastly different. Unlike me, Lisa is no-nonsense and rational. She's decisive and pragmatic. And tough. She's worked as a consultant on oil rigs in the North Sea, and at chemical plants in Africa and Eastern Europe. She has multiple degrees, an international business career, and is funding her world travel with substantial savings. I, on the other hand, am traveling on dubious instinct, two high-interest credit cards, and a vague notion of what day of the week it is, which is essentially no different from my usual life back in Australia.

"I'm booking a bus ticket tomorrow," she says, turning her head toward me. "I can reserve a seat for you, if you want?"

I groan at the thought. "But then I have to go back to Delhi."

Lisa rolls onto her side and wriggles her back close to me. "Sleep on it, and let me know in the morning."

Her close proximity leaves me unsure if she wants me to snuggle into her or if she does in fact want to sleep. In Lisa's logical female mind, tiredness plus bed probably equals rest. Whereas, in my male mind, woman plus bed equals sex. I take a chance, and lightly brush my fingers against her lower back. There's no response, so I gently nudge her butt with my wrist.

Lisa twitches in annoyance. "What's wrong?"

"Nothing. Just trying to get comfortable."

"I'm not having sex with you," she says firmly. "I don't sleep with guys on the first night. I'm not that kind of girl."

I almost laugh at the cliché.

"And why would you even want to?" she continues. "I was just in the bathroom."

"Right now, I'd have sex with you in the bathroom."

"Go to sleep," she says, effectively dismissing me.

The rebuff stings, so I roll onto my back and stare at the ceiling. My brain is wired from the weed and whiskey, and sleep is elusive.

Within minutes, Lisa's breathing becomes audible, indicating that she's dozed off. Wide awake, I trace the outline of her form in the low light with my eyes. I don't even know why I want to sleep with her. Is it because I'm horny? Or is it because I want to email the news about my sexual conquest to Elliot, in the naive hope that he'll forward my exploits onto Emma?

It's both, of course.

I want sex but I also want Emma to feel like she means nothing. That she is as forgettable to me as I am to her. I want her to know that I hate her. For making me love her.

I barely complete this thought when an irrational shift in mood takes hold of me. Suddenly, I want Lisa to leave. I want Emma's sleeping silhouette beside me instead. I want to admire *her* shoulders, her back, her hips, her ass, her…

Jesus Christ, get a grip, idiot.

I'm obsessed with someone I never even slept with. I never even saw Emma nude, not even in silhouette. What kind of man thinks like this? What kind of fragile fool falls in love so easily? What kind of male believes in fairy tales, fantasies, fortune-tellers, and happily-ever-afters? A weak man. A childish man.

A boy.

I take a deep breath and try to relax. But I can't. Sparked by drugs, alcohol, and a rampant libido, my brain synapses fire in quick succession, launching me into a neurological orbit that is light years away from sleep, sobriety, or sanity. My erratic mind merges fantasy with reality in a string of chaotic thoughts. The present jumps to the future. Future slips to past. Lisa turns to Emma. And, inevitably, Emma brings me back to the woman I want to forget.

Claire.

I close my eyes in an attempt to dismiss her. But I fail. Unable to rein in the effects of the drugs and alcohol, my overactive mind spools up a memory from the past.

The scene comes back vivid and clear, like it happened yesterday.

Our first kiss.

A PENSIVE CLAIRE IS PERCHED, cross-legged, on an old recliner in the lounge room, her fair skin framed by the evening darkness beyond the bay window. Music is playing, sombre lyrics over a hypnotic electronic beat—a song of lament for a melancholy mind and heavy heart. I glimpse a CD case that proclaims itself to be something of *Substance*—an album created by a *New Order* that failed to overthrow the old rock establishment of my youth.

It's a Friday night.

But Claire is lost in her *Blue Monday*.

Not wanting to intrude, I sit on the couch furthest from her. The song finishes and I start some aimless and awkward conversation that fails to dislodge the room's solemn mood. It's obvious Claire is despondent and unapproachable, but something inside tells me to persist with a friendly advance.

I muster some uncharacteristic courage and walk over. "You look like you need a hug." I extend my arms, beckoning her. "Come on, I won't bite."

Claire shakes her head and remains seated.

"Don't worry," I say, doubling down. "It's purely platonic."

"I don't want a hug," she says flatly.

Her rejection hits hard and humiliation blooms on my cheeks.

"Just offering because you look like you need a friend."

"I don't," she says. "I just need to be left alone."

The barbed dismissal finds its mark. "Okay, leave you to it then."

Without another word, I retreat to my room, furious with both Claire and myself. I close my bedroom door and stew on what just transpired. Regrettably, I've crossed a line, and now there will be a lingering awkwardness between us as a result.

A second later, there's a knock on my bedroom door. I open it to find Claire.

"I'm sorry for being a bitch," she says gently.

My heart warms in an instant. "You weren't being a bitch."

"Yeah, I was." Her tone is laced with contrition. "I didn't mean to be. I'm just really stressed about my health."

I recall the photographs of a digestive disease she'd recently shown me. The images of horrific cancer-like ulcerations of the human bowel were confronting.

"That's why I offered the hug."

"Can I still have one?"

I pull an incredulous face. "No! That would just be weird."

"Don't worry." She grins. "It's purely platonic."

I smile at her wit, then walk over and participate in an awkward embrace that is cold and formal and, well… weird.

"That wasn't awkward, was it?!" Claire jokes.

I smile once more at her humor. Claire then departs for bed, leaving me to wonder if my feelings really are just platonic. I crawl into bed and stare at the ceiling. My thoughts tumble, attempting to grasp what my true intentions are and if Claire's mirror them. After ten minutes, I leave my room and knock on her bedroom door to make sure she really is okay.

"Can I come in for a second?"

"It's unlocked."

I edge the door open and through the darkness see Claire's outline on the bed. A full moon beyond the casement window highlights tears on her cheeks.

"Are you all right?"

The concern in my voice is real and instantly deepens when Claire suddenly starts to sob.

I walk to her side. "Hey, what's wrong?"

"I'm so scared," she says, voice quavering with emotion.

I sit on the edge of the bed to comfort her. "It's going to be okay," I say, promising the unknown. "Things will get better."

"What if they don't?"

"No offense, but you're a pretty stubborn chick. I'm pretty sure this won't beat you."

"Then why am I crying?"

"Probably because you're exhausted from being ill. Not because you're mentally weak."

Claire studies my face, which is both disconcerting and thrilling at the same time.

"Why did you want to hug me?" she asks. Her voice is quiet and calm.

"Because I care about you."

"In what way?"

I pause briefly. "In lots of ways."

We stare at one another as that monumental truth hangs in the air. After an eternity, I extend a hand and stroke Claire's forehead. Miraculously, she doesn't flinch.

"I'm not sure I need this kind of confusion at the moment," she says, but her words carry little conviction. "My life's complicated enough."

"So what would you do if I kissed you?"

"I don't know," she whispers.

Without a second thought, I lean over and gently kiss her lips. The moment hangs, electric, before passion takes over. The action marks the end of Claire and me…and the start of *us*.

The thrill of connection levitates my heart and I immediately overwhelm Claire with roaming hands, and a desperate mouth. There's no subtlety, just lust. Delirious with desire, I bombard her with affection until her defenses crumble. I move to undress her, but Claire hesitates.

"I need to get some sleep," she says finally.

Desperate for more, I try to dissuade her. Because woman plus bed equals sex.

Claire holds me at bay.

Finally, I reluctantly accept her reticence and cease the foreplay, then I kiss her good-night, gently close the door and retreat to my room.

In bed, I fantasize about Claire's body beside mine—her outline silhouetted in the moonlight. My mind races, searching for a valid reason not to go back and hold her for the rest of the night. Unable to contain my emotions, I grab pen and paper, and write a naive letter declaring my feelings. Then, like a love-struck teen, I silently pad towards her bedroom door and slide my words of love beneath it.

It takes just ten minutes for the doubt to arrive. Self-preservation kicks in, and I question why I've shown Claire all my cards. Fearing further humiliation, I return to her bedroom door and peer beneath it. My letter is still there, unopened. I pinch a corner and gather in my vulnerability.

Back in my bed, I re-read my naive words with a critical eye. The experience is harrowing. Every mortifying juvenile sentence undermines any masculine strength and highlights my fragile, over-emotional soul. Filled with shame and embarrassment, I tear the letter up, and resolve to keep my true feelings for Claire in the dark.

Forever.

In case I lose control of my heart.

In case I lose control of my life.

Chapter Twenty-Five

A REPEATED door knock disrupts my sleep.

After several nights of fractured slumber from a stomach bug that has revealed more of my inner self than I care to see, I struggle to fully rouse.

Again the knocking.

Reluctantly, I roll onto my back and open my eyes.

More knocking, this time with my name being called. Finally, I surrender, stand up, pull on a pair of *Wallace & Gromit* boxer shorts—which were a novelty birthday gift—and shuffle my aching body toward the door.

"The Dalai Lama's here!" Lisa squeals.

My light-sensitive eyes narrow in the morning sun that streams through the open door. "What…?"

"The Dalai Lama's in town," she repeats, breathlessly. "He's doing a prayer session at eleven."

A relationship has developed between us since her uneventful sleep-over two days ago. Unfortunately, it's purely platonic—just conversation, shared meals, and no chance of sex, which is a fate I wouldn't wish on my worst enemy. Ironically, my worst enemy is myself.

"What time is it?" I ask.

"Ten."

The cogs in my head grind into gear. "Shit! My bus leaves in a few hours."

"I know. I came by earlier and tried to wake you."

"Did you end up changing your ticket?" I ask.

Lisa shakes her head. "No seats left. I'm on the next bus, so you'll have to find us a guesthouse when you get to Delhi."

"One room each?" I ask, then, trying to sound casual, I add: "Or do you want to share a double?"

"Get a double," she says. Her gaze drifts to my *Wallace & Gromit* boxers and a flicker of doubt crosses her face. "Or maybe two singles. Whatever's easiest." The disturbance passes and she returns to her most pressing concern. "Do you want me to wait or should we meet at the temple?"

"You go. I need to get dressed and pack."

"Near the prayer wheels. Quarter to eleven, okay?"

I nod in agreement and watch her leave. Closing the door, I survey the disaster that is my room, then begin the process of packing; a chore that is offset by the thrill of a new adventure. Personally, I thought this moment would never come. I've been wanting to leave for the better part of a week but McLeod Ganj truly is like the clichéd *Hotel California*—it's easy to *check-out*, but harder to leave.

Once packed, I vacate my home of two weeks with a spring in my step, and merrily make my way to the temple complex. I stroll past fly-encrusted cages where Muslim butchers provide meat for Buddhists who avoid killing, past roadside drains clogged with plastic water bottles discarded by eco-minded tourists, past limbless lepers and disfigured beggars whom I ignore en route to my daily bakery breakfasts. On any other day, these hypocrisies would erode my soul. But today, I'm immune. Today, every face, shop, and sign, looks beautiful.

My awareness, and sudden acceptance, of these contradictions could be a sign of spiritual growth and maturity. But I know better. I know my blissful outlook is only due to one reason: I'm always happiest when leaving.

It's during this state of elation that I run into Tova and Ruth exiting a local cafe. I'm surprised to see them because I'd almost forgotten about their self-enforced exile. Both girls gush about their meditative rebirth as soon as they see me.

"You should have stayed," Tova says, her voice a hushed whisper. "It was life-changing."

In the way she speaks, for starters.

Ten days of silence have left Tova with an almost inaudible whisper that would escape the ears of an elephant. And although her new persona seems calm and spiritually collected, I liked the old Tova better; the one who giggled unashamedly and had animated conversations. She was effervescent, like champagne, now her personality is like bottled water—purified and still, but essentially bland and flavorless.

"I heard you were at a rave party," she says. "With a girl."

The comment makes me marvel at the scope of the Israeli backpacker grapevine. Mossad has nothing on these fuckers.

Her words are colored with an accusatory tone, but given her personality's recent slide into beige, it's not an altogether unwelcome development.

I refrain from defending myself, because, well…because I just couldn't be bothered. Tova's too far gone. She's spiritually *McDonald's-ised*—half-cooked after ten-days of meditation, seasoned with a new-found purpose, and wrapped in a thin layer of self-awareness. So I cut my losses and leave to find the rave party girl.

My heartbeat quickens when I see Lisa waiting outside the temple. Normal Lisa. Effervescent, courageous, determined, excitable Lisa. Unique Lisa.

"All packed?" she asks.

I give her a thumbs up as we fall into line behind dozens of worshippers and begin a clockwise walk around the temple's perimeter of prayer-wheels. We spin the cold, heavy cylinders with our hands until we reach a main hall where scores of bodies sit on the concrete floor, patiently waiting for their spiritual leader to arrive. Lisa and I tip-toe past the sun-weathered local faces and find a space among the pale complexions of European travelers.

Minutes later, His Holiness arrives.

Like a band groupie, I crane my neck to see the icon as he makes his way through the congregation to sit behind a microphone. His maroon and saffron robes, perversely, remind me of McDonald's corporate colors. It's an unwelcome association that threatens to cheapen the experience, so I scan the crowd around me. There's a mishmash of tourists from all walks of life but, for the first time, I see the Dalai Lama's true devotees—the Tibetans.

Many are everyday men and women of Buddhist faith, some are elders steeped in scripture, and others are monks and nuns who have committed to life-long vows. All are the real deal. These are not fast-faith customers. These are souls who draw spiritual sustenance by chewing the hard gristle of their beliefs…unlike those of us who only want to swallow the soft palatable bits.

The Dalai Lama begins his prayers, delivering them in hushed tones that enchant his audience. His words are calm, reflective, and, after thirty minutes, incredibly monotonous. By the half-way mark, my patience is well and truly tested. I'm ready to run. I can't even maintain a cross-legged pose on the floor. I'd sell my soul for a Christian's hard church pew or a Muslim's worn prayer mat.

Thankfully, after what feels like the earth's longest hour, the Nobel Peace Prize winner wraps it up, and his appreciative attendees quietly disperse into the surrounding streets. Despite their muted departure, everyone appears in high-spirits. I'm over-joyed too, and not just because the prayer session is finished. I'm happy because my McLeod Ganj tick-list is complete.

I've seen the Dalai Lama, which means I can finally check-out and leave.

Chapter Twenty-Six

OH, *shit*... I need to find a bathroom. *Fast.*

The bus door opens and I dash into Old Delhi's morning traffic in search of a half-decent guesthouse. After twenty futile minutes checking rooms, I reassess my ambitious accommodation 'want' list—no bed bugs, working air-conditioner, running hot water, lockable door—and instead focus on my present 'need': a room with a toilet.

I pay upfront for the next room I find. Then, with the urgency of a woman about to give birth, I unlock the door with fumbling fingers, bolt inside, discard my backpack, drop my pants, and charge into the bathroom. Sweet relief arrives—unfortunately, just a fraction too soon. After twelve butt-clenching hours on the bus, my sphincter gives up, and a torrent of putrid liquid tans my legs and the cream floor tiles. In horror, I slump onto the toilet seat, surveying my sickening surroundings as wave upon wave of bowel spasms punish me. The stench assaults my nose, but there's no retreat available. Finally, the stomach contractions cease and I reach for the toilet paper. But, of course, there is no toilet paper, just the usual hose and spray nozzle to wash your butt. I spray my backside and the floor, then stand unsteadily to my feet, and cautiously skate my way through the slippery mess to the shower. The ghastly task of scrubbing clean every inch of myself and the bathroom then follows.

Suffice to say, it's a pretty crappy start to the day.

One hour later, I have cleaned up the bathroom and returned from emailing Lisa the address of the guesthouse. Utterly exhausted, I slump onto the bed and let *Men are from Mars, Women are from Venus* loll me into a fitful, feverish sleep.

In a repeat of the previous morning, a relentless knocking wakes me.

"How was the trip?" I croak, opening the door.

Lisa shoulders past and drops her rucksack. "I'm shattered. Yours?"

"Truly shit," I state, without elaborating.

Lisa fans her sweat-drenched shirt. "I need a shower and some sleep."

I stay silent about the literal shit show that took place earlier.

"What have you been up to?" she asks, unpacking her toiletries. "Go anywhere?"

"No, just been shitting my insides out."

"On the bus?"

I shake my head. "On the bathroom floor."

"Great. And now I have to go in there."

Her tone isn't disgusted, just resigned, which makes me wonder if every backpacker in India has had a similar experience.

"Is it clean?" she asks.

"Probably cleaner than it's ever been. I scrubbed it for half an hour."

"What with?"

"A bar of soap. And a whole bottle of shampoo."

She cringes, then steps cautiously into the bathroom. I hear the shower run and the scent of shampoo wafts into the room, which is a lot more pleasant than the previous aroma.

Lisa emerges ten minutes later, towel-drying her hair.

"Make sense?" she asks.

I give her a vague look.

"The book. Does it explain why we're different?"

I dog-ear my page and close the book. "It explains why we're both misunderstood."

"What's to misunderstand? Women want love. Men want sex. End of book."

Her summary jogs a memory.

"Speaking of men and sex," I say. "Have you checked the browser history in the Internet cafes? There's some serious porn addiction in India."

"Can't be any worse than Pakistan. A guy ran up two grand on my credit card."

"Jesus… Did you get it back?"

She nods. "The bank covered it."

"How the hell did he spend that much on porn?"

She hangs her towel over the bathroom door and lies beside me on the mattress. "Apparently, he bought memberships to dozens of sites."

I shake my head in disbelief. "Imagine the cash you could make with a local porn site."

"Who would pay for it? It's free online."

"And yet someone ran up two grand on your credit card."

"But no one has credit cards here—that's why he used mine."

"They have cash though," I say. "Just do a membership card and sell it in Internet cafes. Make it valid for a month. Charge fifty rupees." I toss my book onto the bedside table. "How many men in India?"

"Half a billion," Lisa says.

"Get one percent of that market. Now multiply that by one U.S. dollar."

"Five hundred thousand," says the finance wiz.

"A *month*," I say, letting the figure sink in.

"Isn't porn illegal here?"

"Isn't marijuana?" I counter. "It's not an issue if the site's hosted on overseas servers."

"How come you know so much about Internet porn?" she says, a hint of suspicion in her voice.

I laugh self-consciously, then mention a school acquaintance who programs for a company raking in millions each month from online porn. Unbelievably, they don't produce any adult content, they simply buy it from others and market it.

"He could help set up something like this."

Lisa leans forward, all business. "Why don't you do it then?"

I shift uncomfortably, surprised by her enthusiasm for the idea.

"I don't have the money." Then, as an afterthought: "Plus, there's the ethics of it."

Lisa dismisses my concern. "If you don't, someone else will."

The last thing I need is someone to encourage me to do dumb shit, because, frankly, I'm more than capable of that myself. Truth is, I loathe this side of my personality—the wannabe hustler, get-rich-quick merchant who wants a life on easy street. The shady character who lives in a fantasy world where ill-gotten cash is redistributed to worthy causes like family, friends, kids with terminal illnesses, and people in need. Or my chosen charity case: Claire. Always Claire. As if me crediting her bank account could somehow debit all of my guilt.

Lisa sits up. "How much money would you need? Fifty thousand? A hundred? I'll be your silent partner."

Her offer shocks me, especially, since porn isn't my passion—it's just something I turn my hand to occasionally, so to speak.

I wave her off. "Forget it. It's a dumb idea."

"How do you know? Do a business plan. If there's something in it, prove the model locally, then scale it."

Her wildcat focus unnerves me. Lisa's unemotional business mind might be crucial to survive the male-dominated world of corporate banking, but after two weeks in a Buddhist backwater with spiritual empaths, she seems possessed by evil spirits.

I look for an exit.

"I'm sure it's harder than I make out."

"Everything worthwhile is. You just have to commit."

Like everything in life, unfortunately, I think to myself.

"I dunno."

Lisa lowers her head onto a musty pillow and reverts to her go-to solution. "Let's sleep on it," she says. She catches the glint in my eye. "Let's *go* to sleep," she clarifies. "Not sleep with each other."

With any hope of sex dashed, and a long rail journey looming, I reluctantly lie my head beside hers. We stare into each other's eyes for a moment, then, ruthlessly, I channel all my powers of telepathy and instruct her to undress, straddle my hips, and ride me like a rough overland train all the way to our next destination of Jodhpur.

Lisa shuts her eyes instead, and slips into a deep sleep.

Chapter Twenty-Seven

OUR TRAIN PULLS into Jodhpur station. It's eight o'clock in the morning and I feel like shit.

"I feel like shit," I tell Lisa needlessly.

My equally exhausted companion hoists her backpack.

"I need to find a bathroom," she says, ignoring me as she heads for the carriage door.

I shadow her brisk stride outside, then across the platform to a bench seat outside the station's restrooms. She slips off her pack and quickly disappears inside. A few minutes later, she re-emerges, relieved and visibly excited.

"They have hot showers," she exclaims.

I give her a mischievous smirk. "Wanna share one?"

She eyes me with a sardonic look. "Are you going to shit in it?"

"Haha, very funny."

A cheeky, grin appears on her face, accentuating two cute dimples on her cheeks.

"Can you watch my bag?" she asks, coaxing a change of clothes from her crammed backpack.

I nod, then watch her go.

A lifetime later, she returns, looking completely revived. Her face glows, and her shoulder-length hair—pulled into a tight ponytail—

reveals a slender neck circled by a crisp red bandana. She smells like soap and cheap shampoo, which is to say, she smells like a well-scrubbed Delhi bathroom—not the perfect perfume, but undeniably more pleasing than an *unscrubbed* Delhi bathroom.

We swap roles, and I head off for a shower.

"There's a cloakroom at the ticket office," Lisa says when I return.

"Any time limit?"

She shakes her head. "You can leave luggage all day."

This is great news since we're only in Jodhpur until a midnight train takes us to Jaisalmer, a remote desert town near the Pakistan border. With that in mind, we check our backpacks into the cloakroom and venture into the street, where the usual Indian circus of touts, traffic, and turmoil is in full swing.

Jodhpur is a paradise for addicts of soft furnishings—or, as I like to call them, 'females'—so, naturally, Lisa's priority is to sample the city's merchandise. We climb into an auto-rickshaw, and give the driver an address. The man then performs the classic Indian parlor trick of taking us everywhere but where we actually want to go.

After half an hour of frustration and angry ultimatums, we arrive at a street lined with ramshackle timber buildings. The rickety warehouses display bright piles of textiles outside—cushion covers, table runners, bedspreads, and wall hangings, all folded and stacked to create rainbow towers that lure passing shoppers.

Lisa takes the bait and reels me into a nearby store. The establishment's owner greets us with an effusive welcome, offering hot chai and a cold sales pitch. He directs us to a couch, then, with the help of an assistant, unfurls a dozen vivid items that make a kaleidoscope seem drab by comparison.

I note Lisa's besotted look. She only has eyes for what her heart truly desires, which is soft cashmere scarves, throw rugs made from vintage Rajasthani wedding dresses, sequined cushion covers, and bedspreads detailed with silver wire, embroidery, and appliqué.

She looks like a kid in a toy store.

The owner, Uday, drapes a fine pashmina shawl across Lisa's palms.

"You see this, Madam—number one quality. My best product, kept for special customers. Not sold in New York, London, or Paris. In Jodhpur only."

"It's so beautiful," Lisa gushes.

"If you like, I can make a deal," Uday says. "If you don't like, no problem. But if you like and don't buy now, then many problems. You will be having regrets for always."

Lisa nods as if hypnotized. "I like everything. But there's not enough room in my bag."

"Madam, I can ship anywhere in the world," says Uday.

"But will it arrive?" I ask cynically.

"Absolutely one hundred percent safe, sir," he says emphatically. "We do this every day."

Lisa looks to me for guidance. "What do you think?"

"Up to you." My words do little to solve her dilemma, so I try again. "What are the chances that you'll ever be back here?"

"Probably zero," she says.

"There's your answer. Go crazy while you can."

She bites her lip. "I didn't budget for this, though."

"It won't be cheaper back home," I say, knowing full well it isn't my money she's spending. "Make the most of it."

Lisa gives me a look that suggests she's swallowed an aphrodisiac that has rendered me instantly attractive. And I wonder why I didn't encourage her to go shopping a week ago, instead of trying to seduce her with my personality.

A minute later, she abandons fiscal self-control—not sexual, sadly—and I'm left to watch her repeatedly stroke lengths of fabric throughout the warehouse.

Despite my distaste for unchecked consumerism, Lisa's shopping spree brings me joy. Her ball-busting businesswoman armor has dropped, revealing a softer side. Right now, I'm seeing anything but a merger and acquisitions broker. In fact, judging by the prices she's agreeing to, I'm seeing a terribly inept negotiator. And yet, I can't help thinking that whatever sum she spends, it's a cheap price to pay to see her happy.

Deal done, Lisa signs the shipping docket with trepidation, and we head to our next destination.

When it comes to tourist attractions, Jodhpur's Mehrangarh Fort is impossible to miss. The five-hundred-year-old fortress looms over the city, standing atop a mountain of angry *terra firma* that looks like it erupted from the bowels of hell. Its stone walls tower hundreds of feet above every other dwelling, casting an ominous shadow that makes me question my earthly significance—or lack thereof. As an architectural statement it's singularly masculine and just a tad intimidating to new arrivals, which is the whole point of a fortress, I guess.

It's a different story inside the citadel. We join a palace tour and discover feminine touches everywhere—opulent apartments, gilded cradles, elaborate costumes, ancient paintings, and a heap of fancy historical stuff that I lose interest in after half an hour. Lisa's attention span drifts in unison with mine. Stifled by desert heat, travel exhaustion, and castle claustrophobia, we escape outside for fresh air. Roaming aimlessly, we stumble upon a set of handprints cast into a sandstone entrance.

Lisa sighs heavily after reading the accompanying plaque. "What is it with this country?" she asks, voice thick with emotion.

"What do you mean?"

"The way they treat women," she says.

According to the inscription, the *sati* handprints mark the sacrifice made by widows of a nineteenth-century Maharaja. After his death, his fifteen wives, draped in jewels and finery, left vermilion-stained prints on the wall, then—in an act that boggles my mind—walked through the gates and threw themselves onto the Maharaja's funeral pyre.

"It's just a historical—"

"No, it's not," Lisa snaps, before I can finish. "This stuff *still* happens here, Chris. They still burn brides." She quietens so as not to raise attention from local tourists. "And the police and courts do nothing."

From a foreigner's perspective, it seems that way. News outlets report on women being set alight in 'kitchen fires', stabbed by spurned lovers, and scarred by acid attacks. Disturbing accounts of honor killings perpetrated by family members or in-laws are in newspapers; stories of rape, domestic violence, and unpunished deaths. As an outsider, it seems Indian society is okay with this insanity—as if women must yield to the whims and advances of men.

Suddenly, a cold dread seeps into my thoughts. Was this the insanity Emma experienced with me? Is *still* experiencing? Do I really believe she's unjust for spurning me, just because I'm convinced we're meant to be? Just because I'm convinced she *belongs* with me.

Belongs *to* me.

That horrifying thought knots my gut, tightening discomfort to nauseating self-recognition.

I hate when this shit happens. I really do. I hate being confronted with truth…when I'm peddling lies. I assume all my relationships are equal, and yet I dominate and manipulate partners to my will. I encourage their dreams, yet prioritize mine. I push for open communication, yet dismiss their views.

Because I always know best.

Always.

Lisa and I walk in silence to the ramparts overlooking the city. A sea of azure houses stretches out, earning Jodhpur its 'Blue City' nickname. Exhausted by the midday sun, we squat in a sliver of shade cast by an old cannon. The heat radiating off the steel and stone is ferocious. To combat it, Lisa loosens her bandana, soaks it with water, then dampens her face. I drain my water bottle, wishing its content were iced instead of tepid.

"I think I'm done with the fort," I say.

"Me too," Lisa replies.

She lights one of the clove cigarettes she's partial to, and inhales deeply. The scent of the smoldering spice reaches me as a middle-aged Indian couple passes. The husband glares at my traveling companion, muttering tersely in his native tongue. No doubt he sees Lisa as the embodiment of everything that is disrespectful of tradition: sitting on the ground, bare skin exposed in a tank-top, smoke hanging from her mouth. She is exactly the kind of woman who he'd like to pull into line. What he doesn't see is Lisa's exhaustion, travel frustration, strong heart, and generosity—all the sensitivities and vulnerabilities that make her a woman. The things I never saw, or appreciated, in women.

I ignore the locals and write them off as ignorant, intolerant, and lacking in empathy. They continue on their way out of our lives—until the man abruptly stalls, turns his attention to Lisa, then mimes a back-handed slap. At first, I think it's a joke until I realize it's not. In an instant, a murderous anger surges through me and I want to grab the prick by the throat and launch him off the wall.

But I don't stand up to him.

Not because I'm scared, lack chivalry, or that I'm a foreigner in another man's land. I stay silent and unmoved because of an unspeakable secret:

I know I've done worse.

I'M in a duel with Claire.

It's mid-afternoon and we're in the bedroom, firing cheap shots at ten paces.

"Do you still like her?" she asks, sharply.

"As a *friend*." The last word is stressed and not just with emphasis.

"Does she know about us?"

"Of course she knows." The irritation in my voice is unmissable.

"So you told her?"

"*Yes*."

"When?"

"I dunno. Ages ago."

"And she was okay with that?"

I look at my girlfriend as if she's a fool. "Why wouldn't she be?"

"Because it's obvious that she still likes you, Chris."

I launch into defense mode. "She came over to get feedback on her writing."

Claire doesn't buy it. "What exactly did you tell her when we started seeing each other?"

"I told her that you and I were seeing each other."

"Then why is she still calling?"

"Because she's a *friend*."

Claire shakes her head emphatically. "Girls don't stay friends with an ex unless they want more."

"Crap."

"It's true. You keep giving her hope by leading her on."

"How am I leading her on?"

"You never told her that you were breaking up."

"There was no need. It just faded. We were focused on our own stuff. She wasn't hung up on me."

"How do you know?" she asks. "You showed a lot of interest at the start."

Instantly, I regret all the conversations Claire and I had back when we were just housemates.

"You used to drive two hours just to sleep with her," she continues.

"It was just sex." I want the words back as soon as they leave my mouth.

"Did Paige know that?"

There's no point arguing with Claire when she's like this. Her medications and illness are messing with her emotions. She's exhausted, irritated, and too close to the truth.

I look out the casement windows, past the chipped-paint, wishing for an escape. There's a storm brewing in here, but the day outside is perfect. Sunlight pierces the jacaranda tree, warming the *Celtic Cross* printed bedspread and touching a set of drawers topped with scented candles, incense, *potpourri*, and, disconcertingly, a framed photo of Claire's adoring parents.

"Trust me," I say, offering the *real* truth. "*Our* relationship is different."

"Because I'm your housemate?"

"No, because I share everything with you."

"You had sex in this house with her. Do you know how that feels for me?"

"I had sex with other women before Paige."

"Not here." Her distrust kicks in. "Well, not that I know of."

The comment riles me. "Jesus Christ, it was just casual sex. Everyone does it."

"I don't," she snaps. "Lots of women don't. This is why it's so hard to be with you. I don't know if I'm your girlfriend or a friend with benefits."

"Of course, you're my girlfriend."

"Is that what Paige thought? Or did you assume she knew it was casual?"

I rub my forehead in exasperation. "This just goes round and round. It doesn't even matter what I say. How about, 'Yes, Paige knew it was just sex'. Happy?"

She isn't.

"If it was just sex, why does she still contact you?"

"Are you nuts?! I told you she wanted to discuss the play she wrote."

"Explain the drunk midnight calls."

I turn my palms up, baffled. "Everyone does that."

"Only when they're hung up on someone," she says.

I stare blankly at her. She's right—I might not be sleeping with Paige, but I am fucking with her.

"I give up. What do you want me to say?"

"Can you acknowledge how hard this is for me?"

"Sure. I get it. This is hard for you." I add a damning disclaimer. "But you make it harder than it has to be."

Claire's nostrils flare.

"Because I'm the one answering her phone calls, seeing her in my house, watching her sit on the couch with you. Do you know how hard it is to trust you, knowing what you're like around women?"

A switch flicks inside me. "And what *the fuck* am I like around women, Claire?"

She flinches. "You flirt constantly."

"Seriously? Give me a fucking break."

"Have you slept with her since you've been with me?"

"What? When?" I look at her in disbelief. "When could I have slept with her? You and I hardly ever leave the house."

"What about the night you went out in her car?"

I think back to the night in question. Paige felt lonely. She wanted to go for a drive, talk about dreams and aspirations—writing, acting, music. I felt alone too, and in a moment of weakness, I wanted uncomplicated sex. But Paige refused. Out of respect. For Claire.

"You had your friends over," I say defensively.

"So what?!" she snarls.

"We couldn't hear ourselves think."

"So you left with her and made me look like an idiot," she screams. "In front of my friends."

My gaze drops to the floor like a chastised child.

"Where did you go?" she asks.

"We just drove around. Talked. Then came back."

"After you finished fucking?"

"No," I say, viciously. But what I really mean is: *How dare you keep questioning my lies*. "We came back because we ran out of things to talk about. We ran out of things to talk about years ago."

Claire begins to cry. "Then why does she still call you?"

"Because she's a *friend*."

"I don't want to do this anymore." She wipes her eyes with the heel of her palm. "I don't want to end up like her."

"Claire," I plead. "I share a house with you. I share a bed with you. I share everything in my head with—"

Claire interjects. "Then why keep her hanging on?"

"I can't just ignore her."

"You obviously still like her if you're reading her play. Otherwise, you'd give her closure."

I shake my head in exasperation. "Fuck this. I'm done. This shit is all in your head."

"It's not in my head," Claire shrieks.

"Fine. I'll tell her I'm not allowed to talk to her. Okay?"

We stare each other down and a silent beat passes.

"Would you drive two hours to see me if we weren't living together?"

"Oh, for Christ's sake, Claire. The sex wasn't even that good. Just ask her. I'm sure she'll tell you. And do you wanna know why?" I glare at my girlfriend as if she were my mortal enemy. "Because I didn't do it for her, Claire. I couldn't get her off. Are you fucking happy now?"

Silence.

Claire breaks the deadlock. "She probably didn't know where she stood. That's why."

I send her a deadly serious look. "Just leave it, okay?"

"You should call her," she says, quietly. "She's still hung up on you."

"Claire, she's not hung up on me."

"Do you know that for sure?"

"Would you stop?"

"Did you make it clear—"

"Claire—"

"—or did you let her think she had a chance? Like with me?"

"Enough, already," I warn.

Claire continues, unrelenting. "You need to call her and give her closure."

"I'm not *fucking* calling her," I bellow.

"So what do I say next time she calls?"

"Nothing," I yell. "Don't fucking say anything."

"I'm serious, what do you want me to—"

"JUST FUCKING STOP," I roar.

In a flash, I lunge forward, instantly breaching her personal space. My lover recoils in terror, but I grab her, and shove my face against hers.

"I said *fucking* STOP!!" The words seethe through my gritted teeth.

Claire's body fights my hold, her eyes flickering in distress at first, before widening in unblinking defiance. Unexpectedly, her body relaxes, and her entire being gives way to a calm, welcoming acceptance of my grasp. She presses herself into me, as if inviting the fingers of my hands to force deeper into the soft skin of her…

Neck.

Suddenly, the moment registers and the magnitude of the situation dawns on me.

I am *choking* her.

Strangling her.

In horror, I release my grip and step away.

We stare at each other.

In total silence.

Claire looks different. Like a wild animal—aggressive, defensive, cornered.

In shock, I retreat to the door, cursing repeatedly as the devastation sinks in. There's no escaping what has happened. A line has been crossed. And it was me who stepped over it.

Me.

Or was it Claire?

"Why did you push me?" I shout, slamming a palm against the door jamb. "Why do you *always* push me?!"

Claire stares at me, loathing in her face. She looks completely and utterly in control of her emotions. Terrifyingly so.

I storm into the bathroom, slam the door, and lean against the vanity. I look at the mirror, my chest heaves and my cheeks glow with fury. My dark eyes reveal an evil impossible to dismiss. I'm a portrait of wrath. A hideous identikit drawn from a bottomless well of hate for the world. An ever-burning furnace that was smoldering deep inside, but has now branded Claire's stony face, with handprints that can never be erased.

In a fit of self-loathing rage, I drive a fist through the wall. The punch explodes the fibre cement sheeting into sharp shards that lacerate the webbing between my fingers. Instantly, my hot blood runs free into the sink. I submerge the 'damned spot' under running water. The flow fails to stem the bleed, so I grab a bath towel and wrap the wound. The dull throb calms me.

But I see no way out.

I lean against the wall and slide to the floor.

An eternity passes before I am brave enough to slink into my bedroom. *My* bedroom. Unlike Claire's bedroom, where 'we' exist, my room is virtually barren. Outside of clothing, there's no piece of me here—no books, photos, pictures, or paintings. No life. No depth. No outward clue of who I am, simply because who I want to be exists only in the dreams, aspirations, and fantasies within my head; a beautiful collection of elusive future possibilities that I am convinced will one day transform my ugly present.

I lie down on the thin foam mattress, another, supposedly, temporary fixture in my life.

An hour later, Claire tentatively enters in silence, and sits at the foot of the bed. My head falls in contrition.

"I'm sorry," I murmur. "I can't believe I did that."

We search for hostility in each other, but find only self-revulsion.

"It wasn't all your fault," she says. "It takes two—"

"Please don't say that."

Even to my ears, her words sound like an attempt to bandage over the gaping truth; the one that will end our current life as we know it.

"It was me that did that," I say. "Not you."

"But I pushed you. Like you said."

Another bandage. Justification through self-blame.

"I had my hands around your throat, Bub," I say, addressing her with the pet name that we long ago bestowed upon each other in lieu of 'Hon', 'Sweetie' or 'Babe'.

"How do you know I didn't want that?" she whispers.

Her words confuse me. "That doesn't even make sense."

"Subconsciously," she says. "Maybe I wanted to feel something from you for once. Something real."

Her explanation leaves me speechless. It's almost as if we're acting out any number of domestic violence articles we've both read in newspapers and women's magazines. It takes me a full half minute to digest that horrifying fact.

Claire looks me deep in the eyes. "What are you thinking?"

"I don't know. I don't know what to say. I've fucked everything."

Claire's brow furrows with concern. "What does that mean?"

"I can't undo this. There's no going back now. You know that."

She jumps in quickly. "You just need to promise that it won't happen again."

The ultimatum sickens me, because we're fast becoming a textbook case study where Claire is the victim who won't leave, and I am the perpetrator who is forever in control.

"You don't know what it's like," she says, quietly, "to be scared of men."

Instead of prompting sympathy, her statement irritates me, and, inexplicably, I feel the urge to challenge her assumption. Once again I believe that *I'm* the wronged one in this scenario. That *I'm* the broken one. That *I'm* the victim. Not her. I want to tell her that I know exactly what it's like to be scared of men…because I've feared men since I was a little boy.

Feared *real* men.

Men who were workers and sportsmen, drinkers and jokers. Men who dominated, controlled, and demanded unquestionable respect. Men who competed on unequal footing to undermine strengths, just so they could mock weakness. Men who ridiculed the soft, the emotional or those who lacked hair on their balls. Men who branded the sensitive as girls or pussies or fagots or a mummy's boy. Men who hid insecurities with bullshit and bravado, who had chips on their shoulders and words filled with rage. Men who were taught not to love, and to fear all commitment, who built walls that were defenses, impenetrable to everything—except heartbreak and failure and alcohol-induced truths.

These are the men I've been scared of all my life.

The men who ruin boys.

The men who hurt women.

The men who scare Claire.

The men who should have known better.

Men like me.

I steal a look at the florid skin on Claire's neck. Despite my self-centered world view, it's obvious—even to someone as narcissistic as me—who the *real* victim is. The proof is before me. The evidence of wrong-doing fingerprinted on the surface for all to see. And far deeper beneath.

I note the worry on Claire's face. She looks distressed rather than frightened as she studies the blood on my hand.

"I remember something you once told me." she pauses, her eyes study mine. "You said you never wanted to be with anyone who saw your anger."

Her recollection jolts me. Because, suddenly, I realize Claire isn't scared *of* me. She's scared of *losing* me.

"I never wanted them to live in fear." My words are sullen and low. "Like my mother."

She reaches a hand out to mine. The spilled blood, now dry and cracked, begins flaking away.

"So where does that leave us?" she asks.

"I don't know," I say softly.

Claire raises her free hand towards my knitted brow, gently strokes my forehead with the soft pads of her fingertips. The tender gesture is reminiscent of my mother settling me as an anxious child, lolling me into a sleep that ushered in nightmares of a faceless man returning to kill me. The man who violently beat my mother. My namesake—Chris.

"You're not your biological father," Claire says, as if reading my mind.

Her eyes are sympathetic, loving.

"Then why did I hurt you?"

Claire stares at me for a moment, then delivers one final, unarguable, truth.

"You hurt me long before this," she says.

Chapter Twenty-Eight

IN A REPEAT of the previous day, Lisa and I arrive at our new destination feeling like crap. The platform says we're in Jaisalmer but, in the early morning gloom, I see little proof of civilization beyond the train window.

I peer down the carriage. Disheveled passengers rouse themselves from slumber amid audible yawns, morning chatter, and the reverberant growl of throats clearing phlegm. There's congestion in the aisle too, as travelers with full bladders line up for a toilet cubicle that only the desperate—or those short of sense, particularly sight and smell—would brave.

I hastily pull on my shoes, sling my backpack over a shoulder, and turn to Lisa.

"Ready to go?"

My travel-mate gives me a thumbs-up, and we disembark.

A quick walk to the station's main exit brings us into contact with a swarm of auto-rickshaw drivers. It's far too early in the morning to haggle, so we climb into the first yellow-and-black jacketed buzz-box and let the driver sting us for an over-inflated fare to the Golden Fort.

The ride is dull and uninteresting. Without daylight, Jaisalmer and its surroundings are almost invisible. There's no expansive view of the

Thar Desert or glowing vision of the eight-hundred-year-old fortress that is photographed for countless travel articles. There's just vague silhouettes in the darkness; a journey through shadows.

Our auto breaches the fort's entrance as dawn breaks, threads through several narrow, maze-like alleys, and stops at our destination. Lisa immediately notices a problem.

"This is the wrong guesthouse," she says to the driver.

"Your guesthouse closed, madam," he replies in clipped English. "Too early. This one better."

Lisa responds sharply. "Take us to the one I asked for, please."

"Madam, very best room is here." He climbs out of the cab. "Come. See."

An exasperated Lisa looks to me for help.

"May as well check it out while we're here," I say, somewhat resigned to our fate.

My answer excites the driver. "Yes, very good, sir. Please, come. Is good room. I promise."

He leads us to a cramped reception area and introduces the manager. Miraculously, the room is perfect for middle-of-the-road nomads like us—not too flashy, filthy, or fashionable. Its rustic, bohemian charm makes an immediate impact. It reminds me of the earth-walled homes I've long admired in owner-builder magazines—masculine yet feminine. Its decor is simple and homely. The floor is covered in heavy rugs, and aged tapestries hang from sandstone walls that are so thick they create nook-like window sills wide enough to lounge on. In an effort to sell the room's virtues, the manager demonstrates the firmness of the double mattress, then shows us a rudimentary yet spotlessly clean bathroom. Satisfied with our exclamations of approval, he then swings open the window shutters with a flourish, as if to seal the deal. Lisa and I draw a sharp intake of breath as a majestic view of the Great Indian Desert fills the aperture. The cost for this priceless outlook is fifteen bucks a night.

Sold on the room, we retreat to reception and pay our dues. Once done, the manager urgently instructs us to leave his presence.

"Please go, quickly," he implores, gesturing to a set of stairs that lead to a rooftop terrace. "You must see the sunrise. It is most special."

Obeying his order, we clamber upward as the sun crests the horizon. The orange orb rises above the sand and warm light spills across the desert toward us. The rays touch the living fortress's sandcastle-like bastions, turning the sandstone a brilliant gold.

My attention swings to Lisa. Her face glows in the sun. She looks radiant, content, and free of travel frustration.

"This place is amazing," she gushes.

"I could almost live here," I say.

"You should. You're a writer, you can work from anywhere."

A voice in my head disagrees. *I can't. Not without Emma.*

Sleep deprivation finally forces us from the rooftop and into our room. We flop onto the bed, staring at the exposed ceiling beams, lost in thought and sunrise-induced serotonin.

"I wanted to be a writer," Lisa says, offhandedly.

I stay quiet, sensing there's more to her story.

"When I was a kid I lived in London," she continues. "Near a huge park that had hundreds of acres of woods, and fields, and ponds." Her tone softens at the recollection. "My father and I used to spend hours there. I always wanted to write a book about our adventures."

"You should," I say.

"I will. One day."

I roll to face her. "Why not now?"

Lisa sighs. "Life. Work. Not enough time." She pauses, then, as if savoring the thrill of seeing the printed book, she says: "*On Hampstead Heath*. That's the title."

It sounds quintessentially English to my antipodean ears.

I roll onto my back again. "I couldn't think of anything worse than writing a book."

"But you're a writer."

"There's a million other things I'd rather do than write."

"So why do it?"

I cringe, recalling my embarrassing 'write or die' admission to Joe, the network's head of drama.

"Because I have to," I say, sheepishly.

"For money?" she asks. "Or because it's cathartic?"

"Door number two," I say. "Cheap therapy."

"You must be a decent writer if they hired you."

I laugh at her assumption. "My script editor would disagree."

"Is that the girl you told me about? The one you quit your job for?"

"Yeah, she was going through my script a few months back—"

Lisa cuts in. "Wait." She props herself on her right elbow. "I'm confused. When did you break up with Chloe?"

"Claire. About twelve months ago."

"So you've known this new girl for how long?"

"Eight months or so.."

I catch the bewildered expression on her face.

"Yeah, I know," I say, addressing the obvious. "I'm nuts."

Lisa's eyebrows rise. "You think?!"

I let the rhetorical question slide.

"Honestly," she continues, "from a female's perspective, it's kinda creepy that you quit your job to stalk her overseas." She waits for my excuse, but none is forthcoming. "Anyway, keep going. She was going through your script…"

I take a deep breath. "And I saw it sitting on her desk the day after. So I grabbed it when she wasn't looking—"

Lisa frowns. "So you went through her personal belongings?"

"No, it was just sitting there," I explain. "Next to her computer. Technically it was my property anyway."

"*Technically* it was the network's property," corrects the contracts lawyer.

"I wanted to see if she'd written anything complimentary."

"Did she?"

"No, she tore it apart."

"What did you expect? She's an editor. That's her job."

"I know. But I'd never experienced that before."

"Surely it wasn't that bad."

"I had a scene where a character was selling a jigsaw puzzle at a church fundraiser. But a piece was missing, which was supposed to be a metaphor for her loss. Emma hated it."

"Did she actually say she hated it?"

"She wrote 'Fucking Hell' in red pen next to the scene, followed by three giant exclamation marks."

Lisa laughs. "You'd never survive in my industry. You're too thin-skinned."

"Yeah, no shit."

"You need to learn how to be less emotional."

"I'm not built that way."

Lisa sits upright in a crossed-legged pose and stares at me. "You're a bit of a dreamer, aren't you?" It's not a compliment.

"I have my moments."

"At least you chase your dreams. I got stuck in a corporate life."

"That's fine if that's your dream."

"It's not. I want to travel full-time. I *love* traveling. Except when men max out my credit card on porn or treat me like a slut."

"You haven't slept with me so you're clearly not a slut."

"Tell that to my parents," she says. "They'd be horrified if they knew I was even sharing a room with a man."

Her comment makes me wonder if she had a strict religious upbringing.

"You know, there are worse jobs than writing," she says. "Most people don't get opportunities like that. I had to study and work for a decade to earn mine."

"I worked for mine too," I say defensively. "It didn't just fall into my lap. I was broke and writing for free." I can feel my frustration escalating. "We just have different priorities."

"Some of us have more responsibilities," Lisa says pointedly.

"Responsibilities *you* chose," I counter.

My reply draws a look of irritation from Lisa. Our motivations are different. She'll never be selfish enough to write anything. For her, there will always be something more important—a work obligation, a mortgage, a vacation, a partner. Maybe even a child. That's the difference between us—I refuse to compromise for anything, or anyone.

After a beat, the mood settles, and the edginess in the air dissipates.

"I will write my book," Lisa says. "After I save enough money."

"Good. You should."

"But I wouldn't quit my day job, in case it's unpublishable."

Her writerly self-doubt dissolves my self-righteousness.

"Well, for what it's worth, you already sound like an author."

She bites the nail on her ring finger. "Seriously, though, how do you know if your writing is any good? Besides hiring an editor."

"You don't. You just write for yourself." I pause to ensure I make my next point. "There aren't any rules. I guarantee anything you write will be better than the crap I churn out. You're smart, plus you have an interesting life. Look at what you're doing now. Do you have any idea how your life looks to someone like me?"

She stares at me, expectantly awaiting my answer.

"You're backpacking solo around the world," I say. "As a woman. Seriously, write that story. You have heaps of travel stories—hitchhiking in Africa, getting robbed in Morocco, your Hell's Angels trip in California, that Pakistani porn dude ripping you off."

She's unconvinced. "What's the point? It's all been done before."

"Then write it so you have something to look back on when you're older."

Lisa considers my advice for the full extent of time she thinks it deserves, which is approximately ten seconds.

"You could do the same," she says.

"I prefer relationship stories."

"Maybe Emma could be your new muse," she says.

"Maybe, but I think every girl is."

"So let me get this straight…you hate writing…but your new muse is a girl…who hates your writing?"

I smile weakly. "And you thought your stuff was unpublishable!"

Lisa eyes widen at the absurdity of it all. "My god, imagine how messed up you'd be if you'd actually slept with her?!"

"Tell me about it."

"Would I get a mention in a relationship story?" A twinkle appears in her eye. "Since I haven't slept with you either."

"Sleep with me and you'll get a whole chapter." I say, playing along.

"And yet Emma gets a whole book."

"Yeah, you're right. Get the red pen—I'll edit her out."

Our banter stops for a beat. Lisa stretches her neck from side to side, rolls her shoulders, then straightens her lotus position pose. She brushes her fringe aside and studies me in silence.

"You know you're chasing a mirage, right?" Her lips tighten. "She's just a fantasy."

"Yeah, I know." The admission comes out of my mouth sullen and subdued.

"What's so special about her?"

"I don't know. I guess, we just shared some stuff."

"About?"

"Personal stuff."

My vagueness brings a moment of quiet. Lisa finally breaks it.

"She's not as perfect as you think."

"That's ok. I'm not perfect either."

Her sober eyes meet mine, and I feel the need to change the subject.

"Talking about Emma doesn't solve my current problem."

Lisa tilts her head, curious. "Which is?"

"Honestly?" I hold her gaze. "Right now, I want you more than her."

A charged silence hangs in the air as Lisa sizes me up. Unsure of what to say, she's caught on the precipice of good decision and bad. Finally, her scrutinizing eyes soften, switching from sensible career woman to impulsive traveler. The sexual tension erodes her common sense, and she leans in. We kiss softly. Warmth flows from her lips, sparking further arousal. We fall into an embrace, our desperate hands begin exploring each other's bodies. Lisa grinds her pelvis against my thigh, her heat radiates through to my skin, further igniting my desire. I want her more than anything. More than freedom. More than writing. More than Emma.

Finally, we discard our clothes.

"Do you have a condom?" she asks in a breathless whisper.

I dash to my backpack, hunt through it, and return within seconds. We restart our heavy petting, then couple. Our impulsive thrusts lack rhythm at first, then our bodies relax into a sensual, easy flow. With each motion, my need for Lisa grows, rousing a primal, half-forgotten spirit within me. I sense a rebirth as her staccato cries catch the air. The shallow gasps of pleasure and pulsating spasms from

Lisa's body, gather all the stress, loneliness, and self-hate within me, ushering a release.

Finally, it arrives.

And in that singular moment of enlightenment, I rediscover a missing piece of my own puzzling life.

My masculinity.

Chapter Twenty-Nine

I WAKE up in a room bathed in harsh sunlight. I'm confused and disoriented.

I must have fallen asleep.

I check my watch. It's 9 a.m. Only three hours since sunrise, but already the bed linen is soaked with sweat and clinging to my naked back. I peel the damp sheet off and discover I'm not wearing any underwear. I spy my boxers on the floor, alongside an open condom wrapper. Finally, the pieces fall into place.

Holy shit… I had sex!

I roll over to face my lover but find an empty mattress instead. Scanning the room, I spot Lisa's nude ass. She's bent over, rummaging through her backpack.

"Whatcha doin'?"

The sound of my voice startles her and she turns around, presenting me with a full-frontal view of her breasts.

She self-consciously raises an arm to shield her nipples. "Stop staring at my boobs."

"I was *touching* them a few hours ago."

"That was different. I was distracted then."

"I can distract you now if you want." I jest, ever hopeful.

Lisa wraps a towel around her torso, scuttling all hope.

"I'm going to have a shower," she says. "Then get some breakfast. Do you want to come?"

I do indeed want to *come* but instead of slipping that juvenile piece of sexual innuendo into our conversation, I show uncharacteristic restraint and simply say 'yes' to the breakfast invite. My maturity earns an immediate dividend.

"Can you scrub my back?" Lisa asks, waving an exfoliating glove. "My pores feel like they're filled with crude oil."

I consider asking if she would like me to wash her front too, but I silence my big mouth for the greater good of, well… for the greater good of my sex life, I guess.

Lisa slips into the bathroom. I grab my own toiletries and follow. When I step in, I find her sitting on the toilet. Unfazed by my arrival, she finishes her pee, gathers her toothbrush, soap, and shampoo, and steps into the shower recess. Her movements are habitual and ordinary, yet an unexpected sense of nostalgia hits me. Out of nowhere, I recall trivial intrusions of privacy from the past. Memories of everyday bathroom and bedroom moments shared with Claire: us toweling off post-shower, me squeezing blackheads, her half-dressed make-up application, our wearing of dubious underwear that had seen better days—all the routine moments of real-life romance that seem so unattractive or insignificant. Until they are gone.

Lisa adjusts the shower's water temperature. Satisfied with the mix, she edges under the steaming cascade, savors the soaking for a minute, flicks back her saturated hair, then lathers shampoo into her locks. I watch the excess foam streak down her breasts, over her stomach, and past her thighs. The vision instantly prompts my body to siphon several cubic inches of blood from my heart and redirect it towards a lower life source.

I join her in the shower, positioning myself behind in an attempt to hide my erection. Lisa passes me the glove, oblivious to my arousal, and I dutifully rub soap into her toned shoulders, her glistening back, then her curvaceous ass. I discard the glove and gently massage the suds over her thighs, her stomach, and, finally, I glide my slippery palms over her breasts. Lisa moans agreeably and before she can say 'this feels like a clichéd low-budget porno', we are engaged in a scene reminiscent of exactly that. Unfortunately for Lisa, it's a short scene that lacks a satisfying climax. Well, at least for her.

We towel off, dress, then venture outside in search of breakfast. The fort's alleys are quieter than expected, with only a few locals and the obligatory cow. Wandering the yellow sandstone lanes, we pass stores gearing up to sell jewelry, handicrafts, desert tours, and camel safaris. I ignore the advertised bargains and extend a hand to the rubbled masonry walls. The weathered surface stimulates my fingertips, making me feel like an inquisitive child.

Our exploration ends when we reach a courtyard cafe that curiously markets itself as an Australian-owned business. We take a seat at a terrace table and order Vegemite on toast.

"Do you want to do a camel safari?" Lisa asks between bites.

"When's your flight to Nepal?"

"Wednesday. That gives me three days before I have to be back in Delhi."

"Is that enough time?"

"Maybe for a two day safari."

"We can do that, I guess," I say, even though the prospect holds no appeal.

Lisa takes a sip of her tea. "Sure you don't want to come to Nepal?"

Our impending separation meant little to me prior to us having sex this morning. But now I have more to lose.

"I won't come back to India if I leave."

"Then hang out with me in Thailand as well. You're going there anyway." She licks a fingertip, then dabs several stray crumbs of toast off her plate to eat. "When does Emma get to Thailand?"

"Four weeks."

"So what's the problem?"

"I can't afford it. I need to stay in India to make my money last."

"I'll loan you the cash."

I veto that idea immediately, because if I tie myself to Lisa I'll lose my travel independence and do whatever she wants. The truth is, I don't need Lisa. I like her. But I don't *need* her. Right now, I don't need anyone. Not Lisa. Not Claire. Not even Emma. I just need freedom.

Says the man who has had sex twice before breakfast.

My self-worth and confidence always soar after sex, and the

insecurities I feel when I'm lonely vanish. Instead of being obsessed and dependent, I become bulletproof and aloof. This is a sign that the old me is slowly returning, which, I know from experience, is both a blessing and a curse.

We finish breakfast and make a bee-line for the nearest Internet cafe to catch up with loved ones. I log into my email account, which proves to be a frustrating endeavor because when it comes to immediacy, data delivery speeds in Jaisalmer rival bottled messages floating in the Atlantic ocean.

Finally, my inbox appears. It's a barren wasteland of previously read emails. There's no contact from friends, family, Claire or Emma. Oddly, I'm unbothered by this fact. I peek over at Lisa, who is busy answering multiple enquirers. She spies me in her peripheral vision, briefly turns in my direction between keystrokes, and flashes a genuine smile. Her face is radiant and attractive, and suddenly, I feel pleasant sensations and deeper emotions coalesce inside me. I'm unsure if it's lust or love, or just the thrilling prospect of a fresh start. A new beginning, maybe? With Lisa.

I quickly shake the insanity from my head, turn back to my computer, and type four letters into the inbox search bar.

A lifetime later, the query returns a list of every email I've sent to, or received from, Emma. The result leaves me flushed with embarrassment because it's glaringly obvious that this love affair has been one-sided. The realization makes me feel like a fool, and I suddenly wish I could break free and scrub her from my life. I notice the date stamp on each message. Many emails have been sent on the same day. It's like a timeline of insanity. The embarrassment is palpable and my newfound confidence starts to slip. Unable to face anymore, I move the mouse cursor with the intent to log out. But then I stop. I redirect the cursor to the box alongside the first email. I select it. Then I select another email. Then another. And, finally, I select all the rest. Then I do what I should have done long ago.

I hit 'delete' and consign all trace of Emma to the trashcan.

Chapter Thirty

DÉJÀ VU...

I wake up in a room bathed in dim moonlight. I'm confused and disoriented.

How long have I been asleep?

I check my watch. It's midnight. Still six hours until sunrise, but already the bed linen is soaked with sweat and clinging to my naked back. I peel the damp sheet off, roll over to face my lover, but find an empty mattress instead.

Scanning the dark room, I spot Lisa's nude body perched on the wide sill of the open window. Her precarious position tightens my gut with terror. Is she suicidal? I launch myself from the bed, fearing the worst.

"What are you doing?" My voice is sharp, accusatory rather than concerned.

Lisa looks at me, surprised. "I couldn't sleep."

Outside, a pack of stray dogs bay wildly at the moon… or the sky… or the road… or whatever it is that makes Indian dogs bark continuously every single fucking night of their lives.

"Was it the dogs?"

She shakes her head. "Go back to bed." Her voice barely rises above a whisper.

"Are you ok?"

"I need some time to think."

Lisa turns her face towards the vast desert sands. I catch the moonlight reflecting off her moist cheeks.

"What's wrong?"

Lisa folds her arms across her naked breasts. "Nothing. Go back to bed."

"Not without you," I say, concerned about her mental wellbeing and physical safety.

"I just want to be left alone," she says firmly. Her words are a melancholy echo of Claire's initial *Blue Monday* rejection of me in a lounge room long ago.

"Look," I say, refusing to budge. "I need you to tell me what the hell is going on. I'm freaking out here because I'm scared you're going to jump."

"I'm not going to bloody jump," she snaps. "I just need some space. It happens sometimes, okay? Please, go back to bed."

"Is it something I did?"

"No."

A nagging thought creeps into my head: it was terrible sex, I bet. I was being a selfish fuck in the shower, literally.

"I'm not going to bed until you tell me what's wrong."

A long silence stretches between us. Finally, she turns and meets my gaze.

"I feel like a slut, okay?" Her declaration is emphatic and full of self-loathing. "I'm no better than those stray dogs."

The absurdity of the comparison makes me snort. "What? Because you slept with me?"

"Yes," she says tersely. Then, before I can respond, she begins to sob.

I reach out to comfort her but she recoils. I retreat and try a different approach.

"How can you be a slut? It's not like you slept with me the first night."

She bites her lip in an effort to stall the tears. "There's other stuff."

"What other stuff?"

"I don't want to discuss this, Chris," she says. "At least not with you."

Her dismissal stings, and a mix of anger, hurt, and frustration flares inside me, and for a fleeting moment, I entertain the thought of jumping out the window myself.

"*Please* just go back to bed," she pleads.

"How can I?" I fume. "It's the middle of the night, you're sitting on a window ledge, two floors above the ground, crying. Because you slept with me!"

"It's not because of you," Lisa spits. "It's because of *me*." She lets out an exasperated sigh. "I need you to leave me alone. I'll be fine in the morning."

Thoroughly confused, I retreat to the bed, lie down, close my eyes, and try to block out the barking dogs, the relentless desert heat, and the enigma that is my lunatic lover. It's an impossible task.

After several long minutes, Lisa comes back to bed and positions herself as far from me as possible. I extend a reassuring hand in a silent offer of comfort, but she flinches, her body hostile beneath my touch. The rebuff wounds me further, so I turn my back and deliberately create a gaping divide.

"For what it's worth," I say, desperately seeking closure. "I was trying to offer some support because I actually care about you."

My words hang in the air for an eternity.

"Just not the same way you care about Emma," she finally murmurs.

Suddenly, with the unsayable now said, I understand the broader implications of our congress.

"I don't know how I feel about anything," I offer softly. "Or anyone."

Lisa doesn't reply, so we lie in wordless isolation with our backs turned to one another, and a gulf as wide as the Thar Desert between us. The moment is oddly familiar. Like being with someone, yet feeling completely alone.

Chapter Thirty-One

RIDING a camel is like having sex with a crazy person—it seems like a perfectly good idea *before* you mount. Unfortunately, it's only *after* you mount, that you realize that camel riding—like having sex with a crazy person—is a terrible fucking idea.

I know that comparison is neither fair nor chivalrous, since Lisa is the lunatic I'm referring to, but, honestly, after her midnight meltdown, I wondered if she was even more unhinged than me. Mind you, I'm currently saddled to a female who is far more demented than Lisa. In this case, a cantankerous cow who bites, spits, and farts whenever I climb on top. And if that isn't challenging enough, her hairy hump has chafed my inner thighs raw, slapped my ass cheeks black and blue, and beaten my testicles so badly that my ball bag feels like it's gone twelve rounds with an angry octopus trained by Mike Tyson.

Suffice to say, Lisa is a far more agreeable ride.

I glance across at Lisa and her steed, then, with envious eyes, at our boyish camel driver, Sarif. Neither shows any sign of saddle soreness. Hoping to uncover a secret technique, I scrutinize Sarif's riding style. Like a dancer, the little Rajasthani's lithe torso intuitively sways, compensating for his animal's awkward gait. I try to mimic his actions but quickly give up, embarrassed by my lack of coordination. I check out Lisa's form next. Impressively, she possesses the same fluidity demonstrated by our tour guide. Either she's a natural in the saddle, or my rhythmically inconsistent bedroom rides have provided invaluable training. I attempt to catch her eye, but she is lost in her own world—a world that now excludes me, since there's been no communication since last night, and, more disconcertingly, no sex.

I wipe the dust-encrusted sweat off my forehead and divert my attention elsewhere—namely to our next stop, which is a remote desert hamlet a few miles away. The desert sun is ferocious, so the prospect of finding shady respite in the village is enticing.

When we reach the cluster of huts, Lisa and I dismount and explore the adobe buildings. The tiny round dwellings, constructed from mud brick, thatch, rough-hewn timber, and cow dung, speak of a resourcefulness born of necessity. There are dry-stone wall courtyards, and front doors fashioned from flattened cooking-oil tins. Makeshift animal pens formed with stacks of thorny branches, imprison sinewy goats. The human inhabitants attract my attention as well. Women going about their chores are draped in vibrant, printed textiles. Chunky silver necklaces and bracelets adorn their slender necks and wrists. The jewelry, a stark counterpoint to their abject poverty, creates an almost regal air. The imagery reminds me of *National Geographic* photo essays I used to pour over when I was a kid.

Sarif encourages us to photograph anything that captures our eye. I see Lisa interacting with an old man who is perched on a low stone wall. She frames his weathered face through the view-finder of her SLR camera. I focus my cheap Nikon on modest possessions—earthen stoves, bemused chickens. My snapshots capture a life without modern conveniences: No running water, electric lights, TVs or fridges, no kitchen benches, cooking appliances or Ikea tables littered with receipts for caramel lattes, green smoothies or almond croissants. There's nothing but the essentials for human survival in a desert.

Sarif finally summons us back and I reluctantly climb atop my hobbled beast to resume our excruciating journey. An hour later, our camel train arrives at a parched creek bed. Our guide instructs us to take a siesta beneath a cluster of trees while he prepares lunch. I'm grateful to stretch my legs on solid ground. Lisa, however, remains high in the saddle, her face etched with concern as she frantically searches her packs. Finally, she climbs down and approaches my animal. Saying nothing, she gives my packs a once over also.

"What's wrong?" I ask.

"I can't find my camera bag." The distress in her voice is evident. "There's five thousand dollars worth of gear in it."

"Where did you see it last?"

"I put it on the wall when I was with that old guy."

Sarif turns to Lisa. "What is wrong?"

"I left my camera bag at the village."

Alarm registers on the camel driver's face, and he swings into action.

"Quick, quick," he says, stripping weight off his camel. "We must hurry. This village is very bad for stealing. Very, very bad."

He forms a step with the upturned palms of his hands and orders Lisa to scale onto his dromedary. She obliges, settling onto the saddle. A vaulting Sarif follows.

"You stay with camels," he commands to me, as he whips his mount into motion.

The camel gallops out of the creek bed and they disappear from sight, leaving me alone in the desert silence. A touch of concern needles me because I have no idea where the hell I am. Despite hating my cranky camel with a passion, I'm suddenly grateful for its companionship. Hopefully it can lead me back to Jaisalmer if Sarif and Lisa don't return, and if not, I'll happily eat it.

After what feels like an eternity, the adventurers return. Lisa holds her arm aloft, the spoils of their village raid grasped tightly in her hand.

"Got it!" she cries victoriously as they reach the shaded creek bed.

"Very best job," gushes an excited Sarif. "Very, very best job!"

They slide off the saddle, faces flushed with adrenaline and heat stroke.

"The old man pretended he hadn't seen it," states Lisa. "Which was an outright lie." Sarif hands her a water bottle and she takes a deep swig before continuing. "I told his family I'd slit his throat if they didn't return it."

My jaw drops.

"None of them even moved." She takes another hit of the water. "So I snatched a baby from one of the mothers."

Sarif laughs hysterically. "This lady," he says, slapping his thigh. "This lady, she is very best. She hang baby upside down, like this." He reenacts a scene that resembles him holding up a skinned rabbit by its legs. "She yell, 'You give *my* baby back and I give *your* baby back.'"

Suddenly, every impression I had of Lisa being a poor business negotiator evaporates.

Sarif places a respectful hand on Lisa's shoulder. "I never forget you, Madam." His face is filled with awe. "Every time I visit that village, I never forget you."

Lisa is chuffed with his admiration. Me, less so, because I'm secretly horrified that she would use a baby as a negotiation tactic. It changes everything. Any thought of her being a possible substitute for Emma instantly vanishes because her maternal instinct came secondary to her material interest.

"So what happened after that?" I ask, somewhat dumbfounded.

"Nothing at first," Lisa says. "So I told them if they wanted their baby they could pick it up from the police station in Jaisalmer."

Sarif guffaws once again. "They bring camera back straight away."

Lisa turns serious. "Because they knew I meant it."

I have no response to that.

"We stay here one hour," Sarif says, putting us back on track. "Lunch and rest. Then go to sand dunes."

"How far are the dunes?" I ask.

"Three hours only."

It's not the answer I want to hear. However, even the thought of that unpleasant journey fails to dislodge the camera incident from my thoughts. It makes me wonder what Emma would do in that situation. And Claire? Would she grab a baby and hang it upside down?

No.

Claire would *never* sacrifice a baby. I know that for certain.

Not for a camera. Not for a break-up. Not for anything.

Not by choice.

Chapter Thirty-Two

THE DANGER REGISTERS as soon as I see it.

Etched in the sand beside our bedrolls is a trail of Nike-like *swooshes*.

"Viper," the cameleer says indifferently.

"Venomous?" I ask, alarmed by how close it has slithered to our heads during the night.

"Yes, yes. Very venomous. Many venomous snake in Jaisalmer—Viper, cobra…businessman." He chuckles at his own joke.

"Nocturnal?" I ask. My inquiry draws a blank look. "Does it hunt at night?"

"Yes. Night-time hunting only," replies Sarif. "But Cobra anytime hunting." He flashes his fangs in a broad smile. "Like businessman."

His wildlife update makes me hate desert safaris even more, but it also makes me realize that the last place I want to be, is actually the safest place to go—which is on the back of my camel.

We scoff breakfast, strike camp, then mount our mobile shag-piles in readiness for the final day of adventure. Despite the discomfort, I'm looking forward to today's trek, simply because I know it's nearly over. Lisa's enthusiasm for the monotonous desert landscape and its energy-sapping heat has diminished overnight, too.

"I'm so over this,' she comments away from Sarif. "Be glad when it ends."

Thankfully, it does. And far earlier than we expect.

After two hours of riding, we crest a dune and a paved highway appears, mirage-like, before us. Sarif orders the camels to stop and instructs us to board a waiting Jeep. I glance at my watch, it's barely 10 a.m., which somehow makes the early conclusion of our safari simultaneously feel like poor value for money *and* a million-dollar lottery win. Lisa and I smile at each other in relief, the rift between us shrinking as the Jeep ferries us back to the relative luxury of Jaisalmer's golden fort.

In need of new accommodation, we search for a place to stay. There is little vacancy within the fort, so we are forced to settle for a room that overlooks an eyesore of cluttered rooftops, aired laundry, and electricity cables. It's a huge contrast to the romantic lodgings we previously had. Eager to wash away two days of sand and sweat, we both head to the shower.

"Want me to scrub your back?" I offer helpfully.

"No," Lisa snaps, "because you'll want sex."

Her brush-off is a frustrating example of the difference between male and female libidos. Like most women, Lisa needs to be in the mood for love-making. This means she needs a compliment or two, some foreplay, and an emotional connection. In other words, Lisa needs to be in the right headspace for sex. This is entirely different to men—we only need to be breathing.

Forced to find another use for my wandering hands, I start scrubbing several cubic tons of Thar Desert off my aching body. The gritty water flows from my feet to a long drain that follows the base of a wall. Alarmingly, it trickles past a floor-level vent that offers a clear view of the shower to any pervert stationed at the reception desk one level below. I spot three such deviants ogling Lisa as she washes her hair.

"The guys downstairs can see you through the ventilation grate."

Lisa shrugs. "I don't care."

Her casual indifference confounds me, but I let it go and retreat from the shower to towel off in private.

Lisa enters the bedroom shortly after. She's still completely naked when someone knocks on the door. I wait for her to circle a towel around her torso, then partially open the door to reveal a shy adolescent cradling two fresh bath towels. I recognize him from the ventilation grate peep show.

"More towels?" he asks.

"No thanks," I say sharply. "We already have some."

I hear the scuffle and murmur of two older males on the stairwell behind him. Male instinct tells me that the unsolicited 'room service' is an opportunistic attempt to catch a closer glimpse of Lisa.

I close the door on the kid, but before I can walk away there is another knuckle rap. This time it's the guesthouse manager—a thickset thirty-something male who has ample size and confidence.

"Sorry to disturb you, sir," the man says. "Would you and madam like to join us on the rooftop this evening."

He casts a hungry eye over Lisa's exposed legs and shoulders.

"For what?" asks Lisa.

The manager forces the door open a fraction more, allowing the third male to peer over his shoulder. "For drinks and talking, madam. I have whiskey and smoke. You smoke, yes?"

"Sometimes," she replies.

The manager smiles broadly. "Madam, I have the very best ganja and opium in all Rajasthan. It would be an honor to share with you."

"What time?" she asks brightly.

I give her a withering look.

"Anytime that suits, madam."

Finally, I step in. "Thanks for the offer, mate." The man and I trade awkward smiles for a moment, then I close the door and turn on Lisa. "Surely, you don't trust these guys?"

Lisa tosses her damp towel on the bed. "They're harmless," she says, pulling on some underwear.

"They were watching you in the shower. And now you're okay to do drugs with them?"

"It's just pot, Chris," Lisa exclaims.

"And opium, Lisa."

She rolls her eyes. "Don't be such a square."

Her comment triggers me.

"Are you serious? What if it's a set-up and something bad happens?"

Her brow rises. "Wow... You're really uptight."

"Of course I am, because if anything goes wrong—" I pause as a secret fear begins to escape my lips. "—I can't protect you."

Lisa stares at me, bewildered by my sudden outburst.

"You need to chill out," she says.

It's not the advice I want to hear, because I've heard it a million times. *You need to Chill out... Relax... Calm down.* The inference always the same: *You need to act normal.*

"It's an unnecessary risk," I say defensively.

Lisa pulls on a white shirt and fans her damp hair outside the collar. "Then let's do something else," she says casually. "I'd rather go to a restaurant anyway."

"But these guys will be waiting downstairs."

"I'll tell them I've changed my mind." A grin teases her lips, then me. "Or that you're a square."

I return a half-smile, trying desperately to downplay my manic meltdown and appear semi-normal. But it's obvious that Lisa probably now wishes she hadn't had sex with a crazy person.

AFTER AN UNCOMFORTABLY HOT AFTERNOON SIESTA, we do, indeed, go to a restaurant and enjoy relaxed conversation over dinner. Meal finished, we go back to our room. It's early evening, but the desert town's ambient temperature makes it feel like we are being stewed alive in the vindaloo we just ate. Eager for relief, I switch on a fan, but India's notoriously unreliable power supply is currently on vacation. No doubt somewhere cooler. Hell probably.

Hoping to invite a nonexistent breeze in, I open every window, while Lisa lights half a dozen candles. The sunset flames on the waxed wicks imbue the room with a degree of false romance as daylight dissolves to dusk.

In preparation for a night of sweaty humidity and broken sleep, we strip naked and flop onto the bed, but any respite from discomfort is frustratingly elusive due to circling mosquitoes. Seeking a different relief, I gently trace a fingertip over Lisa's exposed stomach.

"It's too hot for that," she protests, slapping my hand away. "How can you even think about sex in this heat?"

"Just built tough, I guess," I say in jest.

She turns away, annoyed. "Go jerk off in the shower."

"What if we did it without touching?"

"What?" she huffs. "That doesn't even make sense."

The unrelenting heat has made Lisa irritated and me restless.

"How can you have sex without touching anyway?" she finally asks.

I prop myself onto an elbow, in an effort to see her face. "I meant no touching except down there. No hands. No kissing. Just eye contact."

"Sounds like some stupid tantric sex thing."

Deflated, I lower myself back onto the mattress and occupy myself by sending kamikaze mosquitoes to heaven as they stray within range. Eventually curiosity gets the better of Lisa.

"Should we try it?" she asks coyly.

I need no further invitation, and soon the sheen of sweat on our bodies turns to pools of perspiration as we engage in a session of uncomfortably awkward, yet surprisingly enjoyable intercourse.

We pull apart, and I catch Lisa's dimpled smile as candlelight shines on her sunburnt cheeks. My heart skips a beat, but I'm unsure if it's a result of the afterglow of sex or if it's something deeper. Lisa interrupts my thoughts as she tenderly strokes my bicep.

"I think I'm starting to fancy you," she murmurs, her mood softening.

I remain quiet, hesitant to echo her sentiment because I'm wary of the midnight cold shoulder, the baby hostage negotiator, and the risk-taker I can't protect. Lisa deciphers my long silence, understanding the deeper meaning of the delay. Her face hardens as she removes her hand from my arm—and in that instant our merger falters and the deal collapses.

"I think you're all right too," I say, belatedly trying to re-engage.

But I'm too late. It's past midnight on our relationship. The sun has set. The camels have gone. Our safari has ended.

Chapter Thirty-Three

DESPITE HAVING the cruising speed of a glacier, my public bus reaches the outskirts of Jaipur on schedule for its 9 p.m. arrival. After ten hours of mind-numbing desert highway, the city's lights lift every passenger's spirits. Two female backpackers, sitting several seats up, even give a celebratory cheer.

I steal a look—not for the first time—at the girls' reflections in their window. The darkness outside mirrors their profiles, allowing me to admire the kind of wholesome, youthful complexions I associate with vestal virgins, vice-free vegans, or the volunteers of some virtuous 'Save the Whales' street team. My gaze drifts from the plain backpacker to her striking friend—a woman whose long blonde hair and sharp features remind me of Robin Wright, the actress who played Buttercup in *The Princess Bride*. For the longest of minutes, I entertain the ludicrous notion that I could be her fairytale prince.

I glance around the cabin to see if anyone has noticed my ogling. Instead, I find a bus full of men, all appraising the same backpackers with varying degrees of subtlety. The girls are entirely oblivious to the attention, having only time for each other—in a hanging-with-ya-bestie, girls'-own-adventure way. Bits of their chatter drifted back to me during the long trip—talk of artists Tracey Emin and Damien Hirst, gossip about Gwyneth Paltrow, and, tragically, off-key renditions of *Spice Girls* songs. I've also heard lots of laughter. The kind that is shared between best friends. The kind that I miss.

Claire and I had that. At the start. Back in the time of the *Spice Girls*. Back when Damien Hirst chopped up a shark and submerged the parts in aquariums filled with formaldehyde. He had another grim piece too—a cow and her calf, sliced in half and torn apart. Separated. He called it *Mother and Child (Divided)*. Claire and I figured his intent was to evoke a sense of tragic disconnection, which was something we'd never experienced ourselves.

As for Tracey Emin, her most famous art installation was an unmade mattress surrounded by dirty underwear and used tissues. If that was art then Claire and I were prolific artists too; our rampant lust constantly producing disheveled bed sheets, discarded knickers, and crumpled tissues.

And Gwyneth Paltrow? Poor Gwyneth. Claire and I cringed during her Oscars acceptance speech for the movie *Shakespeare in Love*. She seemed so young, naive, and insulated…which was, in hindsight, so very much like us.

There were good times, weren't there, Claire?

I look beyond the girls' reflections, into the night. Darkness surrounds me. I'm lost again. In the past, the present, and in an imagined future.

Suddenly, the bus veers off the main highway and a real, rather than imagined, gloom descends as we disappear into unlit backstreets. The suburban detour baffles me—Jaipur's main bus station is in the city center, so the diversion makes no sense. Concerned, I press my face to the window and search the streetscape for signage. But the dark thoroughfares show no signs of anything at all—no people, traffic, or even cows, which is unsettling.

The route change disturbs other passengers too. Several raise themselves from tired slouches and look outside. Their confused facial expressions speak volumes. Clearly, we are on the wrong track.

Finally, the bus driver steers to the roadside and pulls up alongside an eerie park. He extinguishes the headlights, plunging us into darkness. The unscheduled stop perplexes everyone on board and an indignant din fills the cabin. Utterly mystified, I turn to the rotund man sharing my bench seat.

"Any idea what is going on, Vipul?"

The cabin lights come on and I see the big man's forehead pinch in frustration. The cheery demeanor he greeted me with upon first boarding has vanished.

"Everyone must leave," he says bitterly.

"Is it a breakdown?"

"No breakdown," Vipul spits. "This driver and conductor are crooks."

He hauls his corpulent body to his feet then furiously manhandles a bag from the overhead rack. He notices the bemused look on my face. "These men are working with the auto drivers outside," he explains.

I follow his eye line and see numerous figures loitering in the evening shadows. It takes a second, but eventually it makes sense: it's a hustle. Dumped in no man's land on Jaipur's fringe, we're all *fare* game for these predatory men.

"Can they do that?" I ask.

Vipul eyes me apologetically and bobbles his head. "Unfortunately this happens often on government buses."

"So what next?"

"We pay for an auto, my friend. Or walk."

The auto drivers lurk at the perimeter of the bus like expectant sharks circling a shipwreck. I instinctively look at Buttercup and her friend, worried about their safety. The girls are still in high spirits, oblivious to the danger outside.

Their blissful ignorance ends when a handful of auto drivers discover their presence. The men hone in on the girl's and cast a barrage of baiting calls through their window. In the space of several breaths, I hear promises of cheap fares, cringe-worthy compliments about their looks, and blatant demands for sex…followed by outright abuse when the girls ignore the *Eve-teasing*. Whipping themselves into a frenzy, the men turn feral, their vulgar behavior causing the travelers' faces to tighten with alarm. Seeking to avoid confrontation, the women turn away from the mob. The rebuff triggers a backlash, and several auto drivers hammer the flank of the bus with clenched fists. The sound startles the girls, and I watch in horror as intrusive hands grasp their window and slide it open. In a flash, an arm snakes inside the bus and strikes, cobra-like, onto Buttercup's elbow. She recoils in terror, wrenches herself free and quickly retreats into the aisle alongside Vipul.

I watch, stunned, at the unfolding drama because where there is a mob there is rarely any reasoning.

"You guys ok?" I ask.

"It's a bit intimidating," says Buttercup, vying for understatement of the century.

"Do you think they're dangerous?" asks her friend.

I glance at Vipul. "Are the girls safe with these guys?"

"Best to stay near me," he replies. "I'll help you get an auto."

Buttercup swallows heavily. "Thank you so much."

Even under duress, she looks captivating, but right now I wish, for her sake, she was a hideous beast.

We cautiously disembark and are immediately swarmed by a dozen torsos tainted with fetid body odor. Several men crush against the girls in an attempt to grope at their backpacks, breasts, and buttocks. I push to intervene, but the crowd blocks me, and soon I'm separated from Vipul and the girls.

My utter inadequacy and complete lack of power infuriates me, and, suddenly, I hate India more than any country on earth. I hate the profiteering, the scams, and the endless harassment. For the first time in my life, I vaguely comprehend the physical fear and sexual intimidation that women protest about. It's real and legitimately terrifying, and it makes me question my own behavior around women.

I spot Vipul guiding the girls into a waiting auto, and, hopefully, a safe onward journey. I too find escape. Surrendering the battle, I allow a driver to push me into his waiting vehicle. I flop onto the backseat, mentally drained, and ask to be taken to a guesthouse. As we leave, I find a moment to reassure myself with a truth I suspect is hollow. I am *not* like these men. I am *not* a violator of women. The *real* version of me is a good man.

Or is he?

What if I had a risk-free opportunity, an ambiguous excuse, or an anonymous mob?

Chapter Thirty-Four

"CHRIS, YOU FUCK A LOT?"

The question is from a teenaged boy hunched over a computer monitor plastered with hardcore porn images. The pictures are the usual 'blonde with big tits' porn that stopped turning me on at sixteen, which just so happens to be the age of Chandon and his buddy, Rajinder, who are parked next me.

"Jiggy-jiggy all the time, yeah?"

Chandon's words tickle my inner idiot, and I laugh out loud.

Jiggy-jiggy!!

It sounds like a fishing game played by excitable toddlers in backyard kiddie pools. Or maybe the catch-cry of a 1980s aerobics instructor: "Come on, people, step it out. Let's get jiggy-jiggy."

"Not really, mate," I tell my randy enquirer.

"Your last time was when?" Rajinder presses.

"My last...*jiggy-jiggy?*"

The word sounds ridiculous as I utter it, but I mentally store it for later use anyway, primarily to replace the equally silly 'rumpy-pumpy'—a playful term rendered unusable since my split with Claire, along with a list of childish pet names like 'Bub', 'Little Piggy' and 'Stinky Butt Boy'. Words that, in my mind, were ours alone. Words that meant nothing, yet everything, especially once they ceased to be heard.

"Four days," I say, thinking of Lisa, who I've been pining for more than I expected.

"This is very recent," Chandon says.

"This fucking was with Indian girl or Western one?" Rajinder prods, hungry for dirt.

"She lives in Australia."

A smile parts his wispy beard and mustache. "Ahh, same country as you. This fucking is very easy for you then."

"No, it was anything but easy, actually."

Rajinda smoothes the sides of his turban. "Easier than an Indian girl, yes?"

"I don't know. I've never had sex with an Indian girl."

"Western women are much easier than Indian women," chimes Chandon.

I wince at his comment.

"But they only like Western men," he continues. "Not Indians."

"That's probably less about you guys," I reason. "And more about being overwhelmed by the attention they get here. But chicks don't sleep with every dude they meet in my country."

Chandon thinks about this for the briefest of moments.

"But some women do this 'all the time' fucking, yes?"

"None that I know."

It never ceases to amaze me how completely the myth of Western women's sexual promiscuity has permeated India. Although, in some ways it's entirely understandable, given we saturate the globe with suggestive Hollywood films, risqué music videos and Internet porn.

"I'd say there's more sex happening here," I add. "You have a billion people. And the *Kama Sutra*. And sex ashrams."

Chandon laughs. "This is true. We have this ashram in Pune."

"You guys know anything about it?" I ask, hoping for further details.

"It's very expensive," Rajinder says. "Mostly just time-pass for Westerners."

I was 'time passing' earlier in the day when I met Chandon and

Rajinder. I'd been exploring the backstreets of Jaipur, jumping into random games of cricket. Firstly, a match with a dozen kids, then a street game with some teens, and finally a more serious encounter with some older males. This last game was memorable due to a heartfelt cultural exchange where several players taught me some Hindi. To nail the pronunciation, they had me yell words at passing families, which was a liberating experience…right up until the point Chandon rushed over and begged me to quit cursing at people.

To apologize for the behavior of his compatriots or, as he quaintly labelled them 'Those sisterfuckers', Chandon insisted on buying me a ticket to the latest Bollywood release. So, we headed to Jaipur's iconic Raj Mandir cinema, and sat through a movie that had more plot turns than a London cemetery during the bubonic plague.

It kicked off as a romantic comedy set in India, morphed into a wife-swapping drama in Mauritius, then turned into a Swiss murder mystery that quickly escalated into a suspense thriller with numerous fight scenes. It then concluded with a twist that revealed a hundred million dollar insurance scam. All this was punctuated by extravagant song and dance interludes—the last of which took place on a cruise ship… after the bad guy dies…due to being impaled…by an anchor.

Indians refer to this genre-hopping madness as a *masala movie*. Personally, I think these films are the celluloid equivalent of a multiple personality disorder.

Which is probably why I loved it!

The audience loved it too. They laughed. They cheered. They sang. The gorgeous Bollywood starlets were wolf-whistled by excited men, and the handsome lead actors had every female swooning. Everyone hooted hysterically when sexual tension was implied using suggestive metaphors, like the female and male lead characters kneading bread dough together, or the image of spurting showers drenching bodies. These were designed—obviously by a director with tongue firmly in cheek—to appease the government's censorship board.

Rajinder straightens in his chair. "In your country, you find girls how?"

"Mostly through friends or getting to know someone at a party. Or work."

"One night stands too?"

A nerdy youngster several cubicles away, catches my eye as he slips a headset with a microphone on his head. He's maybe thirteen or fourteen years of age. Most likely studying to become a doctor or engineer—the accepted Indian success story. Whatever the case, he probably doesn't need to overhear our carnal conversation.

"Yeah, that happens sometimes," I say, lowering my voice.

Chandon's ears prick up. "You have a fuck buddy?"

"No. Too complicated."

"Because women fall in love easily, yes?"

My mind flashes to me standing at Emma's door—unannounced and uninvited—clutching flowers she never asked for.

"Or they *won't* fall in love," I add.

Rajinder nods solemnly. "*Achha, achha.* This is true also."

"Everyone wants sex," Chandon says. "But I think we are all looking for love."

His observation is the most grown-up thing any of us has said all day. As a result, an uncommon silence falls. Within seconds, the teen with the headset interrupts it.

"I want to fuck you," he says loudly.

I look to see who the lucky recipient of the proclamation is, but discover the kid staring blankly at his computer screen. So much for study. He's obviously connected to an adult chat line. The patchy data connection muddies the romantic poetry of his message, so he repeats it several more times, altering the emphasis and volume of each delivery.

"I want to *fuck* you. I want to fuck *you*. I want to FUCK YOU."

If I were a better man—say, someone with principles—I'd be appalled. Sadly, I'm not a better man. I'm a dubious individual with elastic ethics who also watches porn. So the last thing Indian males need is a moral lesson from someone like me, i.e. another hypocritical, holier-than-thou, middle-class Westerner. What the men of India might need, however, is something to help cure their chronic pornography addiction. Something like education, censorship, and age control.

Either that or they need access to *more* porn. Unlimited porn. On demand.

Preferably via a website hosted in America; a website with low-cost membership options specifically designed for Indian users.

If only there was a selfless visionary who could turn such a fantasy into reality.

If only.

UPRIGHT - Power, action, sleight of hand. #Abracadabra

REVERSED - Greed, poor planning. Wait... who's the sucker here?

Chapter Thirty-Five

THE STREETS around Jaipur's old city teem with 'helpful' locals—hawkers, hustlers, and scammers who test my patience with each step. It begins with the usual 'Excuse me, sir, what is your good name?', followed by questions about my country, some forced camaraderie, and finally, their pitch. In the case of gem scammers, this is always presented as a risk-free opportunity for easy money.

Dodging these con artists is a challenge because kindness is a weakness they exploit. But after enough encounters, most travelers master the subtle art of ignoring advances and walking on. Which makes me wonder how Marten, the Dutchman, fell for their too-good-to-be-true swindles. I guess, he was greedy and gullible.

"Excuse me, sir, what is your good name?"

I hesitate mid-stride and turn to find a heavy-set, middle-aged man standing at the entrance of a carpet shop. His thick mustache, and piercing gaze remind me of a Bollywood villain.—or Saddam Hussein.

"Sorry, I don't need carpets," I say, torpedoing any soft-sell scud before he can launch it. "I don't even have a house."

He frowns. "No house?! Then where do you live?"

"Currently out of a backpack."

"Ah, okay, you are a backpacker. Very good." He motions towards his shop. "My friend, can I invite you inside for a chai?"

I shake my head and attempt to walk on.

"You are from where?" He calls. "America?"

I let his question thwart my progress. "Australia."

"Sydney or Melbourne?"

I stop and face him. "Brisbane."

"*Achha achha,*" he says, nodding. "I know it. I have one cousin in Brisbane."

Of course, you do, I think to myself.

The man presses on. "How long have you been in India?"

"Four weeks."

"And for how much longer?"

"Eight."

"This is a long time," he muses, stepping closer. "I think you will see much of my country."

"That's the plan."

He reaches forward and touches my elbow. "Come inside for a chai, my friend. I would like to hear about your travels."

I smile at the subtle set-up. "Nah, I'm good, thanks, mate."

He raises a hand in surrender. "I understand. One too many bad street encounters, correct?"

"Yeah, a few too many, actually."

"My friend, what if I give you my word? Just one chai and travel talk. No selling."

Against my better judgement, I accept the offer and let myself be led towards the shop.

"May I ask your name?"

"Chris."

He offers his palm for a handshake. "Chris, I am Ramesh." He opens the glass door, and ushers me inside with a hand on my shoulder. The weight of his gold bracelet rests on my arm. "Welcome to my shop," he says proudly.

I look around the marble-tiled showroom. Polished timber shelves, jammed full of rolled rugs and tapestries, line every wall.

Ramesh flicks his fingers at a lethargic employee. "Two chai," he commands, his voice carrying the weight of routine authority. He turns back to me. "For twenty years, I have sold the finest Rajasthani rugs, Chris. It's a shame you don't have a house because I would give you the very best deal."

"I don't even have a rental at the moment."

"So you are living in hotels?"

"Just a guesthouse," I answer. Then, just in case he is on a fishing expedition, I add: "A budget one."

"Because you are saving for travel, yes?"

I nod.

Ramesh studies me for a beat. "Twelve weeks of vacation must be very expensive," he says. "What is your job in Australia?"

"I'm a truck driver," I say, hoping my past life job sounds less affluent than my recent TV gig.

Ramesh squints, as if weighing my words. "In Australia, this pays well?"

"Yeah," I lie. "For a mining company."

"Truck driving is poorly paid in India, but in your country this offers a good wage?"

"Good enough to holiday in India," I say with a smile.

He returns a wry grin. "But not good enough to buy a house?"

It feels like I'm trying to con a con-man so I turn my attention to the piles of rugs around us.

"Is there good money in carpet selling?"

Ramesh smirks. "Enough to own a house."

I laugh at his quick wit, just as his employee returns with our chai.

"My friend," he says, tone measured and earnest as he grabs both cups. "Money comes and goes." He hands me a tea. "But friendship? That endures time and distance."

"You should put that on a birthday card," I say in jest.

Ramesh acknowledges my comment with a forced smile. "But it is true, yes?"

I nod in agreement, sensing that I've embarrassed him.

We sip our chai in silence for a moment, and I try to think of something to add.

"You know, you could make a lot of money *and* friends if you sold Internet porn to Indians instead of carpets to backpackers."

My silly suggestion puts a smile on his face. "*Achha, achha.* Porno is very popular. But I think this is already free online."

"Trust me, lots of people still pay for it."

He gives me a quizzical look. "You know this business?"

For days, I've fixated on a way to make money off adult content in India, so I can avoid going home to a real job. All I need is a local partner. With that in mind, I spend the next ten minutes pitching Ramesh the story I told Lisa: a high-school friend, a millionaire porn mogul, a market waiting to be tapped. By the time we've finished our chai, his interest is aroused.

"And you know how to do all this?"

"Some of it. The guy I told you about can help with the rest."

"My friend, I think we should discuss this in private."

Ramesh signals for me to follow him to a cell-like office at the far end of the building. Once inside the dimly lit room, I notice it is bereft of furnishings. There is no table or chairs, just four stained concrete walls and a tired kitchenette that is home to a large plastic water container, an electric kettle and several teacups. Ramesh gestures to a floor strewn with cushions and invites me to sit.

"So, tell me again—how do people pay for this porno?"

I lay out the business model as best I can. It almost sounds convincing—even to me.

"The only problem is porn is illegal here," I add.

Ramesh waves off my concern. "This is no problem," he says vaguely. "In India, everything is possible." He smiles. "If you know the right people."

"Are you sure?"

Ramesh summons more chai from one of his staff.

"My brother-in-law is the superintendent of police," he adds. "So these things can be handled.

The thought of involving the police tightens my chest.

"Probably still worth being as lawful as we can," I say.

We return to discussing my idea and after a few minutes the gaunt-faced employee arrives with our chai and wordlessly hands us the tea cups. I notice the deference in which he serves his boss, and for a moment, Ramesh doesn't look like a carpet-seller—he commands the room like a Godfather. His presence as heavy as the air between us, belongs to a powerful man with police connections. A chill shoots down my spine, and I feel the unmistakable discomfort of being caught way over my head.

Ramesh regards my silent discomfort with an air of confidence.

"We will start this business," he says smoothly. "Equal investment. You bring the idea, I bring the customers. We share the success."

He raises the tea cup in salute, his gold bracelet catching the dim light.

Chapter Thirty-Six

To: Jonesy
From: Chris
Subject: Porn

Hey, mate. Currently backpacking thru India and have decided to try and do something really stupid—I want to build a porn site for Indian males! I have some local contacts for the business and coding side of things. What I don't have is any adult content. Any suggestions?

—

To: Chris
From: Jonesy
Subject: Re: Porn

Hey, man. Sounds interesting. I can get all the adult content you need. There are gigabytes of it on our work hard-drives. Let me know what you want and I'll FTP it to your server.

—

To: Deependra
From: Chris
Subject: Website development For Ramesh

Hi Deependra, Ramesh suggested I contact you about coding a website. I think he mentioned to you what we are trying to do. Basically, we need two sites. One will have legitimate sex education content on it. The second is a dedicated adult content site that needs to be hosted on servers in North America.

Is this doable with your skills?

Cheers
Chris

To: Chris
From: Deependra
Subject: Re: Website development For Ramesh

Good morning, Chris. Thank you for your email enquiry. What you ask is no problem for me. I have spoken with Ramesh about your project and I am confident that I can complete any coding tasks you require to the highest standards once we have discussed the key points in greater detail.
I look forward to your prompt reply.

Kindest Regards
Deep

Chief Executive Officer
DeepWeb Rajasthan - 'Your one-stop Web Design, Printing & Travel Agency'

To: Aleta
From: Chris
Subject: Dumb brother checking in…

Hey Piehead,

How's life? Ma and Pa driving you nuts? Bet you're really looking forward to Thailand. Mum said you booked your flight to Bangkok for the day after I fly in. Pretty cool 18th birthday gift to yourself!! I'll meet you at the airport so you don't get lost in the chaos.

Not much happening my end, travel-wise. Been stuck in Jaipur for the past week or so because I've been trying to build a porn site for Indian men. Yeah, sounds insane, I know. And, yes, I do understand that I'm not furthering the cause of Indian women by trying to make millions out of selling porn to Indian men…but if I don't do it, someone else will. Does acknowledging a wrong make it right? Probably not. Oh, well. ;-)

Anyway, chat later when I have something interesting to report. Ciao for now.

—

To: Chris
From: Aleta
Subject: Re: Dumb brother checking in…

Nooooooo!!! What are you doing?!!! Please stop with all this crazy stuff already and just have a vacation like a normal person.

—

Chapter Thirty-Seven

MY TAXI ROLLS through a suburban residential development in the low light of evening and stops at the driveway of an Indian-style McMansion. I step out, taking in the imposing structure. It's an uninspiring clone of its estate neighbors, proof that money can't buy good taste. Before I can cast further judgment, the front door opens, revealing Ramesh, impeccably dressed in a crisp button-down white shirt and tailored brown trousers.

"Ah, my friend! You are here at last," he says, offering a firm handshake. His voice carries both warmth and formality. "Please, come in."

My host leads me into a marble-tiled entryway that smells of spicy home cooking.

"I sent the servants home," Ramesh adds with pride. "I prefer to cook myself for special occasions."

"Good timing," I say. "Because today's my birthday."

Ramesh blinks, caught off guard. "You should have mentioned this on the phone," he says, voice unable to mask the inconvenience. "We will need a cake."

"No, please, that's totally unnecessary. Dinner is more than enough."

"I don't think so," Ramesh counters. "I must talk to Priya about this."

We enter the dining room, where his family stands in line to receive me, their expressions polite but unreadable and postures poised as if receiving a foreign dignitary,.

"This is my wife, Priya, my son, Naveen, and my daughter, Zenisha."

I shake hands with each of them, mustering a self-conscious smile as Priya discreetly assesses my ratty backpacker attire.

"How old are you guys," I ask the kids.

Ramesh answers for them. "The boy is eight, and the girl is ten." Then, without pause, he turns to his wife. "Priya, he has a birthday today but didn't warn me."

Priya's eyes widen. "Is this true?" She glares at her husband. "How can I organize a cake at such late notice, Ramesh?"

"Please, no cake," I repeat. "I haven't had a home-cooked meal for months, so dinner is perfect."

Priya studies me, then relaxes. "Perhaps we can make this meal memorable. Do you like kulfi? We have saffron and pistachio flavors."

I tell her that the delicious Indian ice cream is, indeed, a favorite.

With the tension eased, we take our seats at the dining table. Priya disappears into the kitchen and returns moments later with a selection of curries, rice dishes and flatbread, all arranged with the precision of a restaurant spread. I glance at Ramesh—he remains seated, watching her work but making no move to help. The sight makes me pause—did he really cook any of this?

Priya finally sits, and after a short Hindu blessing, I'm invited to eat. Grabbing a piece of naan, I help myself to a few modest portions, then wait for my hosts to do likewise.

"You have been in Jaipur for how long?" Priya asks, spooning fragrant biryani rice onto the plates of her children.

"Two weeks."

She catches Zenisha biting her nails and forcefully pulls the girl's fingers away from her mouth.

"And what have you been doing during this time?"

"Mostly just relaxing."

She raises an eyebrow. "For two weeks?!" A flicker of envy and disbelief crosses her face. "I think you have the kind of life a wife and mother can only dream of." She shoots a sharp glance at her son. "Naveen! No slouching."

The boy straightens instantly. The scene triggers a wave of nostalgic memories of my own childhood dinners, before morphing into something more complicated. An unpalatable sense of shame fills my gut because I'm enjoying the hospitality of a family—alongside a doting wife and young children—while dragging pornography and greed into their world. Why? And why, for that matter, is Ramesh?

Priya fills her own plate last, as mothers do, then steers the conversation toward my family, my marital status, my life in Australia, and my travels through India. It's pleasant but pedestrian. The kids grow restless within minutes. Even Ramesh seems to retreat, nodding absently. The eager-to-please man I met on arrival has faded into a disconnected individual, leaving his wife to do all the social heavy lifting.

Eventually, dinner ends. I volunteer to clean up, but Priya refuses my offer and swiftly clears the table with the help of her daughter. With the women occupied, Ramesh dismisses his son. The boy utters a perfunctory goodnight and flees to his bedroom, leaving me alone with his father.

"Your kids are very well-mannered," I tell him.

"Thank you. I am very proud of them. The girl is top of her class and the boy is working hard to improve his grades. Do you have children?"

"Not that I'm aware of."

He laughs. "Illegitimate perhaps?"

"I doubt it."

Priya returns with two cups of chai, providing a wanted distraction.

"Thank you for the meal and the hospitality," I say.

Priya smiles warmly. "It is my pleasure. Your visit means a great deal to Ramesh." She touches her husband on the shoulder. "He has been impatient for you to come, but apparently, you have been too busy. Relaxing, as you say!" She looks at her husband, who is fidgeting. "But you are here now, so I will leave you men to discuss whatever it is men talk about."

"Nothing interesting," I joke.

The corner of her lips shift to form a subtle smile. "Sport and politics, yes?" she teases, before retreating back to the kitchen.

The air shifts the moment Priya leaves. Ramesh straightens his posture, his casual warmth replaced with something harder to read. He reaches across the table and pinches caraway seeds out of a small bowl.

"How is the website going?" he asks, rolling the natural breath fresheners between his fingers before popping them into his mouth.

"Slowly. But I think we're onto something. Deependra seems to think so too." I help myself to some of the seeds as well. "Have you had a chance to look into the legal stuff?"

Ramesh doesn't answer immediately. He glances at his watch, mind elsewhere. "I think it is best to wait until the website is finished."

"Oh, okay. It's just that Deependra is concerned about it."

Ramesh shrugs, uninterested, leaving me confused, uncertain, and wishing I never suggested this stupid business in the first place.

Starting a porn site has been far more complicated than I expected. Ramesh has done nothing to help. Plus, sometime between witnessing the mob madness on the bus and uploading a thousand hardcore porn images, I've developed a problematic moral conscience.

Ramesh gulps the remainder of his chai. "Come," he says, summoning me to stand. "I will drive you to your guesthouse."

"It's fine. I can get a taxi."

His response is firm. "I will drive you."

Yielding to his wishes, I follow him to the garage and climb into his car. Ramesh slots the key into the ignition, but stalls before turning the engine over.

"Deependra said he requires a progress payment. Did he mention this to you?"

I blink, taken aback. "No. How much?"

"Two hundred thousand rupees. One hundred each. Equal investment, as agreed."

The number slams into me. Over one thousand American dollars —for what? Almost nothing has been built yet.

"When does he need it?" I ask.

"Tonight."

His answer makes no sense. I converse daily with Deependra via email and not once has a progress payment been mentioned.

"We can stop at a bank machine on the way." Ramesh adds.

My chest tightens. This is moving too fast. Way too fast. Everything feels wrong.

"I think that would exceed my daily limit."

Ramesh starts the car. "Maybe just withdraw your daily limit and you can repay me the difference later."

An awkward silence rests between us as Ramesh drives us to a Bank of India branch. My business partner opens the car door and steps outside. I reluctantly follow suit, then walk slowly toward a brightly lit ATM, with Ramesh shadowing me along the way.

At the ATM, my stomach tightens. It all feels too sudden. Too convenient. I insert my credit card, watching the machine's glow cast strange shadows on Ramesh's face.

Feeling incredibly alone and extremely vulnerable, I select 'withdrawal' from the menu, and enter the amount needed. Within seconds, the machine returns my card.

"Transaction declined," I report with relief, hoping this will end our charade.

"Try eighty thousand," Ramesh orders.

I don't want to do this. I don't want to do anything for this guy. I want to run, disappear into the night, and catch the first bus out of Jaipur. But, unfortunately, I'm too polite. So I key in the reduced figure instead.

The ATM screen blinks slowly, stretching each second. Suddenly, I hear the tell-tale sound of notes being counted and collated. The cash gate opens and the machine spews out a wad of rupees.

Someone has hit the jackpot. But it isn't me.

Ramesh is suddenly beside me, closer than before. "It worked, yes?"

He extends his palm without hesitation, and my fingers tighten around the cash for half a second, hoping this is a legitimate transaction or an elaborate joke. Finally, I surrender the notes and Ramesh pockets them like a skilled magician.

The words of Marten return to haunt me: "Indians are smart, man. World-class scammers."

My mind races back over the past fortnight—Ramesh's reluctance to engage in the business, his police-commissioner brother-in-law, the family dinner, the progress payment. Was this all a setup?

Ramesh reads my apprehension. "I can help you replace this, my friend. I have a birthday gift for you at my store." He claps my shoulder, his good humor returning. "The best quality Rajasthani gemstones."

Oh, no… What have I done?

Happy thirtieth birthday, you stupid motherfucker.

Chapter Thirty-Eight

THE BUS from Jaipur spills me onto a dirt road in downtown Pushkar. I pull out my guidebook and consult the vague map and town summary. Apparently the desert hamlet is typically quiet, except for one time of the year when its population swells to epic proportions during a well-known fair that could be likened to a *Miss Universe* beauty pageant—for camels.

Each December, a caravan of ample-bumped models parade their lithe legs and clipped camel toes in front of a bone-headed audience of hundreds of thousands in the hope of gaining dim-witted adoration and a brighter future.

The Pushkar Camel Fair, however, is held in November, which is one week away.

I close the guidebook and venture off in search of accommodation; a task that proves to be near impossible due to the fact that every hotel, hostel, guesthouse, and dog house has been booked out weeks in advance.

The midday heat clings to my skin as I trudge through the town. After twenty humid minutes, I stumble upon a decrepit lodge at the town's edge. It's such a dump that it might actually have a vacancy. Inexplicably, this grungy hovel has one of the town's rarest luxuries—a swimming pool. It also has a vacant single bed. Unfortunately, that single bed is located in an old camel stable. Out of desperation, I check out it out.

Unsurprisingly, the room's decor has a distinctly agricultural feel. The rustic list of features include a heavy timber barn door (which, worryingly, has a padlock on the *outside*), soft natural light (due to no electricity), and an earthy mattress (that is damp and musty). An added bonus is that guests can, quite literally, hit the hay here, because there's actually straw on the floor.

The stable does, however, have a view of the pool. I spy several Indian guys, possibly in their late teens or early twenties, swimming with a female backpacker. Above the splashing, the unmistakable banter of young, oversexed males reaches my ears. Their talk, directed at the girl, is part of a charm *offensive* that includes the evergreen classic 'Do you fuck a lot?', and gems like 'You want some spicy Indian?', as well as the timeless wishful thinking promise of 'I will fuck you all night'.

I pay for the room, then eager to escape the desert heat, head for the pool. Submerging myself into the tepid water at the unoccupied deep end, I resurface to hear the backpacker address her poetic admirers.

"Everything is always about sex with you Indian men," the girl groans, exasperated.

I try to place her thick accent. Middle-Eastern, maybe?

"You are like little boys," she snaps. "Not real men. Not like him."

She points to me.

A guy perched on the pool edge calls out: "Hey, man, what country are you from?"

I tell him.

"Australians are *real* men," the girl says, casting the insult like bait. "Not immature like Indians."

Her words trigger a chase. One of the guys dives after her, wrestling her in the water. It looks playful at first, but her sharp kick to his groin suggests otherwise. He recoils, ducking underwater to avoid further blows, though he stays close enough to leer at her skimpy bikini-clad figure. The girl swims to me, clinging to my back like a lifeline.

"Protect me!" she pleads, wrapping her legs around my waist.

I hesitate. Is she joking? Serious?

"Don't drag me into this," I say lightly.

"What's your name?" she pants.

"Chris."

"Please, Chris, protect me."

One of the guys laughs from the other end of the pool. "Netta wants to fuck you, man. She's easy."

Netta whips around. "I would fuck him before I fuck you."

She swims to the edge, climbs out, and snatches a towel. As she dries off, her bikini strains against her curves. The guys ogle openly.

"Stop staring, you fucking perverts!" she spits.

Then, as if nothing happened, she turns to me.

"Where are you eating tonight?"

"I have no idea."

"You can eat with me." It's not an offer. It's a command. "One hour."

One hour later, Netta leads me into an eatery where the staff greet her by name. I scan the menu, faintly aware of the ominous stirrings in my belly. Netta fires a dozen questions at me during our meal, all of which center on her love affair with Australia, its animals, its landscape, its immigration policy and…its men.

Exhausted from my bus journey, I tell my dinner companion that I'm done for the night. But Netta has other plans.

"Can you give me a massage?" she asks.

Her request catches me off-guard because women are never this forward with me.

"And I will give you one after," she adds.

Her offer of sensual affection is a challenge for me. Since dinner, my stomach discomfort has evolved into the lower bowel rumble commonly associated with multiplying bacteria. The microbes, no doubt, responsible for the fever-like temperature raging in my body, and the vague dizziness messing with my mind. Unfortunately, my penis has its own mind, so I am soon led astray.

We enter Netta's room and she lights several scented candles within the rustic sleeping quarters. The subsequent glow faintly illuminates two wall-hangings as well as a squadron of mosquitoes, who will no doubt launch a million nocturnal sorties from the ceiling. A large window, wide open to counter the oppressive heat, is screened by a lace curtain. The loosely stitched fabric dances languidly in the lethargic evening breeze, as if caressed by an occasional warm sigh or flirtatious whisper. On each breath, I catch a perfume of roses wafting from the thorny garden beyond. My mind briefly drifts with the scent to another time and place.

It's all very romantic and sensual, but I'd rather be asleep.

"Which oil do you like?" Netta gestures towards three bottles of aromatic lubricants on the bedside table. "Lavender, rose or sandalwood."

"Whichever one you like best," I say.

She selects rose, then, without any hesitation, strips off her clothing. My loins stir at the sight of her nakedness as she lowers herself on the mattress. I lather my hands with oil and gently massage it into her shoulder blades, her soft skin gleams in the candlelight. The sensual rush of blood combined with the aromatic oil makes me lightheaded and, once again, my mind drifts elsewhere—the heat, the candles, the curtain, and the *potpourri*-like scent of rose reminds me of summer nights at home. Suddenly, my fragile, feverish mind abandons me and magically I'm transported back to Brisbane.

MY LOVER IS LYING face down on the mattress.

"I wish we could stay in here forever," Claire says.

I gently knead the massage oil into her shoulder blades.

"Me too," I reply.

The room is our safe haven from the real world. The 'incident' between us has been evicted and locked out by another abusive force—Claire's illness. Petty fights have been replaced by sheer exhaustion, and any old resentment is now reserved for new irritations: for doctors and their schedules, for friends too busy for visitation, for family members who are too far away, and, lastly, for people whose lives go on, while mine stagnates and Claire's fades from view.

She turns her head to one side, facing me. "Remember when we used to have sex three times a day?" Her voice is wistfully reminiscent.

"Now we hardly even do it at all." She reaches back and brushes her hand against my leg.

I take the cue, lean over and kiss her cheek. Claire rolls over, beckoning me to return and taste the deep affection that escapes her lips. I do so, and the intensity rises, fueling more desire until she pulls me close to her body.

"I want you inside me," she whispers.

A cheeky smile stretches my lips. "I want me inside you too!"

NETTA AND I UNCOUPLE, torsos glistening with sweat, and roll onto our backs. I reach for the bedside table, grab one of her Marlboros and light it.

"Sorry, that probably wasn't very enjoyable for you."

I pass the cigarette. Netta pinches it between two fingers, wraps her lips around the filter, draws in, then exhales slowly.

"It wasn't so bad." Her free hand palms my exposed stomach, then inches lower. "Do you want to try again?"

I don't. Nor does my one-eyed, single-minded friend.

"I should go back to my room."

"Why?" she asks.

"The guys would have seen me come in with you."

Netta shrugs. "I don't care. They think all foreign women are easy."

"You having sex with me won't change their minds."

She hands the smoke back and I take several tokes before crushing it in the ashtray.

"Stay in Pushkar," Netta says. "Until the camel fair." She rolls her body against mine, then rest her head on my chest. "Afterwards, we can go to Udaipur. Then Goa." She raises her face to look me in the eyes. "Have you been to Goa?"

I shake my head.

"We can get married there," she continues. "Then you can take me back to Australia."

I laugh nervously, hoping her proposal is in jest.

"I will go to the sex ashram with you," she says seductively, returning to a topic of conversation we had during dinner.

"I can't stay. I fly to Thailand in two weeks."

It's a lie.

"Then I will meet you in Thailand," she counters.

I playfully nudge her with my elbow. "Maybe you'll marry one of those Indian dudes first."

Netta stiffens. "I don't want an Indian guy."

She glances down at her hand. The one that is unable to resuscitate my libido.

"What about one of your countryman?" I tease. "There are plenty of Israeli guys around."

She gives up on arousing me and slaps my thigh playfully.

"I don't want an Israeli either." Her fingers comb through my chest hair. "I want to marry an Australian" She tilts her face towards mine. "I want to wake up to kangaroos and koalas…and you."

Her lips find mine. I kiss back, but my heart isn't in it. She notices.

"You have a girlfriend in Australia?"

I shake my head.

"A wife?"

"Nope."

"You are lying." Her eyes narrow. "There is someone."

"Not any more," I say.

"Why not?"

"It was too complicated."

What I don't tell her is that it was me who made it complicated. That my unrealized ambitions were more important than us. That her illness drained her body and my patience. Or how guilt kept me tethered to a life I didn't want, and how leaving made me feel free and… monstrous.

"What made it complicated?"

"It just didn't feel right," I tell her.

Netta studies me, then shifts the conversation. "Did you like fucking her?"

I wince. "I'm not answering that after we just had sex!"

"Don't worry, I'm not jealous." She traces a circle on my stomach. "I just want to know what made it not right."

I hear the sincerity in her voice and relent. "Because it was exhausting." Netta says nothing so I continue. "I wanted an easier life."

Netta places her hand over my manhood again. "Did she make you hard?"

I frown, unable to answer because the topic is so personal and non-sexual to me.

"What about you," I counter, trying to redirect. "Any boyfriend or husband in Tel Aviv that you're running from?"

Her reply is an empathic 'No'.

"Now I can see that you're not telling the truth, my little Israeli friend," I goad.

Her expression becomes serious. "There is no one."

"Come on," I say, cajoling her lightly. "There must be someone."

She removes her hand from my groin, and rolls away from me. In an instant, the desert air in the room turns icy. I prop myself onto my haunches and lean over her body.

"Are you ok?"

Netta shields her face from my view. "I had a boyfriend," she says. A beat passes. "He was…umm, how do you say—" She searches her mind for the English word. Failing, she turns expectantly to me, her eyes moist. "When you are to be married?"

"Your husband."

"No. Before husband and wife. A French word."

It takes a second for me to catch on.

"Fiancé?"

"Yes, *fiancé*. He asked to marry me. And I said 'yes'. But two days later I changed my mind." There's an extended pause before her clipped English fractures: "Then he… suicide with his gun."

The world stops.

"His mother and father—" Tears spring from her eyes. "—I am not welcome in their…" She rolls away, tightly hugs her pillow and begins to sob deeply.

Her reaction makes me want to run a million miles, to flee her problems, as I once fled Claire's. But I don't. Instead, I wrap an arm around Netta, and in silence, we lie together. Two wounded souls trapped in purgatory. Between past and present. Between regret and longing.

Between heaven and hell.

UPRIGHT - Introspective, soul-searching, student of life ... That's cool.
REVERSED - Isolated, withdrawn, depressive sad-ass ... Not so cool.

Chapter Thirty-Nine

JAMES BOND WAS HERE.

In Udaipur.

Doing what, I don't know—chasing skirt, drinking martinis and blowing things up, I guess. Nice work if you can get it.

I haven't seen *Octopussy* in decades, so I don't remember the movie's setting, nor the floating palace that featured prominently. The film is screened nightly in the restaurant next door to jog tourists' memories, but I have other plans. I bypass the outdoor sign advertising the eatery's 007 gimmick and step into my hotel. Unlike the palatial Lake Palace from the film, my budget lodging is crammed onto a shoreline alongside a hundred other guesthouses.

Crossing the foyer's checkerboard floor tiles, I head to a lone computer reserved for guest use. I've been waiting months for this moment—years, really. This is the culmination of so much self-questioning, wondering if I was ever good enough. The suspense has been killing me all day.

To distract myself from the excitement and trepidation, I took a taxi boat to the Lake Palace, a rickshaw to the City Palace, and wandered aimlessly through the city's tangled streets. I even spent time with a copy of *David Copperfield* that I found under my bed (the

Charles Dickens novel, not a clone of the American magician), but I couldn't focus beyond the opening paragraph. My mind was consumed with one thing: the TV episode I wrote. The episode airing right now.

I check the time on the computer screen.

The end credits will be rolling.

I log into my email with anticipation, hoping to find feedback from my mother. True to form, she doesn't disappoint. I smile at the time stamp on the message. Within minutes of the episode concluding, she has sent a response. Her tone is unmistakably proud. She's seen my name on screen before, but this is the first time it's been preceded by the words '*Written by*'. For her, that credit will partially vindicate the patience, belief, and emotional support that parents of losers, depressives, and useless dreamers know too well.

I read her words and my spirits rise. As a result, my anxiety dissolves. Maybe my writing is okay. Maybe I can do this. With my self-confidence on a high, I wonder if I quit television for all the wrong reasons. Why didn't I just 'get back on the horse' like my boss, Bryan, had suggested? Or take Emma's advice and separate my career from my personal life?

Maybe it's not too late.

Maybe I can block out the past. Forget Emma. Ignore my insecurities. And go back to work.

Buoyed by this moment of clarity, I draft an email to Bryan and Elliot. Taking them up on their old offer, I tell them to add me as a writer for next season.

I send the email.

Then I reread my mother's. Twice. Then I refresh the page, hoping to find reactions from friends and family.

An hour later, I'm still at the computer, refreshing my inbox for praise from, well…anyone. But there is none.

By nightfall, no additional congratulatory words have appeared. Which leaves me thoroughly convinced that I have, without question, written the world's worst episode of television.

"I can't write this stuff," I moan to Emma.

She looks up from her computer. "You're doing fine," she says, placating me. "Your second draft was so much better than the first. Like it was written by two different people."

Since my break up with Claire, *everything* I do has been like that. I don't know who I am anymore. Bipolar, almost. I'm either good or bad, right or wrong, *yin* and *yang*, hot and cold. I'm two sides of the same coin. I create opportunities then leave. I fall in and out of love. I love-bomb, accelerating connections with infatuated thoughts, passionate words, and obsessive actions. I'm warm, kind, attentive. I'm loving, complimentary and sensual. I see no flaws in the object of my affection…until they return the attention.

Then the script flips.

The claustrophobia sets in. The walls close. Love is replaced by anxiety, fear, and a desperate need to escape any form of commitment. I withdraw. I turn inward. I become unreachable. And, then, like clockwork, I self-destruct and destroy everything around me. It's a life of extremes. Nothing comes naturally, nor with ease. Especially not writing. I'll never be half the writer Emma is. The gap between our talents are as extreme as my emotions.

"I can't do what you guys do," I tell her. "None of this comes naturally to me."

She looks up from her computer. "What do you mean?"

"You keep things simple. I'm the opposite. I complicate everything." I pause, knowing she needs further explanation. "I only worked that out recently. That's why my two drafts were so different. In the first one I was trying to build the story towards some deeper truth or meaning. That's *why* I write. But in the second draft, I tried to do what you guys do."

"And what is it we do again?" she asks, intrigued.

"You don't drip feed the story to the audience," I say, holding her attention. "You spoon-feed it to them like they're idiots."

Emma's face hardens, instantly providing a small, ugly part of me with the pleasure and pain I secretly desire. My insecurities about her run so deep that I want payback. And by deliberately denigrating my own writing, I've won it, because I've successfully belittled hers.

If she won't give me what I want, I'll *take* something instead.

With bated breath, I wait for her response.

"You're probably more suited to prose," she says coldly. "I don't think TV writing is your thing."

I'M STILL the only guest in the hotel foyer, so I check my inbox one last time. Still no congratulations. Not even from Claire. I draft another email—this time, an apology to Emma for the drama I caused while writing the episode that just went to air.

I send it.

After it vanishes into the ether, I reread it. I realize it lacks context, so I compose another email to her, explaining the previous apologetic email.

Then I send *it*.

On rereading, that email sounds too serious. And borderline mental. (Why I can't pick this stuff up *before* I press send is beyond me.) I compose another email, this time addressing the stupidity of the previous two emails with just the right amount of levity to make me sound normal.

Then I send it.

Of course, as soon I do, I belatedly realize that sending *three* emails in the space of several minutes is anything but normal. In fact, it's probably a sure sign of a mental disorder. So I send another email. And another. And before long, I have left a trail of insanity that I can't erase.

My face flushes with embarrassment at the thought of Emma reading them. I wish I was 007, because if I had a license to kill, I'd use it on myself right now.

I check the time at the corner of the screen. I've been online for two hours but mentally offline for years. Suddenly, I notice the date on the monitor, and my heart aches.

Tomorrow is Claire's birthday.

And here I am emailing Emma.

Two loves, two worlds—a life of extremes.

Claire will have watched my episode, of course. And I know she will watch the next episode as well—the one I don't want her to watch. The one with *our* secret in it. The one written by Emma.

Out of nowhere, a wave of grief roars up from the past, threatening to overwhelm me. A full minute passes before I can resurface and plot my next course.

I draft another email.

To Claire.

Written with a fractured mind, I tell her about my recent travels—the Golden Fort, the camel safari, the baby drama, the porn stupidity. I tell her I'm lonely and want to live on a farm. I tell her I'm still messed up but I think I'm getting better. I tell her I slept with two backpackers but I want to be celibate. I tell her I love her but I'm still hung up on Emma. Then I sign off by wishing her a happy birthday.

By the end of the message, I conclude that just like Indian men who write crazy matrimonial ads, I shouldn't be left unsupervised with sharp objects, computer keyboards, or females.

Thanks to valuable lessons gained from recent experiences, I weigh up whether I should send the message or delete it. Finding no ready answer, I leave it up to God or Ganesh or Allah, or whoever is in charge of decisions that affect life advancement in India, and ask for a sign.

Within seconds, the evening air outside the hotel is filled—like a David Copperfield magic show—with explosions and smoke.

I send the email.

Then run for the door.

I reach the alleyway just as another blast erupts in the darkness. The deafening sound ricochets off the sandstone walls, forcing me to shield my face with my hands. My pulse quickens. Is it a bomb? A gunshot? I scan the street for the source of the explosions.

Then I see them.

It's not terrorists. Not danger. It's a wedding party.

The procession is led by several men. Without warning, they light two more hefty firecrackers and toss them into the night. The ensuing detonations split the air like a thunderclap. The commotion draws a dozen other hotel guests to the foyer, hands over ears, facial expressions pinched with confusion and intrigue. We watch as the matrimonial march approaches—drummers pound up-tempo beats, and more firecrackers are thrown in reckless celebration.

Amid this cacophony, the groom, dressed in white linen with gold embroidery, is perched atop a monstrous elephant. The regal beast, painted from head to toe in bright pigment, is draped in lush textiles bedazzled with sequins and silver.

The dancing wedding party that trails is a living jewel as well, adorned in vibrant robes, shiny bangles, and heavy chains of gold. Their figures sparkle as they walk past shards of light cast from hotel entrances. The spectacle makes the Western wedding tradition of white dresses, tailored suits, and fancy cars seem dull and stiff by comparison.

Neither ceremony is my idea of a perfect wedding, however.

My tastes are simpler—a beach ceremony, a handful of guests, no spectacle, no fuss. All I need is the right partner to stand beside me and say *"I do"*.

For a time, I thought Claire was that person.

"You know, I'd marry you in a second," I once admitted during a storm-filled, midnight phone call, after we had broken up. "If I could get my shit together."

The comment rendered Claire silent for so long, that I thought our connection had been lost in the wild winds that ravaged the distance between us.

"Don't say that unless you mean it," she had whispered. "In sickness and in health."

Her words found their intended mark.

I'd already failed that vow of commitment. Failed the test of love during imperfect moments brought on by sickness that stole her health. I had abandoned Claire. As I would again. Always running. Always desperate to turn the page, and start a new chapter so I could move on from the old. What I didn't know was that the greatest escapes are merely an illusion. And that beginning a new chapter doesn't erase the one before—it only further complicates the story.

The last of the procession passes, and the crowd of onlookers drift away. I follow suit, climbing the stairs to my hotel room, unsure of where I fit or where to begin. Seeking distraction, I pick up the battered copy of *David Copperfield* from my bedside table. I flop onto the bed and turn to the first page.

"I am born." It begins. *"Whether I shall turn out to be the hero of my own life, or whether that station will be held by anybody else, these pages must show."*

Chapter Forty

A ROUGH HAND seizes my arm from behind, wrenching my elbow.

"You should not be here," snaps an angry voice.

The forceful arrest pivots me on the spot, and I find myself face-to-face with a barrel-chested wall of khaki.

"This is very dangerous for you," spits the policeman, his tone abrupt and unpleasant.

Seeking shelter from the man's coldness, I study his face for understanding but find no warmth emanating from his rigid, mustachioed jaw or the fiery eyes shadowed beneath the severe peak of his black officer's hat.

"Sorry, I'm lost."

I meekly hold aloft the *Lonely Planet* guidebook as proof of my innocence.

"Do you know where you are?" he barks, apparently unfamiliar with the meaning of the word 'lost'. "This area is very bad," he adds. "Many people are robbed and killed here."

"Sorry, I—"

"Come with me," he orders, cutting off my excuse.

I hesitate, fueled by distrust, and a litany of travel horror stories involving bribery, police brutality and false imprisonment. In response, the lawman's eyes narrow.

"NOW!!" he shouts.

I obey this command immediately, then follow his strides to what I know is certain disaster. I know this because I'm guilty. Not of a crime, but of lying. The street cop also knows it too—because he's apprehended me in Mumbai's red-light district.

I am innocent on some level, because it wasn't my idea to be here. I blame *Lonely Planet*. I skimmed its pages for 'places of interest', expecting the usual cultural landmarks and historical buildings. But there was an almost afterthought of a suggestion that intrigued me. It said: *take an 'eye-opening' drive through the city's red-light district'*.

"Why are you here?" the cop asks.

"I was walking to the city."

"Walking?!" he scoffs, incredulous. "This is a very bad area. It is not safe for you."

I mumble another apology. It falls on deaf ears.

We press on, in silence, winding through the district's refuse-strewn alleyways until we spill onto a wide thoroughfare that, inexplicably, feels less inviting than where we originated. The fetid main street is lined with derelict buildings that look as if they've been cobbled together with debris salvaged from a hurricane. Standing in the shadows of these structures are scores of sallow-cheeked curb-dwellers, their hyena-like eyes menacing yet wary. The wretched figures are a rogue's gallery of pimps, drug pushers, sex workers, and strung-out addicts, all of whom are framed by absurdly colorful doorways and walls that contrast their lives of abject darkness. The air is thick with the scent of sewage, sin and despair.

Evil lives here.

And Death visits often.

I increase my pace, closing the gap to my unpaid escort.

"You are backpacking, yes?"

"Yes."

"There are warnings about this area in your travel book, correct?"

"Some."

"But you came anyway?"

I stay quiet, unsure if this is a statement or a rhetorical question.

The truth is, I came to satisfy my curiosity. But not my sexual curiosity. My motivations were far cruder—I wanted to be a poverty tourist.

Drawn, as always, to the poor and destitute, I was eager to see how the other half live. I wanted to gape at the human flesh trafficked from dark recesses of India, Nepal, and Bangladesh. To confront the reality of women forced into prostitution against their will. And because of my stupid messiah complex, I wanted to entertain the impossible notion of saving them—every broken, enslaved, beaten life that was in need of rescue. But mostly, I wanted to witness the sense of loss and displacement. So I could fuel my own.

Of course, explaining *that* to a cop would likely earn me a one-way ticket to a padded cell in the nearest asylum.

Five minutes later, we arrive at a small roadside police booth. Several constables glance up as we approach. I note their deferential nods reserved for a worker of higher rank. My captor motions me into the hut.

"This way, please."

For someone who is no doubt corrupt and about to request a bribe, his manners are impeccable.

Inside, he removes his hat and settles behind a lone desk. A nameplate, etched in the local language and English, reveals his identity: Captain Hari Bharti.

Hari.

Dirty Hari, I bet.

Under different circumstances, his name might amuse me. But not today.

"You are in Mumbai for how long?" asks Hari.

"Two days."

"Then traveling where?"

"Pune."

He picks up a pen and scrawls in a notebook.

"Where are you staying?"

"Colaba."

"Hotel name?"

"I can't remember. It's a hostel near Leopold Cafe."

A flicker of distrust in his eyes. "You *walked* from Colaba?"

"I went to the Gateway of India first, then Taj Palace Hotel, then to—"

"*Walking?* To all these places?"

"Yeah. I was trying to get to Maharma—" My mind fumbles for the correct pronunciation. "Marmalah—" I give up. "The big laundry."

"Mahalaxmi Dhobi Ghat."

"That's it. The guidebook said it's the biggest outdoor laundry in the world so I thought—"

"Yes, yes." He nods in the usual Indian way. "This laundry is very big."

"I wanted to see Juhu Beach too."

"These places are too far apart for you. This is two days only visit, maybe little bit more also. You have your passport and visa?"

I nod.

"Give it to me," he commands.

Again, I hesitate. This time, I'm concerned the travel document won't be returned without a bribe. An awkward pause results. Eventually, I squeeze a hand behind the waistband of my shorts, unzip my money belt, extract the slim book, and pass it to the burly policeman. His gaze lingers on the national emblem stamped in gold foil on the cover. He opens it with his beefy hands, studies the photo of the sunburnt face, then flips through the pages until he finds my entry visa. After scrutinizing the dates, he closes the passport. Once again, he stares at the image of the kangaroo on the cover, leaving me to wonder how much it will cost to get the animal back into my pouch.

"Very good cricket team," Hari says, handing back the passport.

Relief floods through me, and, for a second, I dare to imagine that the big boss man isn't going to swindle me.

"You play?" he asks.

"Used to. You?"

"When I was young. Now I am working all the time."

"Do you have kids that play?"

Hari's granite face softens to the consistency of wet cement. "No boys. Girls only."

I take that as a 'no'.

"It's a popular game in India," I say.

Hari's head bobs in agreement.

I return the passport to my money belt, then dig out one of my 20-cent coins and place it on the desk. Hari picks it up and studies the embossed figure.

"Who is this? Don Bradman?"

"Yeah."

His eyes widen as if enchanted. "This is from your country?"

"It's a commemorative coin."

Hari stands, walks to the doorway and summons his constables. Within seconds, half a dozen officers crowd the tiny hut. I hear Bradman's name mentioned in a stream of Hindi as the coin is passed between hands. Finally, it returns to Hari, who offers it back to me.

"Keep it," I say.

Hari stalls momentarily, staring at the relief of Bradman wielding his cricket bat in full flight.

"I can not accept this."

Surprise, surprise. *Dirty Hari* is too clean to take 20 cents!

"Please, take it," I insist. "I have more in my backpack."

The hard man reconsiders. "Thank you," he says quietly. "This means a great deal to me."

I wait for the gathered men to giggle at his display of emotion, but they don't. They simply watch on, eyes full of unspoken envy, like children with hearts on sleeves. I wonder where these men were when I was growing up? The vulnerable, sentimental guys. The blokes who valued mateship and worshipped sport, but still upheld a paternal duty of care—to unconditionally serve and protect all.

Hari breaks the moment, asking a constable to bring chai. We drink, trading the usual small talk about our countries, families, and lifestyles.

Finally, he stands and exchanges words with a constable.

"My men will drive you past Dhobi Ghat and Marine Drive. Then to police headquarters. From there, it is only a short walk to Victoria Terminus."

The offer humbles me. "Thanks, but I'm happy to walk."

He waves me off. "It is already arranged." He grabs his hat. "Please, follow me."

I trail him outside to a Land Rover filled with half a dozen policemen.

Hari extends a hand toward me. "It has been a pleasure to meet you."

I clasp his huge paw and shake it. "You too."

I climb into the rear of the four-wheel-drive. A signal is given.

And just like that, I receive my own personal red-light (and blue-light) tour of Mumbai.

Chapter Forty-One

MY TOUR CONCLUDES at Mumbai's gothic-styled police headquarters, two blocks from Victoria Terminus, the city's largest train station. The rail hub—colloquially known as 'VT' by locals—is the second most photographed building in India (the first being the Taj Mahal). From the outside, the century-old station resembles a gigantic fairy-tale palace, complete with Disney-esque arches, gargoyles, domes and spires. Flanking the grand entrance gate, two impressive statues—a lion and a tiger—symbolize Britain's imperial pride and India's fierce resilience.

Falling in step with peak hour commuters, I pass the feline sentinels and enter the cavernous station to reserve a ticket to my next destination: Pune. The ticket hall teems with hundreds of passengers, ensuring a long, tedious wait. The ordeal is made worse by a steady stream of people brazenly cutting in line directly in front of me. Each time, I bite my tongue, trying to embrace yet another *authentic* Indian experience.

A disgruntled man directly behind me isn't so forgiving. His squat frame brushes past me, and with a confidence befitting someone who actually *looks* intimidating, he loudly chastises the offenders. His rebuke works, and the culprits retreat to the back of the line.

"I apologize for these men," he says upon returning. "But you must tell them to stop. Otherwise, everyone will be held up."

"I wasn't sure if I should say anything," I say, defending my meekness. "Being a foreigner."

"This is why they pick you." He extends a palm in greeting and we swap introductions. "This is my card," he adds, handing over a business card as if to confirm his identity.

Prashant's profession is listed as *electrical engineer*, but his tired clothes, worn work bag, and middle-aged paunch suggest a weary, white-collar battler rather than a rising corporate star.

I glance at the growing peak hour crowd. "Do you deal with this every day?"

He nods. "This is not so bad yet."

"It gets worse?"

"Busier, yes. You are traveling from Australia? Or New Zealand?"

"Australia."

"I thought so," he says, pleased with his deduction. "For how long."

"Three months."

"And where are you going now?"

"Pune."

Prashant clicks his tongue. "My friend, you will wait a very long time. The Pune train is not for many hours."

"I'm booking for tomorrow."

"Ah," he nods approvingly. "And tonight? What are your plans?"

"Just sleep."

"In that case, I would like to invite you to my home for dinner."

I loathe social gatherings—even at the best of times. The thought of an awkward evening of small talk, drenched in sweat from a peak-hour Mumbai train ride, is about as appealing as dysentery. So I scramble for an excuse.

"I wouldn't want to inconvenience you."

"No inconvenience. Meeting you is very good luck for me. You are like a God."

His words catch me off guard. *A God*. Finally, someone recognizes my significance!

With my escape thwarted, I reluctantly accept his invite.

"This is a very good day," Prashant beams. "My family will be most honored."

I smile weakly, then spend the next fifteen minutes trying to dissuade him from buying me a train ticket to his house. Prashant wins, and we make our way to the station's packed platforms.

Victoria Terminus is the world's busiest train station. At peak hour, five thousand passengers cram into carriages designed for a quarter of that number. In transit, commuters cling to exterior siding, dangle from open doors, even ride on rooftops. In fact, so many new passengers try to board at each stop that it's virtually impossible for old passengers to get *off*.

Prashant senses my unease. "Have you been on a Mumbai train?" he asks.

I shake my head.

"Please, stay close," he warns. "You must be fast."

Our train arrives, and a fleet-footed Prashant pushes forward against the flow of disembarking passengers. I follow, my body propelled by the crush behind me. Within seconds, the carriage is jam-packed. Late arrivals continue to squeeze onboard—even as the train jerks forward—compressing every inch of space until there's barely room to breathe.

As the locomotive gains speed, feeble gusts of air funnel through open windows, diluting the thick musk of body odor and easing my growing claustrophobia.

From my six-foot-high vantage point, I spy three children from the wrong side of the tracks weaving through the throng. The beggars—two girls and a little boy—solicit goodwill as they go. After several station stops, the kids finally reach Prashant and me. Their dirty, disheveled appearance tugs at my heartstrings, rendering me the softest of targets.

"Money?" the eldest girl asks, hands outstretched.

I reach for my wallet, but Prashant blocks me.

"Please do not give," he says firmly. "These children work for criminals. They are forced to beg."

The revelation doesn't come as a shock, but I'm still consumed by guilt that can only be lessened by giving. In an action that contradicts his own advice, Prashant retrieves two coins from his pocket, places them into the girl's raised hands, and ushers her away.

"This is not your duty," he explains. "It is mine. This is my religion. It is good karma for me."

The girl moves on, leaving room for the little boy to step forward. He can't be more than five years of age. Mimicking the older girl, he raises two expectant hands and stares at me like a dependent toddler. In an instant, the urge to lift him up and wrap him in my arms overwhelms me. I want to whisk him to the safety of a mother. His mother. My mother. *Any* mother.

Claire.

The child looks at me with pleading eyes, begging me to make good on my silent promise.

"I wish I could save you," I relay wordlessly to him. *"So I could save me."*

But I can't.

To do that, I'd need to believe that life could get better. That every tomorrow could begin with hope instead of remorse. That happiness lay beyond every corner instead of disaster. That karma was a reward for right instead of a punishment for wrong. That everything bad in the world wasn't my fault. And not all of its problems were mine to single-handedly solve.

Problems like his. Problems like mine.

Problems impossible to resolve.

Prashant breaks the spell the child has on me. With a firm hand, he shoos the boy away. My heart aches as I watch the child vanish before me.

For the rest of the journey, I remain silent, observing Mumbai life through the window, trying to comprehend how twenty million inhabitants coexist in this city.

"When the train stops, you must move fast," Prashant tells me. "There are twenty seconds only."

Despite his warning, I am completely unprepared when we reach his station. Scores of waiting commuters clamber onto the train before it even stops, and suddenly I realize I am at risk of being trapped in the carriage. Leading by example, Prashant charges through the crowd like a bull and exits onto the platform. I try the same approach, but the tide of new arrivals surges against me, restricting my progress.

Precious seconds slip away.

In desperation, I call to Prashant. "I can't get off."

"You must push," he shouts. "Push!"

More seconds pass as additional bodies block my escape.

The conductor's whistle blows.

With renewed determination, I shove my torso against the wall of passengers. I gain a single footstep. Then another. Two more. I'm just a body length away from freedom when I feel the carriage shunt.

And the train moves.

Chapter Forty-Two

PRASHANT LEAPS INTO ACTION. With a forcefulness that belies his unassuming demeanor, he muscles his way back onto the moving carriage, creating a man-sized gap between passengers. In one desperate dash, he grabs my arm and hauls me through the opening, and together we escape onto the platform.

I'm unscathed but shaken.

Prashant, however, is grinning.

"*Now* is peak hour," he says with a sparkle in his eye.

With hurried strides, we exit the station and emerge onto a street. Prashant sets a relentless pace, and I struggle to keep up with the little engineer as he weaves through congested human traffic with an ease I envy. In every direction, people scrutinize me as I pass, their expressions switching between curiosity and bemusement at the oddity in their presence.

Leaving a main thoroughfare, we veer into an alley that snakes us through a patchwork of concrete buildings, their facades aged by weather and grime, and the touch of a million passing lives. The sheer density of living is overwhelming, as is the visual intensity. Nothing looks uniform. No single color or architectural style dominates. Everything is chaotic yet functional, makeshift yet permanent. Above us, worn tarpaulins stretch from high balconies, serving as shade. Fresh laundry clings to ropes strung between buildings. At ground level, children play cricket on any vacant flat surface, while elders spectate from shadowed doorways, their weary eyes watching over a world they no longer shape.

The area is not a slum, but it's a world away from middle-class comfort.

Prashant pushes on to yet another precinct, where I sense a discernible change. The laneways are quieter. The buildings squat, simple and homely. Underfoot, a cleanliness exists that wasn't evident before. The concrete here is swept—kept—an unspoken declaration of pride.

Finally, Prashant stops at a modest door set into a blue-rinsed wall. "This is my home," he proudly announces.

A fresh wave of apprehension washes over me as I study the small concrete abode.

"Are you sure I'm not intruding?" I ask hesitantly.

Prashant's chest swells slightly as he pushes the door open. "This is the opposite of intruding," he reassures me. "This is perfect timing. Because today we break our fast."

The significance of his news tightens the knot of discomfort in my gut. He and his family have spent the day in ritual fasting, yet he has chosen to share their evening meal with me—a stranger from a train station.

"I really don't want to impose," I try again.

Prashant waves away my concern and ushers me indoors.

Inside, the interior is dimly lit, save for the flickering glow from a television and the dull radiance of two incandescent ceiling bulbs. Watching the TV from a couch are two elderly figures—his parents, no doubt—while a pair of preteen children sit on the floor. Seeking to add details, my other senses kick in. There's a coolness here, a natural byproduct of rendered concrete walls and low ceiling. But what captures my senses the most is the robust aroma of turmeric, cinnamon, and cumin—spices that champion the virtues of home-cooked food.

Prashant calls to his wife, announcing my arrival.

The woman, clad in a scarlet sari and slim bangles, abandons her position at a small gas stovetop and approaches us. Her husband introduces me to her and his other family members. Their names blur together in my mind, impossible to recall, let alone pronounce. So I smile like the dimwitted foreigner I am. Thankfully, a conversation begins between the four adults, and I gain an unguarded moment to further absorb my surroundings. There are two main rooms—the living space we currently occupy and an adjoining bedroom. A single doorway leads to a tiny washroom, which Prashant points out with evident pride.

"Our home is small," he says, sensing my judgment. "But extremely comfortable."

His words reverberate in my head, highlighting the chasm between our lives. Back home, no one would consider this a 'comfortable' home. There's no guest bedroom, no ensuite, no study or media room. No sprawling backyard. No pool. And yet, here stands a man who is genuinely content with what he has. So many of us have more than Prashant will ever have, yet it never feels like enough. We don't just want a good life—we want a perfect one.

We continue to chat, broaching topics like real estate prices, wages, and the cost of living in our respective countries, but soon, Prashant's wife beckons us to eat. It's only then that I notice the house has no dining table or chairs. Dinner, it seems, will be served on a large woven floor mat.

Following the family's lead, I lower myself into a cross-legged position around a generous offering of dal, rice, chutneys, and bread; all presented on a communal metal *thali* plate and in multiple bowls. There are no forks or knives in sight and, suddenly, it dawns on me that I will be eating with my hands. Or rather, eating with one hand. The *correct* hand. The one that isn't used for toileting. Unfortunately, I have no idea which hand that is.

Prashant finishes his grace-like prayer. When he lifts his face, he turns to me and gestures towards the food. "Please, eat," he says warmly. "You will break our fast."

Filled with apprehension, I spoon food from the communal plates as the entire family watches on. Then I cautiously reach towards my meal with my—right hand. I wait for objections or looks of disgust. There are none, so I clumsily squish grains of rice and chutney into a loose wad between my fingers and ferry it to my mouth. It's awkward and messy, but the food is delicious.

"Do you fast regularly?" I ask between bites.

Prashant nods as he grabs food, also with his right hand. "For many gods," he says. "This one is for Ganesh."

He points towards one of the many large religious posters that dot the lounge-room wall. The vibrant cartoon-like artwork depicts a family of three, consisting of a blue-skinned man, a light-skinned woman, and a child with four arms and the head of an elephant.

"Ganesh is the child," he explains. "He is god of prosperity and protector of families."

The reverence in his voice is unmistakable. It's obvious that Prashant is a man devoted to family and faith.

I hand-build another food ball. "I'm sorry about what happened on the train," I say, seemingly out of nowhere.

My host waves a dismissive hand before scooping dal onto a shard of roti. "It is no problem. Mumbai's trains are very crowded."

"I meant about giving money to the kids," I clarify. "I'm an easy target. Probably too soft for India."

Prashant lowers his bread and eyes me, his expression suddenly serious. "You can never be too soft for India," he says earnestly. "In this country, you must *always* think with your heart."

Prashant's father clears his throat. "You are a Christian, Chris?"

I shake my head while breaking bread—roti bread. "I'm not religious. But I believe in the principles."

Which is true. I do believe in them. I just rarely live by them.

Prashant picks up the thread of conversation. "My family is very religious," he says. "It is our way." He mops up some chutney with rice. "Have you heard of dharma?"

"Karma?" I ask.

"*Dharma*," he corrects patiently. "Dharma is—" He pauses briefly. "Duty, perhaps? Living right. These things together, but more also."

"A virtuous life?" I ask.

"Yes. Good morals." He pauses again. "This is important in Samsara."

Samsara. I've heard of this. The Wheel of Life.

"I thought that was Buddhist?"

"This is in my religion also," he says. "Our journey is continuous, connected to the universe."

I don't fully comprehend what he is saying and it probably shows.

"Do you believe in fate, Chris?" His eyes rise to meet mine. "Or do you think we shape our destiny?"

"Probably a bit of both."

Prashant considers my ambiguous answer. "You know good from bad, yes?" He watches my head nod in affirmation. "Dharma is our path. Our intention. Karma is different. Karma is actions. Every choice, good and bad and in between, shape fate. And all have consequences. It is why you are here, Chris. Why you met me. You know this, yes?"

I think back to the choices and actions that led me to this moment. The detours. The mistakes. The domino effect of constantly straying from the right path. The good intentions but bad actions.

"Without good dharma and good karma," Prashant says, still sermonizing, "our universe is in chaos. Life has no harmony. No balance. No direction. Without it we are lost."

And in that moment, I finally understand.

Call it karma. Call it destiny. Call it fate.

It's all the same deal. The message is universal, no matter what the religion.

You reap what you sow.

Chapter Forty-Three

A PALM SLAMS onto my table.

"You are fucking racist, man. One hundred percent fucking racist."

Up until twenty minutes ago, I had been enjoying a quiet lunch in an upmarket restaurant in Pune. Since then, I've had my solitude interrupted by a sociopath who swears more than I do.

The aptly named Harsh continues his rant: "My family is worth fifty-million U.S. dollars, man. Fifty fucking million." He boasts. "I build high-rise apartments all over Mumbai, but your racist fucking government won't give me a visa because I'm Indian."

A very unlikeable Indian, I think to myself.

Harsh and I are the only patrons in the restaurant, so I have to endure his company and digest his distasteful life story alone. He's the stereotypical rich kid—spoilt, arrogant, overbearing, and super-confident. He wears his wealth and has little patience for the opinions of others. It's obvious that time is money for Harsh, because his watch probably cost more than Prashant's home in Mumbai.

"I don't think it's Indians in particular," I say diplomatically. "Australia's immigration process is strict for everyone. Used to be worse in the 1950s. We actually had a 'White Australia' policy back then."

"You are worse than America," Harsh snaps.

Again with the generalized 'you' accusation. Hopefully, he means Australia as a whole, rather than me personally.

"You don't let anyone in," he continues. "You're so fucking insular and obsessed with how the world sees you."

On second thought, maybe he is talking about me.

I mean, I do actually worry about what others think of me. And I am insular. Especially as a traveller. In fact, I'm so insular that even after two months I still think all Indians live in poverty. Because that's mostly what I've seen…but only because I haven't opened my eyes. The *real* India is far more expansive than my limited view. There are lifestyles and aspirations in this country that mirror, and even exceed, my own.

Many locals in Pune seem exactly like me—same unrealized dreams, frustrations, and aspirations. They frequent upmarket cafes, plan overseas vacations, and immerse themselves in new trends. There are teens obsessed with shopping and celebrity, and affluent businessman and tech-entrepreneurs driven by BMWs, Bentleys and billion dollar visions.

"Everyone in the West is the same," Harsh continues. "You care only about yourself. You think every Indian is an uneducated peasant or some sister-fucking Muslim terrorist." He leans forward, almost spitting the words. "It's fucking racist, man. Every movie and TV show with an Indian, all racist. Always eating curries and talking with a stupid accent. I don't speak like that. None of my friends speak like that. We're better educated than you backpackers. You're the peasants, riding buses and trains while I'm driving a two-hundred-thousand-dollar Mercedes."

Harsh's *marque* of success.

"Half your luck," I say. "They're nice cars."

A flicker of something unexpected flashes across Harsh's face.

"What do you drive, man?"

"Holden Kingswood. Old Australian car."

"Classic?"

"Kinda. 1976."

"Two or four-door?"

"Four."

"V8?"

"Straight six. One previous owner. Cost me eight hundred bucks."

Unsurprisingly, my deal of a lifetime doesn't impress Harsh.

"Fuck classics, man. You'd love my AMG."

Indeed, I would. But Harsh doesn't get the appeal of my car. He obviously hasn't experienced the joys of steering a tank-like sedan that has the handling characteristics of an ocean-liner. Old-school cruising isn't about money, technology, or even engineering. It's about feeling—windows down, AM/FM radio on, cool vinyl upholstery, lazy gear-shifts, and a clutch pedal so firm it could put quad muscles on the tentacles of a jellyfish.

I went on a night cruise the day I bought it. Claire beside me on the bench seat, one hand on the steering wheel, the other around her shoulders. Simple. Uncomplicated. Like the car. Smooth, trouble-free motoring that, for a moment, idled back the complexity of our life.

Harsh glances at his watch. "I gotta go, man." He pushes out his chair and stands to leave. "How long you in town?"

"Two days. Just long enough to check out the resort."

"Fuck that place. You won't get any pussy there. The bitches are ice queens. Fucking racist too."

I chew on that advice for a second or two, trying to regurgitate a suitable reply.

"I'm not one hundred percent sure I'll stay there."

"It's a waste of time. Easier to get a hooker. But whatever." Harsh reaches his hand out across the table. "Anyway, nice to meet you, man."

"Thanks," I say, shaking his hand. "You too." Though the truth is completely opposite.

The Mumbai millionaire departs the restaurant, leaving a bad aftertaste.

I push my plate aside and signal the waiter for the bill. It's time for me to leave as well. I have an appointment—a tour at the Osho International Meditation Resort.

Or, as everyone calls it: *The Sex Ashram.*

Chapter Forty-Four

THE OSHO INTERNATIONAL Meditation Resort could double as the set of a utopian science-fiction movie—a futuristic brave new world built from clinical black marble, opaque glass, exposed concrete, and obsessively manicured gardens. The setting is both serene and surreal, a meticulously ordered realm designed for peace-loving aliens, ethereal wanderers, and trippy space-cadets. Clad in maroon robes, the resort's inhabitants float about, their facial expressions hinting at a drug-induced euphoria. They look like free-love advocates from the 1960s, captured in a permanent post-coital glow. The resemblance isn't entirely misleading, given that the resort spawned from the so-called 'Orange People Sex Cult'.

"Are the red robes compulsory?"

The query comes from Carlo, a Spanish traveller who seems far less interested in meditation than in the abundance of nubile, free-spirited woman who traipse around the joint. He's one of five people in my lunchtime tour group.

Our guide, Edward, turns his thin, pale face towards the movie-star-handsome Spaniard. He swallows nervously like a virgin in a brothel. "Yes, the maroon robes are worn every day," he explains, with the crisp cadence of a London private school boy. "It helps unify our collective meditation experience and reduces unnecessary distractions."

"Like sexual distractions?" Carlo asks, ever hopeful.

The middle-aged German couple and shy Korean girl in our group shift uncomfortably.

Edward's features twitch in barely contained irritation. "*Spiritual* distractions," he corrects. "Meditation requires mental discipline. The fewer intrusions in our mind, the more energy we can dedicate to understanding self."

Carlo accepts the explanation with a respectful nod, then asks: "Underwear or no underwear under the robes?"

Edward's lips thin. "Guests are free to wear what they want beneath their robes."

"Are they free to have sex, too?" the cheeky Iberian adds with a grin.

Edward glares at him. "You'll have to join to find out." With that, he turns abruptly and resumes leading the tour.

I drift toward Carlo, sensing that he's the only one who finds all of this as amusing as I do. He has a sharp wit, and his wicked mind fits the setting perfectly. Ironically, his instincts aren't far off because the Osho's spiritual founder, Bhagwan Shree Rajneesh, was fixated on similar distractions himself. In short, he believed humans could find enlightenment through meditation…and free and easy sex. In his case, lots of free sex. With lots of easy female followers.

Edward leads us up the garden path, passing an impressive circular auditorium. Through expansive windows, we glimpse a meditation class in session. Over a hundred students sit in silence, legs pretzeled into lotus positions as relaxation music hums through the space. It looks disappointingly normal and, sadly, there's not an orgy in sight. After an exhaustingly detailed explanation about meditation from Edward, the tour moves on. We pass a modern bistro and resort-style pool before stopping at a striking black-marble building capped with a glass pyramid roof.

"This is the Osho Auditorium," Edward announces with reverence. "The largest meditation hall in the world."

Carlo leans in and whispers to me, "Sex central."

Edward continues, "Each day, a different meditation class is held here. We offer dynamic meditation like dance and shaking. Laughter meditation, whirling, humming…" He smiles self-consciously. "Today's session is Gibberish Meditation."

Unsure if I have heard correctly, I peer into the cavernous studio space for clarification. Inside, scores of people wildly flail their arms and convulse their torsos in spasmodic movements that make them look insane. In addition, the entire class is speaking in tongues like feverish monkeys on cocaine. There is, quite literally, a stream of gibberish spewing from their mouths.

It looks like one of those agonizing corporate team-building exercises designed to break spirit, embarrass colleagues, and erode all self-respect. But promote good mental health, apparently.

I turn to Carlo and slap him on the shoulder. "So, you gonna sign up, mate?"

Carlo's eyes widen. "I don't know, man. This place is *loco*."

And yet, for all its eccentricity, the Osho resort exudes an air of exclusivity. The clientele are a mix of bored backpackers, wealthy hippies, and meditation enthusiasts with disposable income.

"Lots of women," I say.

"This is true," Carlo admits. "You going to join?"

I shake my head. "You couldn't pay me to do gibberish meditation session."

"But people do pay," Carlo says. "So maybe there's something in it." His eyebrows rise and a wry smile appears. "Would you sign up for sex sessions?"

I return the wry grin. "Don't know. I'd have to meditate on that."

Our chatter draws a disapproving glance from Edward, so we relocate to a grassed area nearby and watch maroon-robed Westerners pad about in sandals, their semi-smiling faces vaguely blissed-out. It looks like a Buddhist monastery where the monks and nuns have suddenly woken to find themselves reincarnated as spiritually stoned millionaires in a ClubMed resort.

A flustered Edward reappears at the pyramid entrance, spots his two missing tour members, then closes in on us.

"Please, remain with the group," he commands, his voice carrying a note of exasperation. "We all have to stay on the path."

And therein lies the problem of the Osho International Meditation

Resort—you must stay on the path. Wear the same robes. Meditate in groups. Let go of self. Conform.

But that's not who I am.

Paradoxically, there is a part of me that truly does ache to surrender to something greater than me—to follow, chant, sing, and lose all my debilitating inhibitions so I can lurch about like an epileptic antelope. But that part of me is buried far too deep within.

Eventually, my sex ashram tour ends, fittingly, in an anticlimax.

Chapter Forty-Five

MEDITATING on my dislike of meditation, I stroll to a nearby German bakery eager for outside distraction—namely coffee, cake and company. The rigid control of the ashram has left me restless, craving external pleasures to escape my own thoughts. The realization unsettles me, and confirms a troubling suspicion I've had lately: maybe my overseas journey isn't a quest to find self, but rather a mission of self-avoidance. If that is the case, it explains why yoga classes and meditation retreats hold no appeal. There's too much time to think. Too much rumination. Too much baggage to unpack.

Best to keep moving.

I order a cappuccino and slice of cheesecake, then make my way to the eatery's outdoor dining area. The decor is a blend of East meets West. Batik wall hangings and posters offering spiritual wisdom, watch over a diverse clientele who are enjoying a taste of European cafe culture. Some are locals, some tourists, some are even Osho followers, who look surprisingly animated and normal outside the walls of the resort.

Seeing no vacant table, I single out a lone diner and ask if I can join him. His sullen demeanor is an instant red flag—because right now, I'm in need of light conversation—but I sit anyway and extend a hand in introduction. He reluctantly clasps it, unenthused.

"Do you live here," I ask.

Ashok nods. "You at the Osho?"

"No. Guesthouse down the road. Just did a tour there, though." It sounds like I've survived the Vietnam war.

"Should have stayed there, bro," he says in a monotone. "That's where all the chicks are."

I glance around the bakery. "Plenty here too."

Ashok's face betrays his morose mood, and he almost smiles. "That's the only reason I'm here."

I cast an eye over his slight frame, noting the button-up shirt, neatly combed hair, and boyish face. He has the air of a first year uni student—innocent eyes, awkward body language, and the circadian rhythms of someone who prefers to wake at the crack of noon. There probably isn't a girl in this bakery who would let him stoke her fire, let alone put a bun in her oven.

"So, you do okay here?" I ask, already knowing the answer.

"Nah, man." His head dips towards his coffee mug. "Foreign chicks aren't interested in me."

"Just wear a robe and pretend you're spiritual," I joke.

My attempt at humor falls flat and Ashok's gaze wanders.

"See her?"

He gestures toward a Western woman sitting alone at a shared table nearby. She's at least five years older than him, possibly even ten, which is around my age. Judging by her single-status, intense expression, and brand new *Lonely Planet* guidebook, she's a new arrival deep in culture shock.

"Chicks like that don't even look at Indian guys," Ashok says. "We're invisible to them."

My attention returns to him. "What's wrong with Indian girls?"

"You don't know my country, bro," he scoffs. "Dating here is all about jobs and money, and family background. That's why I want a foreign girlfriend." He drains the last of his coffee, then glances at my left hand. "You married?"

"No."

"Playing the field, yeah?"

"If I am, I'm the world's worst 'player'."

Ashok smirks. "Come on, man, don't be modest. Give a bro some pointers."

"Sorry, mate, I got nothing."

"Seriously, man, give me *something* to work with."

"I am serious." I tilt my head in the blonde's direction. "You're better off asking her."

"That's never going to happen."

"Why not? Just talk to her."

Ashok's shoulders slump. "Bro, this is the problem. I don't have anything to talk about. Got no job, no cash, no life." His eyes drop to his mug. "I've been here for an hour with one coffee. It's fucking embarrassing."

Jesus Christ, no wonder he was sitting by himself. The miserable prick makes me look like a court jester by comparison.

I drink my coffee in double time. "You up for another one? My shout."

Ashok declines.

"Come on, cappuccino or latte? Otherwise, you'll go home and I'll have to sit here and chat up hot chicks by myself."

He frowns at my shit-stirring jibe but eventually accepts my offer.

I go order and return with the drinks, our conversation still on my mind.

"Ok, here's my advice: show interest and be yourself."

Ashok huffs. "Being myself *is* the problem."

"Don't be so hard on yourself. Just relax and try not to feel so self-conscious."

He shakes his head, skeptical. "Easy for you. You're tall, confident, and traveling the world. I live with my parents."

I do understand, of course. After all, I'm trying to become more windswept and interesting for Emma.

I glance over at the blonde tourist, who is still immersed in her guidebook and looking very unapproachable.

"Should I invite here over?"

Panic instantly flashes across Ashok's face. "No. Don't, man… please."

Ignoring him, I turn to the woman. "Excuse me…"

She looks up, her expression wary, the guarded look of a woman who has learned to anticipate unwanted advances.

"Do you speak English, by any chance?"

She nods, still cautious. "Not so good." Her accent is European.

"Can I ask you a quick question?"

"Sure. It's okay." She closes her guidebook. "If I can answer."

"We were just talking about what women like in men. Ashok thinks he needs lots of money and a good career. And I think good communication and just being yourself."

"I'm sorry, you mean, which men do *I* like?"

I nod, suddenly wondering if she is even attracted to men.

"Both, of course. But mostly the second."

"So what do you like specifically?"

She thinks for a moment, then points to the spare chair beside me.

"Can I sit…?"

"Yeah, please." I pull the chair out and she moves to our setting. "I'm Chris by the way, this is Ashok."

I stare at my Indian mate and raise my eyebrows as if to say "See, *bro*, she fucking invited herself".

"I am Sofia."

"What country are you from?" I ask.

"Italy."

I sit upright. "Ahh… okay."

Sofia laughs, transforming her face. "This is a problem?"

I note the sparkle in her eye and instantly know Sofia has a good sense of humor.

I turn to Ashok. "I made a mistake, mate, don't talk to Italian women. Because they're all *crazy*."

Sofia's mouth opens in feigned outrage. "This is a lie. We are *not* crazy."

"Yes you are," I quip. "And *I* know, because my family's Italian."

"You are making this up," Sofia rails. "You are not Italian."

"I swear to God. I have a Nonna."

There's still a look of disbelief on Sofia's face.

"From where in Italy?" she challenges.

"Not far from Venice."

"I am from the south," she says.

I give Ashok another look of dismay. "Sofia's from the worst part of Italy. Where all the poor people live."

She slaps me playfully. "How do you know this? You have been to my country?"

"Jesus, no." I recoil in mock horror. "Too many Italians to deal with."

Sofia looks to Ashok and raises the palms of both hands in surrender. "He is right. This is why I come here for my vacation."

"Are you at the ashram?" Ashok asks.

She nods. "For two weeks of meditation courses."

"Sex meditation, probably," I interject, crudely channelling Carlo the Spaniard.

Sofia's cheeks redden and she eyes me with curiosity for a heartbeat. I see the lines on her forehead pinch, but her lips open slightly in vulnerability, then I feel a brief but unmistakable spark jump between us.

"This is none of your business," she says flatly. Then, with a suggestive smirk, she coyly adds: "But maybe."

My groin twitches involuntarily and suddenly I am short of a witty retort. I wait for Ashok to say something to further his chances but he's struck dumb as well.

Sofia palms her hair back in a subliminal act of preening. "You are at the ashram too?"

"No. It's not my thing."

"Why not?"

"Honestly? It scares me."

"What scares you?"

"Chanting, shaking, and speaking gibberish in public."

Sofia assesses me, and correctly diagnoses me as control freak. "That is to help you relax your body and mind," she says. "So you can just be yourself."

Ashok smirks at the irony of the tables turning on me.

"I know. I just hate that stuff." My voice sounds far more serious than I want it to.

"This is why you should do it," she says, with authority of a meditation practitioner. "It means you have something inside that must come out."

Sofia stares at me for an extended moment, her direct gaze unnerving me. It's unconsciously compassionate, and I recognize it in an instant, because I've seen it on women before—the one's who want to save me.

"You should come to a meditation with me," Sofia continues.

I sip my coffee. "I don't know. I'll think about it."

I glance at the silent Ashok, who surely must think I'm the world's worst wingman.

In my peripheral vision, I catch Sofia's eye line drift to my forearms and hands, appraising me. I know what she wants. She wants to gently point me back inwards where I don't want to go—lead me to self-discovery through free love.

Encourage me to find 'release'.

UPRIGHT – Oh, fuck... Wake up, motherfucker. Shit is about to get real.
REVERSED – Time for a shake-up. It's okay... it's for your own good.

Chapter Forty-Six

I ELBOW my aching body upright, peeling myself from the damp sheets. My limbs protest as I stagger through the darkness towards the bathroom. With each step, my pace quickens until I find—

Release.

My stomach convulses, and I projectile vomit all over the toilet bowl, cistern and floor. A sharp cramp doubles me over, and I clumsily mount the toilet before a stream of crimson liquid involuntarily explodes from my backside. My fevered body trembles as multiple spasms wrack my frame, painting the porcelain with blood.

So much blood.

A familiar fear, of anxieties past, flickers in my mind.

Jesus Christ, when is this nightmare going to end?

Finally, the attack subsides and I list into the shower. I'm lava-hot and utterly exhausted. Every joint and muscle aches, every breath hurts. My head pounds with a migraine so vicious it warps reality. Feverish hallucinations infect my mind, distorting time and space with alternative realities of torment and terror. Like clockwork, the same ungodly cycle repeats every hour: spew, shit, shower, and sleep. I don't even know how long I've been trapped here. I remember leaving the bakery a few hours before my first attack, but I can't recall when that was. Yesterday? Or the day before?

"Meet me at the front gate at seven," Sofia had said.

My heart sinks as I picture Sofia waiting for me to show. Expectation turning to frustration, confusion, then doubt and, finally, to hurt as she realized I wasn't going to be there.

I'm sorry I wasn't there, Claire.

I catch my feverish thoughts as they falter.

Sofia.

The mental lapse coincides with my legs failing me. Depleted of strength, they fold and I slide down the tiles. I lean forward, hugging my knees to my chest, and let the cascading water from above massage my shoulders. The cool fall stimulates my skin, providing welcome relief. Like entering an air conditioned room in summer. Like slipping hands beneath pillows. Like sliding naked beneath fresh sheets.

I feel myself mentally slipping away again.

I need to rest. I need to sleep.

Forever.

"We need to operate right now."

I hear the words I thought would never be spoken. Male voice. Calm but firm. Professional. Clinical.

Surgical.

"We can't reach the specialist." This update from a newly arrived female.

The doctor stares at the nurse, decides in an instant. "Wheel her to surgery."

His command punctures my hope like a scalpel, releasing nausea-inducing bile into the back of my throat. Claire's mother, Grace, meets my gaze as I struggle to swallow the horror. Her ashen face mirrors mine.

Jesus Christ, when is this nightmare going to end?

For Claire, there is no escape from her ungodly cycle of shit, shower and sleep—unless they operate. The weight of that truth brings me to the point of fainting. Not wanting to create a scene, I flee the hospital ward and double over in the hallway, gasping lungfuls of air to avoid collapsing. Embryonic tears blur my vision.

Please, don't do this," I silently beg. *"Please, don't cut her open."*

Bowed in supplication, I wait for equilibrium and composure to return. Finally, I steady myself, take a deep breath, and peer through the glass divide that separates me from the unfolding disaster. Hopelessness washes over me. I have no solution for this imperfect moment of life—no plan, no skills. No control.

I watch my skeletal lover rise with help from the bed. Her loose hospital gown barely conceals her naked emaciated frame, but she doesn't care. Claire's inhibitions, like her flesh, have been consumed by the illness devouring her. She is twenty-five years old but frailer than an octogenarian.

The nurse guides her to a nearby bathroom, mimicking the endless trips Claire has taken each day at home, for months on end. As she disappears into the cubicle, the doctor looks to Claire's mother. An unspoken exchange passes between them. A truth that makes me sick to stomach.

Claire is dying.

I FEEL close to death as my fever intensifies.

The nausea builds to the point of no return, and I slap a hand over my mouth, then race to the toilet once more. My gag reflex fires and a burst of acidic fluid erupts from my mouth. Again and again. Several dry retches follow long after there is anything left to give. I slump to the floor, drenched in sweat, gasping for breath. Uncertain of my whereabouts, I look around the bathroom.

Fuck...

I'm still in India.

Which means there will be no respite ahead.

Burning up and depleted of energy, I crawl back into the bedroom. My hazy vision betrays me as I go. The walls shimmer, the floor undulates, and my mattress drifts on an imagined ocean. The hallucinations are so real that I don't want to close my eyes. But I'm so tired. Then I see a familiar figure lying prone on the sheets. The beauty beckons me closer.

CLAIRE SMILES at me from her post-op hospital bed, her face soft and angelic from the residual anesthetic. Her eyes are vivid with life because death has finally been excised.

"Hey," she says. Her voice is tired and depleted.

I gently clasp her hand, feeling her reassuring pulse. "How you feeling, Bub?"

"Pretty good." She holds up her IV controller with a mischievous smile. "But it might be the morphine talking."

I can't bring myself to laugh. "Did they tell you what happened?"

She nods. "They told me before I went in." She catches my downcast expression. "I'm sorry."

The apology puzzles me. "For what?"

"I know you didn't want this for me. But I wanted it out."

I force a thin smile. "They saved your life, Bub."

They also destroyed it, I think to myself. Because the physical and emotional implications are now monstrous. Incomprehensibly life-changing. Nothing will ever be the same.

"Look at this," she says, opening her gown.

The action reveals a raw scalpel cut that runs from the base of her sternum, past her navel and through to her pubic bone. A score of metal staples bite into her soft porcelain skin, jawing the massive wound shut.

"Holy shit…" I gasp.

"Big, hey?"

My eye catches another other obvious incision and addition. Permanently sewn onto the right side of her abdomen is the end of her small intestine. The organ that was once connected to her colon now deposits fecal matter into a clear plastic ostomy bag.

I feign nonchalance. "Better than dead, though."

Claire doesn't respond. In silence, my mind races as I entertain what comes next in life. I need to make changes at home. So she can recover.

I need to make changes in me.

"I love you more than anything," I say, as an unexpected flood of emotion threatens to sink me.

Claire squeezes my hand. "I know." Another quick squeeze follows, then a vague, medicated glance. "I'm so sorry, Bub. I can't talk anymore."

I lean over for a goodbye kiss. "Just rest, beautiful girl."

Our lips touch and I kiss her deeply, desperate to pass on my unconditional love. I gently disengage and her eyelids flutter as she slowly fades.

"You going to be all right?" I ask, stroking her forearm.

Claire nods weakly. "Morphine," she says with a brief smirk.

I plant another kiss. This time near her ear. "See you tomorrow, Bub," I whisper.

But I'm too late. Claire is already fast asleep.

An alarm rouses me from my dreams.

I force my eyes open and study the surroundings. My body still burns and the acrid scent of puke lingers in the humid air.

The alarm chimes for my attention.

Disoriented, I try to triangulate its location with ears and eyes that strain to function. Narrowing the source to an unzipped pocket on my backpack, I spot the cubed outline of a travel clock beneath the polyester material. I must have accidentally activated the alarm while hunting for painkillers during the night. I reach across and silence the beeping. Then with a heavy head, I roll back onto the bed and my eyelids close.

I sleep in beyond my usual rising time.

But when I wake I feel unexpectedly revived. It's a new day, a brighter one—the better tomorrow I prayed for during the previous days of drama.

Claire's new life begins today.

In high spirits, I forgo breakfast for a quick shower, then drive to the hospital. With luck on my side, I score a car park half a block from the entrance. A short walk with a spring in my step, puts me in an already waiting lift that delivers me to Claire's floor. The door opens to reveal the nurses' station and I merrily stroll to the ward.

But Claire's not there.

Nor any trace of her belongings.

Confused, I return to the lifts and check the floor number. I'm in the right place so I ask a nurse for Claire's whereabouts.

"There were some complications," says the solemn-faced woman.

Her news spikes my heart rate.

"She's in ICU. I'll take you down."

The nurse ushers me into the lift and I feel my feet fall beneath me. The doors part and reveal a sign that says 'Intensive Care Unit'. Wordlessly, the nurse leads me down a hallway and into a waiting room where I find two distressed parents.

Grace looks old beyond her years, and the ever-talkative Trevor has been rendered silent, which hints at something ominous.

"She developed pneumonia overnight," Claire's mother says, addressing the perplexed expression on my face.

My blank response broadcasts my continued cluelessness, forcing Grace to spell it out.

"There's an infection in her lungs," she explains.

Creeping anxiety sneaks in. "Is she all right?"

Grace takes a long vibrato breath, trying to gather her emotions. "It's not looking good."

I scan her face, needing further clarification. Finally, it arrives.

"She's on a life-support ventilator," she adds.

Grace's words reach me as an emotional whisper but reverberate deep inside me like a primal howl. Suddenly my eyes redden. Desperate to maintain a show of masculinity in front of Claire's father, I try not to cry like a little boy.

"Her body can't fight the infection," Grace continues. "The immunosuppressants she was on are now working against her."

I stand stoic, in control. I'm shaken but I'm absolutely, positively certain that Claire's mother truly doesn't know what the fuck she is talking about. There's obviously been some mistake. Claire was fine yesterday. She was fine twelve hours ago.

Grace eyes me with maternal concern. "Would you like to see her?" she asks. "She's in an induced coma, but I'm sure she'll know you're there."

I nod. Then, in silence, I follow Grace to the ICU ward.

She palms a buzzer beside the sealed door. Seconds later, it swings open and we enter a controlled environment populated with a handful of scattered beds occupied by patients. Looking down on these bodies is a congregation of tall, electronic medical instruments. Like guardians, they watch over someone's heaven-sent with vital sign monitors, ventilation units, and syringe pumps—man-made inventions to stall godly intervention. The quiet hum and intermittent beep of these saviors are the only sounds in the room. I smell antiseptic, hope and fear.

Grace turns to the bed on our immediate left and slips between it and the wall. She announces my arrival to the unresponsive figure beneath the white cotton blanket. Intrigued, I direct my focus to the comatose form.

But it isn't Claire.

A large tracheal tube invades the unfortunate soul's mouth, strips of tape and plastic obscuring their facial features. I look at Grace, who is brushing the patient's hand. Then I look back to the patient. Grace has the wrong person.

It isn't Claire.

It just isn't.

It isn't the girl I kissed last night. It isn't the friend I always wanted to hug. The woman I gave nightly foot massages to. The love I withheld that embarrassing letter from. This person is someone else. Someone unconscious, machine-run. Someone in need of life support.

I look again.

No…

No, no, no…

It's Claire.

"The doctors said they can't oxygenate her at this saturation level for too long," says Grace in an undertone that's inaudible to her child. "She needs to start breathing for herself."

The implication is understood: Claire needs to breathe…or die.

Suddenly, my own breath stalls, and the panic grows. Unable to compose myself, I once again abandon Claire and Grace. Without warning, I exit the ICU and dash into the hall, but there's nowhere to go. Behind me is a broken mother and ahead, an anguished father.

I stand rooted to the spot, lost in transit.

Grace arrives to comfort me. One look at her face and I begin to sob uncontrollably.

"I love her so much," I blubber through streaming tears. "I love her *so so* much."

Claire's mother places a hand on my shoulder. "And she loves you," she says, her own eyes now glistening. "And she knows you're here for her."

I nod in silence, unable to tell her the truth. Unable to tell her that *I* did this. That *I* brought Claire here. Because despite what Grace believes, I've never ever been there for her daughter. Not completely. I complicated her life. I exacerbated her illness. I infected her. It was all me. And even when she seemed better, it was *my* lips that poisoned her. With *my* kiss.

I look at Grace; a person of virtue and strong faith. Calm, resilient. Unlike me.

I immediately make a vow—a promise of commitment—to stand religiously by Claire's bedside each morning until she gets better. Then I utter a prayer to a deity I don't believe in.

Please, God, please… Please, save Claire.

I repeat it again and again, desperate for a sign or acknowledgement.

"Chris?"

A loud voice beckons me and I stir awake.

"*Chris?*"

The voice is insistent, the accent familiar. But it doesn't make sense because God sounds—

Indian.

A pounding at the door.

"CHRIS?!"

My eyes reluctantly open and slowly adjust to the darkness. I see four concrete walls, some spartan furniture, and a set of louvered windows.

India.

I'm still in fucking India.

"CHRIS," bellows the persistent voice. "Open up!"

I stand to attention, my naked body swaying unsteadily.

Again, the thumping at the door. The drum-like sound amplifies in my room and threatens to split my aching skull.

"Hang on," I shout.

Stripped of inhibitions, I stagger to the door, naked, unsteady. A familiar face edges into the frame as I open it. But it's not God.

My saviour is Ashok.

He takes one look at me and his expression darkens. "Bro, I've been looking for you for two days. Sofia said you never turned up. I've been to every guesthouse on the street."

"I need medicine," I grunt, as a countdown to my next internal release begins. "Antibiotics."

Concern flicks across Ashok's face. "Let me call a doctor, bro."

"No." I shake my head, not wanting anyone near me. "Please, just antibiotics. I'll give you some cash."

I cross to my wallet, teetering on the edge of consciousness, then return to the door to thrust a wad of rupees into Ashok's hand. "Sorry, I gotta go."

I slam the door shut, bolt to the bathroom, and endure another round of hell. Then for the umpteenth time, I shower and stumble back to bed. Depleted of life, I lower my body onto the mattress.

Alongside Claire.

I ROLL over and look at Claire. Radiant and beautiful, her pixie-like features draw me in. I lean forward and taste her lips. Claire smiles mid-kiss and my heart swells.

After months in hospital, Claire is finally home.

With me.

I lift her shirt gently and marvel at the scar that's smooth and silken beneath my touch.

"I'll have to learn how to face the real world again," Claire says.

"No," I say, dismissing her statement with an emphatic shake of my head. "I'm looking after you."

"I'll need to look after myself at some point."

"Sure, but not right now. You need to rest and get better. It's my turn to take care of you."

"You say that, but for how long?"

"Forever. Things are different now. I promise."

Claire rolls her eyes. "Where have I heard that before?" She sees the hurt on my face. "I'm joking." There is kindness in her eyes, not spite. "But I do know what you're like."

"I don't want to be like that anymore. I want to be here for you."

She smiles and we kiss again, then, after several long months, renew our intimacy. Minutes after climax, we fall asleep. It takes the sound of afternoon traffic outside the bedroom window to disturb my dreams. I resist opening my eyes, enjoying Claire's presence as she snuggles into me.

"You were in my dream," she whispers into my ear.

I smile because I had the same dream.

I turn my face towards her and open my eyes—

But Claire isn't there.

No one is.

It's just me.

Alone.

In India.

Chapter Forty-Seven

IN NEED OF A FRESH PERSPECTIVE, I take a six-hour bus ride to put my Pune nightmare behind me. My destination: Aurangabad, a city that serves as a transit hub for Ellora and Ajanta Caves—two renowned tourist sites that showcase ancient temples that have been carved directly into cliffs.

As we near the city limits, a thick, cloying smog hangs heavily in the air, clouding my outlook. If my life was a melodramatic movie—which it often is—this arrival would serve as a visual metaphor: the hero, trying to move on, finds no clear sky.

I hate Aurangabad before the bus even stops. It's hot, busy, and located in the middle of nowhere. My lack of enthusiasm doesn't surprise me, however, because I left it, and about ten percent of my body weight, in a bathroom in Pune.

I trade my bus seat for a room in the first budget hotel I stumble across. I don't consult the *Lonely Planet* or let touts lure me astray. I simply walk into the nearest place that has a spare mattress, hand over my money, and collapse into a deep sleep.

By morning, my body is still sluggish, and my head hazier than the local skyline. Wasting an entire day in bed seems like a perfectly reasonable plan. Unfortunately, that brilliant plan is foiled by a stupid decision I made when I checked in—I booked an organized tour for today. "Last chance, sir," the manager had proclaimed. "Only one seat left."

Reluctantly, I drag my lethargic ass onto the tour bus, bracing for a day of inevitable boredom. The travel cliche about temples being like churches—you've seen one, you've seen them all—rings in my head. Today, I've signed up to see *sixty-fucking-three* of them.

My cynicism dissolves as soon as the bus stops at Ellora. A hush falls over passengers, amplifying the sheer scale of the landmark that looms before us. The caves aren't simple burrows into the earth; they're a breathtaking collection of hand-carved temples hewn directly from rock. One structure in particular steals my breath—the Kailasa Temple. Longer than a football field and taller than a ten-story apartment block, it commands my awestruck attention. Intricate carvings adorn every surface of the monolith—staircases, pillars, latticework, figurines, entire rooms—all chiseled, top-down, by hand, over hundreds of years, from one single lump of granite. The logistics are mind-boggling. And the result, truly spectacular.

As I trail my fingertips over the rough texture of the basalt, something stirs in me. A profound sense of insignificance. A stark realization of my own shortcomings. I could never commit to something of this magnitude. I can't even build a long-standing relationship. I don't have the stamina, selflessness, or unwavering sense of purpose—for anything.

I think of Claire.

She possessed all those traits, not me.

Her life was tough, harder than granite. In the span of a few short years, she'd gone from a prize-winning journalism graduate to a clinically depressed department store employee. Her body had betrayed her, leaving her with a lost bowel, no confidence, and a future she could no longer plan. The dramatic shift unleashed a litany of challenges. Her days were a constant battle against chronic fatigue, recurring infections, never-ending side effects of medication, and a revolving door of doctor visits. Socially awkward accidents became a source of intense anxiety and shame: bag leaks, embarrassing smells, involuntary noises from her stoma that sounded like loud flatulence. The psychological trauma hammered at her day after day, year after year. But at least she had me.

Briefly.

Until it became too much. I craved a normal life with a normal partner, preferably one who wasn't irreparably broken. I didn't need a *perfect* life anymore. But I desperately wanted an *easier* one. A life *I* could control.

Claire wanted the exact same thing.

I enter the basement of the temple, where a ring of massive sculptured elephants bear the weight of the world on their backs. The symbolism isn't lost on me: a monument to devotion, resilience, and strength stands before me. Qualities I never possessed.

But Claire did.

"You excluded me from your doctor's appointments," I say, my voice betrays the sting of that memory. "Like you didn't want me there."

Claire catches my reflection in her make-up mirror. "You were always busy."

"You could have told me."

"It wasn't deliberate," she says gently. "I just didn't want to be a burden."

She sets down her eye-liner and turns to face me directly. Eye to eye. Me sitting on the edge of the bed. Her on an office chair.

"I love you," she continues softly, "but I knew I couldn't rely on you. You were always at the gym, or film school, or hanging out with the boys."

"But I *was* there for you."

"*After* my surgery," she gently corrects. "Not before." She sees the remorse on my face and moves quickly to soften the blow. "And I'm grateful for that. You kept me going, Bub. But I knew it wouldn't last. You were focused on our own stuff. But it's okay. I understand." She smooths her shirt over her ostomy bag beneath. "You didn't sign up for this life."

I close my eyes and sigh. When I open them again, they are downcast with regret.

"I don't know how to fix this anymore," I say solemnly.

"Fix what?"

"You. Us."

Claire leans forward and places a hand on my thigh. "Bub, you did fix it. You took care of me when I came home from hospital. You babied me. But now you need to stop. I truly love you for everything you've done, but you need to let me control my own life."

My hackles rise. "I'm not trying to control you."

"I know you're not. But you do. That's not love. That's obligation. You can't just stay with somebody because you feel sorry for them."

"I can't just leave. Who would look after you?"

"I'm a big girl. I can look after myself." Her gaze is unwavering. "I don't want you to be with me out of guilt and pity. I want you to be with me because you love me." Then, in the calmest of voices, she adds: "But I know you don't love me."

Claire's newfound strength frightens me. She has chipped away at tragedies that seemed insurmountable—her health, our relationship, the future—and built herself a temple of independence.

"I do love you," I insist.

"You love me," she echoes softly, "but you're not *in love* with me."

A long beat of silence passes as I stare directly into her sky blue eyes.

"So what do we do?"

She holds my gaze. "I don't know," she says. "I just know I can't do this anymore."

"What do you mean?" My voice tightens.

Claire has always been there for me. My rock. But suddenly, I feel my world crumbling.

She exhales, steady, resolved—and, undeniably, herself.

"It means I want to leave."

Chapter Forty-Eight

I HOLD out the coin to the pre-teen in the bus seat beside me.

"Don Bradman," I tell the boy. "He was the world's greatest batter."

The bemused kid reluctantly drags his attention from his magazine to the offered coin.

"You can have it if you want," I add.

He takes it from my fingers, studies both sides, then, unable to make head nor tails of its importance, attempts to hand it back.

I wave him away. "Keep it. I've got plenty more."

Nonplussed by the gift, the child dismisses Bradman to a trouser pocket and returns to his reading. The brief, almost dismissive, exchange amplifies my sense of isolation. It's been weeks since I played cricket, and I'm missing the social interaction. Without that contact, it's difficult to distract my mind from the crowded introspection that accompanies solo travel.

Outwardly, I'm still gregarious but, inwardly, I'm withdrawing. India might be a country of one billion people, but sometimes it feels like the loneliest place on earth. Which leaves me with an unsettling feeling that my particular journey may never have an end.

We arrive at the Ajanta Caves soon after, and the bus empties.

Stepping out, I am immediately confronted by tour guides, each thrusting brochures in an effort to procure business. I take a pamphlet out of politeness, but decline their services, then walk towards the entrance of Maharashtra's most popular tourist destination.

Passing through the gate, the site's allure is immediately apparent. Dozens of hand-carved, cathedral-like temples are etched into a mile-long cliff face. Curiosity piqued, I consult the brochures, suddenly seeking information the persistent tour guides would, no doubt, have provided. According to the hand-out, the elaborately carved façades I see before me extend deep into the imposing granite escarpment, forming cavernous underground Buddhist temples.

I follow the pathway alongside the ancient lava flow and begin exploring the numbered caves. The monasteries are as impressive as Ellora, yet distinctly different. The expected architectural grandeur is present—carved columns, vaulted roofs, reclining Buddhas—but unlike Ellora, these caves boast a million detailed paintings.

The frescos, in various states of disrepair, chronicle daily life through images of regal kings, mischievous children, and drunken revelers. Thousands of painted figures tell stories spanning millennia. In one cave, dedicated exclusively to celebrating women, a mural features a fifteen-hundred-year-old nativity scene, illustrating the birth of Buddha.

I move from cave to cave with scores of tourists, relishing the cool respite from the Indian heat. The air carries the smell of damp stone, the echo of tour guide commentary, and the hushed awe from pilgrims.

After exploring a dozen temples and monasteries, I've had my fill. Looking to recharge, I take a time-out on the shaded portico of a distant cave. My arrival coincides with that of a foreign couple and their local guide. The chaperone, a wiry man in a full-sleeve button up shirt, leads them to a wall adorned with the remnants of a painting that resembles a gigantic, partially eaten pizza—it's missing slices consumed by Mother Nature, Father Time and greedy souvenir hunters.

"On this wall," the guide announces, his English precise and practiced, "is the oldest known painting of samsara."

His words grab my attention, and I move closer to the flaking artwork.

Samsara.

The *Wheel of Life*.

The image reminds me of Prashant and his Hindu devotion. As well as Dolma and her three Buddhist poisons.

The diagram symbolizes the perpetual merry-go-round of existential bullshit we're all familiar with; a depiction of endless suffering, eternal wandering, and the relentless churn of dharma, karma, birth, and rebirth. Of rights, wrongs, revelation, and growth. Breaking free from these supposedly leads to enlightenment. To nirvana. It's an impossible quest for any human, least of all me.

The tour guide ushers the couple into the cave, leaving me alone on the porch to study the faded mural. The painting is in severe disrepair, but thanks to Dolma's hill-top teachings and my Buddhist books in McLeod Ganj, the missing pieces of this spiritual jigsaw are already embedded in my head.

For instance, I know that in the bullseye of this spiritual dartboard should be a pig, a rooster, and a snake. These animals represent Dolma's three poisons of ignorance, greed, and hate. Encircling them, should be Prashant's dharmic deeds in the form of good and bad humans walking on a path towards enlightenment or darkness. The next ring is a land of ghosts, demons, and hell. Unfortunately, the painting in front of me is missing all these pieces. Worryingly, what *is* present, seems specifically preserved for me—a woman giving birth, and a fragmented blind man on a journey of ignorance.

I close my eyes, inhale deeply, and attempt to swallow the bitter taste of my own past.

Fucking samsara.

Turning from the painting, I walk to one of the giant stone pillars at the cave's edge, and stare into the clear blue sky. The harsh sunlight sears my skin, triggering a reminder of an Australian summer, and an unwanted memory from home. I retreat into the shade and glance back at the painting, my gaze lingers on the chipped area where the broken man stumbles. Then, my focus shifts to the figure on the left.

To the woman giving birth.

"I have to tell you something," Claire says, her voice grave.

She appears deeply unsettled, despondent; a stark contrast to the vibrant blue sky that fills the window frame behind her, or the bright sunlight that bathes her in an ethereal glow.

"What's wrong?" I ask, immediately concerned for her physical health.

Claire wrestles her inner censor for a moment, before releasing her bombshell.

"I think I'm pregnant," she whispers.

Her words instantly shrink my universe to the size of a pinhead. My lungs constrict, and my heart hammers against my ribs. Synapses in my brain fire repeatedly, short-circuiting my mind with a discharge of random, nonsensical thoughts about Claire, me, childbirth, hospital wards, emergency operations, life-support, fatherhood, failure, work, mortgage, depression, suffocation, death.

I take several quick gasps and come back to the land of the living.

"Are you sure?"

Claire nods. "I did two tests. Both were positive."

My breathing escalates again, and my eyes dart around the room, suddenly hyper-aware of details previously unnoticed. I see doorways, but no exits. I see cobwebs on the corner of the ceiling, trapping the spineless and unwary.

"How many weeks?" I ask.

"Six, I think."

Six weeks.

Which makes it several weeks before Claire said she was going to leave. We were almost free. I feel the chains of commitment and responsibility biting into my future, but I also feel something not entirely unwelcome: a sudden sense of pride. Probably akin to what a father might feel.

"I shouldn't have stopped taking the pill," Claire states.

Her lament hangs in the air, reminding us of our stupidity. We'd agreed to stop contraception in an attempt to sever connection and create distance. Yet desire had overridden logic.

I place my hands on my head, trying to process the impending disaster. "Jesus, what the hell were we thinking?"

Claire's head dips in anguish as she fights back tears. "I'm so scared."

Finally, I look beyond my own fears and truly see Claire.

"Your stomach?" I ask in a panic. "Your scar will split open."

She begins to cry.

Reaching out a hand, I gently pull her free from the chair, and hug her tight. Drawing her head close to my chest, I feel her tears seep through my shirt and onto my heart.

We stay mute for minutes, crippled by shock. There's an elephant in the room—smaller than a grain of rice—stomping on plans that once had no limits.

Eventually, we part.

"I'm sorry," Claire says, wiping her eyes with her shirt. "But I don't think I can do this."

Me neither, I think to myself. I'm not ready for this. But it's not up to me. It's up to Claire. I have no control over what happens next. This is her body, and ultimately, her decision.

"You need to have an abortion," I say. The words sound cold and detached even to my own ears.

Claire doesn't respond, despite her earlier misgivings. We're both pro-choice but suddenly all our black and white beliefs muddy into infinite shades of grey.

She looks me in the eye, uncertain. "But what if I did keep it?"

Her about-face throws me. "You can't. It would put your life at risk."

"Women still give birth after colectomy operations," she quietly challenges.

"Yeah, but how soon after?" My tone is sharp. "Not six months, I bet."

"My operation was twelve months ago," she states firmly. "*Prior* to conception. It'll be more than a year and a half by the due date."

Her information isn't lost on me. Claire's already done the calculations. Already entertained the idea of keeping it.

"Bub, I've got no money, no job, nothing. I can't even get my own shit together let alone raise a child."

"Who said you have to raise it?"

Her question lands like a punch.

"So… what? I just have no contact? Like my biological father? That would just mess a kid up. I don't need that in my life."

"But maybe *I* need this in mine," she says. "It might force me to get *my* shit together."

"You just said you couldn't do this."

"I can't. But what if this is my only chance to have a baby?"

"Why would it be your only chance?"

"What if I need more operations and I can't have kids?"

Her answer suddenly makes me aware that her post-operative life has been filled with a series of 'what if' questions that have never crossed my mind.

"How would you afford it?"

"Other single mothers manage."

In two weeks we will be packing up our lives and relocating to separate dwellings—Claire to a spare room at her aunt and uncle's house, and me to my grandparents' basement. We're twenty-something-year-old children who can barely care for ourselves.

"You can't stay at your aunt's with a baby."

"Then I'll move in with my parents."

Back to the home of her Catholic upbringing, pregnant, unwed, and abandoned.

"Your body needs to heal, Claire. Not go through childbirth."

I truly believe the words but in the back of my mind, I'm plagued by something else. A nagging doubt, triggered by a recent documentary I watched about a Buddhist ceremony in Japan. It showed young parents mourning children who were caught in limbo—lives lost through stillbirth, miscarriage, or abortion. The heartbroken mothers had sought guardianship from a deity who was a protector of children. Cherubic statues hand-carved from rock, were propped on temple altars by the women as an offering to redress grief, guilt, and the fear of karmic retribution. I'd been touched by their anguish, but it held little relevance to me as a childless male living in Australia. Until now.

"I can't deal with this right now," I say flatly.

Claire looks at me, her expression a mixture of despair, anger, frustration, and utter exhaustion.

"I can't either," she replies sadly. "But unlike you, I can't run away."

UPRIGHT – The truth hurts. In fairness... you deserve it. And then some.

REVERSED – Dodgy deeds and dishonesty ... never hurt anyone. Oh, wait...

Chapter Forty-Nine

From: Claire
To: Chris
Subject: Re: Udaipur…!!

Hey Stinky Boy,
I know that you're not going to like what I have to say, and it's probably the last thing you want to read while on vacation, but I think it's for the best.

After some serious soul-searching since your last email, I have come to the conclusion that I need a clean break from you. A proper one. So I would prefer it if you didn't contact me anymore. I hope you understand this decision and can see it from my perspective. I know you still want me in your life as a friend but the reality is good friendships, like relationships, take commitment and work. Two things I'm sure you will agree you sorely lack!! ;-)

While I understand why things in our life have happened, the pain doesn't hurt any less. I've been trying to hang on to my best friend, but deep down I have always known you would disappear.

I will always miss you. You are my soul mate and the love of my life. But I can never be your safe haven again.

I truly hope all your dreams come true and you find whatever it is you are searching for.

Claire xo

—

From: Chris
To: Claire
Subject: Re: Re: Udaipur…!!

Please don't do this, Bub. I think about you every single day of my life. And everything that happened. I know you've earned the right to hurt me after what I dragged you through. I know you *deserve* that right. And I know I deserve this. But I don't know what to do. I don't know what to say. I don't even know where to go anymore. My head and heart are bursting, yet I feel so empty inside.

Fuck… I'm actually crying in an internet cafe. Jesus Christ, how do I stop this fucking crying bullshit all the time?! Sorry. Forget it. I gotta go.

I need this to end.

—

From: Chris
To: Elliot; Bryan; Emma
Subject: Howdy

Hi Guys,
Firstly, thank you for allowing me to be involved with the TV series. You made my long-suffering mother very proud. The joy in

her message after my episode aired was priceless. So thank you for making real that miracle.

Secondly, please grab your writers' list for the show and scratch me from it. I'm a bad bet. And it's best that I tell you this while you're deliberating over the arrangements for next season. Truth is, if I came back to write I'd be doing it for all the wrong reasons (money, namely!) and I don't want to pull another stunt like last time. So I guess this marks the end of what is possibly the shortest TV writing career ever!

Bryan: Thanks for having the balls to hire me from out of nowhere and thanks for placing your trust in me. I'm so sorry I disappointed you.

Elliot: You truly are a kind man. Your sense of humor is contagious and you tell some crazy-ass stories. Best of luck with everything.

And Emma: Thank you for being a great sport. The success of the show is certainly a reflection of your talent. You're a class act. It's just a shame you weren't the gorgeous woman Bryan and Elliot promised. ;-)

Cheers
Chris

UPRIGHT - Shadows, self-destruction and sex... sounds fun. Be a devil.
REVERSED - Lose yourself. But in a good way. Song and dance, perhaps?

Chapter Fifty

I'M DRUNK.

It's early evening and I'm in Khajuraho; a remote town renowned for its ancient temples of erotica.

It took twenty hours of well-planned travel to get here, but I'm more lost than ever. Claire's email has knocked me off course. After three months of physical travel, I've finally accepted that my spiritual compass is well and truly broken.

I take another gulp of my whiskey and Coke and re-engage with the two English backpackers who share my outdoor restaurant table.

"See the guy screwing the horse?" I ask Evan and Russell.

The stone sculpture in question is one of thousands that adorn the town's famed temples. The carvings depict scenes of daily life from a millennium ago—farming, dancing, worshipping, making music, making war, and making love. Naturally, it's the perverse rather than the mundane that titillates tourists. The most salacious sculptures portray men having intercourse with livestock, ample-breasted nymphs riding partners reverse-cowgirl, and women performing oral sex. There's also scenes of orgies, as well as a sexual spit-roast.

"I didn't even notice the erotica, to be honest." Evan replies in a clipped English. "I was more interested in the architecture and engineering."

His comment makes me feel like an uncultured porn-addict, and for a brief moment, I regret befriending him on the bus ride in. But I find solace in the fact that Evan—despite his intelligence and eloquence—looks fucking ridiculous. And I'm not just being subjective. Clad head to toe in a garish tie-dyed hippie ensemble, he draws amused looks wherever he goes. The brightly-colored threads are at complete odds with his strait-laced, preppy bearing and flouncy, golden locks. He appears less like the spiritual backpacker he thinks he is, and more like a pampered corgi who has crawled up the ass of a parrot in an attempt to mask an identity crisis. Suffice to say, it's a truly jarring vision.

Russell, on the other hand, does look like a bohemian traveller—albeit less free-spirit nirvana and more *Smells Like Teen Spirit* Nirvana. He has a thick beard and his shoulder-length hair falls over two protruding ears that have probably earned a double-major in the music appreciation of melancholy artists like Radiohead, The Smiths and Nick Drake. The boys' accents and educated speech suggest privileged backgrounds. Both are quick-witted and intellectually deep, which makes idiots like me feel increasingly insecure and incredibly dumb.

In spite of this, we've regaled one another with travel tales and opinions, our true selves being revealed the drunker we become. Evan is risk-averse and slightly judgmental, while Russell is more relaxed and spiritually grounded. And me? I'm awkward, manic, and slowly unravelling. Again.

The conversation is entertaining, until it veers to the unfamiliar. The shift is almost imperceptible at first, then suddenly every topic is about architecture, engineering or mathematics. Then their talk drifts to history, politics and philosophy. This is the problem with drunk intellectuals—their already complex conversations become utterly impenetrable.

My whiskey-drenched brain struggles to keep pace, so I tune out, letting my thoughts drift back to the erotic temples.

Evan is right, even without the porn, the buildings are impressive, especially spiritually. There is symbolism everywhere. A stroll around the temples reveals a sculpted story of three intrinsic Hindu tenets—righteousness through duty, desire through fulfillment, and purpose through work. But no matter how many times you embark on this circular trip, the fourth tenet of liberation remains illusive. By design, it can only be found when you enter the heart of the temple. Only then will the story of self-realization and enlightenment appear before you.

Nearly all of Khajuraho's temples are a shrine to the family of gods pictured on Prashant's wall poster. Ganesh, the elephant-headed god of prosperity, dismantler of selfishness, and remover of obstacles. Parvati, goddess of harmony, fertility, and cosmic mother. And, finally, Shiva, god of destruction, flawed husband, and reluctant father.

Their family tale is well know in India: A husband repeatedly abandons his partner for his own pursuits. His wife, seeking purpose, sculpts a child from clay and breathes life into it. The new born, forever grateful and loyal, vows to be her protector. So when the selfish boss man returns after another of his errant distractions, the guardian son bars his way. In a fit of rage, Shiva beheads the child. Mother Parvati, grief-stricken and angry, demands her idiot partner right his wrong. Chastened, the man is left with no choice, because without his wife he is nothing but a weak and incomplete fool. To make amends he replaces his son's head with that of the first animal he encounters—a sacred elephant. Thus Ganesh is reborn, and balance is restored, and the family live happily ever after in the hearts of a billion Indians.

Luckily, the kid didn't grow up in my family, otherwise he'd look like a guinea pig.

I rejoin Evan and Russell somewhere mid-conversation.

"It's about quality of life, man," Russell says.

"Ahh, but *what* is quality?" I ask, convinced that I sound incredibly philosophical and a little bit smart.

The conceptual question isn't mine, of course. I borrowed it from a book I stole from my school library when I was a teenager. It was a fictionalized autobiography about a guy who went traveling with his child after he lost his mind and destroyed everything around him. Telling, that kind of story resonated with me even back then.

"*Zen and the Art of Motorcycle Maintenance*," Russell says with a smirk. "Pretty unoriginal, man."

Busted.

Exposed as the fraud I am, I shrink back into my seat, face burning from embarrassment. My humiliation grows in the awkward silence until rage sets in. With one derisory comment, Russel has awoken the devil inside me. In an instant, all my insecurities roar to the surface—my fears of conversing with Claire's educated family and friends, my failure to complete university, my inability to maintain employment, and, of course, my repeating of other people's ideas to make me appear more clever than I actually am. Suddenly, the urge to smash my glass of whiskey against the wall and destroy everything around me, including my new friends, overwhelms me. My hate knows no bounds and I feel a frightening, but not unfamiliar, sensation of violent desire stir within.

And it gets worse, because despite *Zen and the Art of Motorcycle Maintenance* being one of my favourite books, I'm actually too stupid to understand most of it. Or whether the *quality* of its content is actually good or bad.

"*Zen* is a terrible book," says a cynical Evan, inadvertently undermining me further. "The whole 'metaphysics of quality' concept was absolute nonsense."

Russell agrees with the babble that I'll never comprehend. "The only readable bit was his take on fixing bikes."

I take a deep breath, calm down, then turn my attention to the restaurant's other patrons instead. Apart from us, there are three other groups of foreigners dining on the verandah, including two female backpackers who attract prompt service from every single male staff member. The brunette has her back to me, but the blonde catches my eye and smiles. Embarrassed, I quickly look away, but my confidence swells. I pivot back to the boys, and scull my drink. It's refill time, but the bottle is empty.

"Up for another round?" I ask the geniuses at my table.

They are, so with unsteady legs, I set a trajectory for the liquor store next door, passing the backpackers as I go.

Returning with two whiskey bottles in hand, I near the girls' table once more. Throwing caution to the wind, I say a prayer to the god of new beginnings and try my luck with the two goddesses.

Chapter Fifty-One

"SORRY TO BOTHER YOU, LADIES," I say, trying hard not to slur my words. "But would you be interested in joining three drunk idiots for some cheap whiskey and incredibly boring conversation?"

My sudden approach elicits a look of alarm on the girls' faces. In silent consultation, they trade glances, no doubt communicating about a 'rules of engagement' agreement only they understand. After a beat, the blonde settles it with a shrug of her shoulders.

"Why not," she says, her Nordic voice throwing caution to the wind. "Should we come over now?"

Thrilled by her eagerness, I nod, then, with masculine pride, introduce them to the masterminds at my table.

The arrival of the girls immediately dissolves the boys' intellectual pretensions. Any boiling resentment I hold also simmers as the new social dynamic takes effect.

Anna and Olivia are great company. The Swedish duo radiate confidence, their easy banter and sharp wit making them more than a match for any playful ridicule and verbal sparring. As a result, an hour disappears in the blink of an eye, along with a bottle of whiskey. I crack open the next bottle to prolong the good times.

Russell leans forward. "Should I go grab my guitar?" he asks.

The tinny, strained Bollywood melodies drifting from the restaurant's sound system prompt a vote of encouragement from all.

"You girls are going to be so disappointed." I warn, with a faux grimace. "Because Russell doesn't actually know any ABBA songs."

Olivia groans. "Why do people only think of ABBA when they think of Sweden?"

"Because that's the only memorable cultural export you've had since the Vikings," Evan quips.

Anna cocks an eyebrow. "And what culture has your country given the world?" she challenges. "Fish and chips?"

Evan spreads his arms with theatrical exaggeration. "Well, just off the top of my head..." He pauses for effect, glancing around our environment with ironic pleasure. "Colonialism."

His dark humor lands well in our whiskey soaked minds.

"Outside of that," he continues. "I offer you Shakespeare, Dickens, Orwell—"

Russell follows his lead and adds: "The Beatles, The Stones, Fleetwood Mac—"

"They're American," Anna interjects.

"Originally from the UK," Russell corrects, gently.

Too gently for my liking.

A sardonic grin appears on Evan's face. "And his country," he says, pointing at me, "gave the world *Neighbours* and *Crocodile Dundee*."

I shake my head. "Here we go."

"Which I believe," Russell adds. "Is actually a documentary about Australian males."

The girls giggle at my expense.

"Yep, it's true," I admit, trying to maintain a sense of humor. "We're a nation of tough, funny men."

Evan chuckles, a dry, knowing sound. "All of whom like a joke," he remarks. "As long as it's not about them."

The comment stings, thus proving his point.

Anna interrupts the cock-fight. "How long are you all traveling for?"

"Four weeks," Evan slurs, holding op three fingers.

Russell stands, stretching, in preparation to fetch his guitar. "Only two for me." He lightly touches Anna's shoulder. "And for the record, I actually like ABBA."

Instinctively sensing that I'm in a 'first to bed Anna' challenge with Russell, I quickly add my contribution in an effort to impress her. "Three months in India, then one in Thailand."

Anna tilts her head. "That's a long time. What do you do for work?"

"I write television," I say, casually. "What do you do?"

"I'm a nurse."

Her revelation has an instant effect on my whiskey-addled brain, and, suddenly, it's not just lust I'm feeling, it's *love*. Not only is Anna attractive and intelligent, she, quite literally, cares for others, which convinces me that Anna is the perfect woman for me. Of course, it's not lost on me that the only reason I'm here in India, is due to the fact that I think Emma is the perfect woman. And, if I'm truly honest with myself, I once thought Claire was as well.

What the hell is wrong with me? Why do I fall in love with every woman who shows the slightest interest in me?

As our conversation continues, I silently size Anna up with a compatibility checklist to see if she truly is 'The One'. Is she:

a) Morning person or a night owl?
b) Church wedding or beach ceremony?
c) Screen addict or book lover?
d) Moderate voter or extremist agitator?
e) Compassionate human or intolerant nut-job?

It's hardly a foolproof test, given that I've identified with all those traits myself during any number of manic meltdowns this past year. Often at the same time.

Before I can successfully tick off all of Anna's attributes, Russell reappears with his guitar, no doubt hoping the instrument will give him an edge in our show of male one-upmanship. I glance at Olivia, hoping she might be an option for Russell instead of Anna. Unfortunately, Evan has already cast some kind of improbable love-spell over her. Either that or she's been hypnotized by his tie-dyed shirt.

Russell shakes out his hair like a rock poet and plucks some arpeggios to warm up. The crisp fingerpicked chords draw appreciative looks from the girls, proving that the addition of a guitar does, in fact, give him a slight advantage in our competition for Anna's affections. To my dismay, Russell is good. Not 'Certified Gold' or 'Platinum Record' sales good, but definitely worthy of a late-night gig in a restaurant playing to a drunk audience of four.

After a few covers, he clears his throat. "This next one's an original," he announces.

As he plays, I find myself keeping time with my shoe. The melody tugs at my memory, and in my whiskey-haze I try to recall the faint echo of a song I can't quite place.

Russell finishes the song and we offer raucous applause. Anna suggests he should release an album, which I silently dismiss as the absurd words of a drunk. But, hey, what do I know about *quality*?

"That was great, mate," I say, alcohol now firmly in control of all decision making. "Sounded familiar."

"Just an old original," he says, offhandedly.

I wrack my brain trying to identify the source. "I'll think of it in a second."

He smiles weakly, then turns to Anna.

After another minute is hits me.

"Elliot Smith," I blurt out, suddenly recalling the artist who contributed songs to the movie *Good Will Hunting*.

A movie about a *math* genius!

A twitch of uncertainty disrupts one of Russell's eyes, making me secretly pleased that he ridiculed my earlier comment about the *Zen* book.

It's payback time.

I've prodded Russell's artistic insecurity by questioning *his* originality. And by the look on his face, I may have just struck gold.

Possibly even platinum.

Chapter Fifty-Two

A LOCKED, security gate separates us from the temple grounds.

"Let's climb the fence," Anna says as a glint of mischief flashes across her eyes.

Evan points to a nearby sign. "No alcohol allowed."

Anna's Swedish partner in crime shrugs indifferently. "It's midnight," says Olivia, tossing her half-bottle of whiskey over the fence. "No one will see."

Two hours ago, Olivia was the most reserved member of our group, but any inhibitions have since been drowned in alcohol, transforming her into a bit of a delinquent.

I look back at the Raj Cafe and Restaurant, hoping the staff that just asked us to leave won't witness our trespass. But there are no staff. Everyone has gone home.

By the time I turn back, Olivia is already scaling the fence. Russell and Evan hold her steady as she reaches the top, and with surprisingly good coordination, she lands gracefully onto a cushion of lush turf. Russell passes her his guitar, then our alcohol. A minute later, we all follow, celebrating our unlawful entry with drunken cheers and laughter.

Russell, guitar back in hand, launches into a lively rendition of *Mamma Mia*. Olivia, clinging to the last vestiges of sobriety, is the first to succumb to the music, dancing with abandon. The previously conservative, but now incredibly drunk, Evan, joins in—head bobbing and arms flapping from his parrot costume in a manner that resembles an avian mating dance. Anna and I are more low-key, and very off-key, squawking into our respective whiskey bottle microphones. By the time the second chorus arrives, our flailing and swaying make us look like participants in an Osho meditation class.

In this ridiculous state, we stagger toward a distant temple, crossing a large expanse of grass. It takes the mauling of two ABBA hits by three men, and the chasing of a dozen fireflies by two women to get halfway.

We get no further.

A barrage of shrill, high-pitched sounds pierces the night air, and a squad of flashlight-wielding police officers swarm from the shadows. The men, repeatedly blowing emergency whistles, sprint across the lawn and surround us in a loose ring. I take in the scene through double vision, trying to work out what the hell is going on. Apart from the annoying metal whistles, not a single one of the over-enthusiastic constables is armed, which means as enforcers of the law, they're no more intimidating than a squad of junior soccer referees.

Eventually, a stern-faced officer strides toward us, sporting a ranking officer's cap and the prerequisite mustache. He also has a holstered revolver…but, thankfully, no fucking whistle.

"What are you doing here?" he demands.

"Just walking through the park," Evan says with surprising casualness.

"How did you get in?"

"Through the front gate," Olivia says, lying like a career criminal.

The cop turns and addresses one of his constables in Hindi. Satisfied with the answer, he returns his gaze to us.

"This gate was locked." His eyes land on Olivia, then the bottle in her hand. "This is alcohol, yes? Whiskey, yes?"

"Barely," Evan mutters. "More like moonshine."

The officer frowns. "No alcohol. This is very disrespectful." He gestures vaguely at the temples surrounding us. "This is a sacred site."

Anna steps forward, her tone genuinely apologetic. "We're sorry, we didn't know. We'll take it outside."

The policeman studies Anna for a moment, his brow softening. "First time warning. You can go, but I must confiscate this alcohol."

I smile conspiratorially, then, in a mistimed attempt at levity, say, "So you can share it with the boys, right?"

The officer shoots me a deadly look. "No. This is the law." He holds out his hand toward Anna. "Pass me the bottles, please."

Anna reluctantly relinquishes her whiskey, as does Olivia.

"You also." He grabs the neck of my bottle and wrenches it from my grasp. "My men will escort you out now. Please, do not return. Otherwise, this will be a very big problem for you."

He grunts an order and three young constables step forward. With zero urgency, the men motion for us to follow them on a casual stroll back to the park's entrance. They unlock the gate, then, with beaming smiles, bid us farewell with handshakes and well-wishing. It's all very surreal.

With no desire to end the evening, we wander aimlessly until we find a bench seat in the street. I quickly sit next Anna, while Evan smoothly settles beside Olivia. The pairings effectively leave Russell to finger his guitar in the moonlight. Finally, after a night of stolen glances, Anna and I have a chance to talk alone.

"What kind of TV do you write?" she asks.

Our shoulders touch, the bare skin of her upper arm resting against mine. She smells of whiskey and perfume.

"None actually. I quit before I came here."

She asks why. I consider lying, to present a less pathetic version of myself, but I've drunk a whole bottle of truth serum, so my lips are loose.

"I had a bit of a meltdown," I say matter-of-factly.

Anna assesses me quietly.

"Because of the job?" she asks, her voice soft and interested. "Or because of a relationship?"

I look directly at her. "Is it that obvious?"

She smiles kindly. "Just from some of the things you said earlier tonight."

I try to return the smile, but it fails to appear on command. "I'm not good at relationships."

"Not many people are," she says.

"I *am*, however, very good at making bad decisions," I add brightly.

She presses for an example.

The one that instantly comes to mind isn't something that should be told under the influence of alcohol, nor with truth or honesty, because it leads to hell. So I change tack and head for safety.

"Hanging out with drunk Swedes who break into sacred temples is a fine example," I say.

Anna shunts my leg with a knee bump that threatens to burst my already full bladder.

"That wasn't my idea."

"Yeah, it was. And it was a supremely dumb idea." I see the lightness fade from her face, so I return the playful knee bump. "I'm only joking."

Anna's eyebrows rise. "I know that," she says, nudging my shoulder forcefully. "Do you think I'm blonde and stupid?"

"No, I think you're blonde and beautiful," says the whiskey.

The Scandinavian stunner blushes.

"So what next?" she asks.

"When I get back to Australia? Or now?"

"Both," she says, softly.

I let out a sigh. "I don't know what happens when I get home." I pause briefly to build courage. "But I know that I'd like to kiss you."

Anna's eyes lock onto mine. "Maybe you should."

The invite breaks our inhibitions, and we kiss. Her lips are sensual, full, and sweet, like rose petals, marshmallows, and bubble-gum lollipops. She's tastes of a brighter future, which is the sustenance I desperately need—a fresh start, new beginnings.

I reluctantly break away.

"I really need to pee," I tell her. "Don't go anywhere. Especially near Russell."

She laughs and promises not to.

As I stand, the full force of the night's alcohol slams into me. I stagger toward a darkened building, searching for a private place to pee. Finding one in the shadows, I step over a low concrete ledge and onto solid ground.

But there is no solid ground.

In fact, there is no ground at all.

I pitch forward into the empty space. A rocky protrusion catches my heel, twisting my ankle with a sickening *pop*, and a lightning bolt of pain shoots through me. Despite the numbing effects of alcohol, my mouth fills with saliva in readiness to throw up. I try to crawl out of the hole, but my leg has the tensile strength of hot custard. So I yell for help. Evan and Russell rush over and haul me free. Slinging my arms around their shoulders, they guide me back to the bench.

Anna's brow is furrowed with nurse-like concern. "Are you okay?"

"Yeah, I'm fine," I rasp.

I'm *not* fine, of course. I'm living in an apocalyptic world of hurt. Plus, I still need to pee. So, despite desperately wanting to spend the night with Anna, I am faced with the unwelcome reality that I need to go straight to my hostel room and pass out.

"I'm going to go take some painkillers and sleep it off," I tell Anna. I look to the others. "I'll see you guys tomorrow."

Flush with embarrassment, I balance on my good foot and carefully step forward onto the injured one. The torture is light-years beyond my threshold for pain and I wince audibly.

"You need help?" Evan asks.

I wave him off, then under their scrutiny, I limp into the night, my awkward gait becoming more exaggerated with each step, until it finally deteriorates into the trademark hobble of a rum-soaked pirate with a peg-leg.

After several more paces, my foot can endure no further punishment. I do need Evan's help. But when I turn back, the sight of the blonde Anna and her brunette friend, sandwiched between a clean-shaven Evan, and a bearded, guitar-strumming Russell, silences me.

Fuelled with bulletproof male bravado, I turn back towards my hotel and do the only face-saving thing I can think of, which is hop down the road on one leg, like a maimed kangaroo. The pain and humiliation is overwhelming. But not nearly as traumatic as seeing my new love huddled in a cozy quartet that looks disconcertingly like a 1970s pop group.

Specifically, ABBA.

UPRIGHT – Just surrender, dude. Let go and see a new perspective.
REVERSED – Indecision and resistance will imprison you. Forever.

Chapter Fifty-Three

THE DOCTOR OFFERS me an apologetic look.

"We're short-staffed tonight due to Diwali, so no chance of an X-ray."

His English is impeccable, as are his neatly pressed clothes, groomed hair, and complexion—all of which make him seem out of place in the spartan, government-run medical clinic.

I'm here after receiving advice in Khajuraho to get an x-ray in Varanasi, which was an hour's flight away.

"What do you recommend then?"

"It presents as a severe sprain," the medico says, assessing my purple foot. "Not a fracture. So just continue with painkillers and a compression bandage. And elevate the leg as much as possible."

His quiet advice is followed by a string of loud firecrackers exploding near the front window. The sharp crack of detonations makes me jolt in fright, sending fresh spikes of pain through my injured foot.

Fucking Diwali.

"How long does this go on?" I ask, my ignorance of all things India once again on full display.

The doc, carefully wrapping a new bandage around my foot, replies, "Only five days."

Only?!

India doesn't do things by half measure that's for sure. From what I've seen, Diwali seems like Christmas, New Year's Eve, and an Independence Day celebration all rolled into one. The festivities border on fanatical. Here in Varanasi's old city, tens of thousands of people flood the streets, leaving not a single space free of humanity, sound, color, or chaos.

"Is it like Christmas with the whole gift-giving thing?"

The doctor bobbles his head. "Similar." Then, with a hint of nostalgia that hints at his middle-age, he adds, "It used to be different." With a tilt of his head, he gestures towards the street. "See all the lights?"

I nod. They're impossible to miss. Thousands of tinted bulbs, neon tubes, LEDs, and oil lamps, illuminate the night in every direction. The festive beacons adorn buildings, roads, street signs, cars, motorbikes…even people. The mighty Ganges River that flows past the city is also scattered with floating lanterns.

"That's the true meaning of Diwali," the doctor continues. "It's a reminder that enlightenment keeps darkness away. Consumerism has taken over. It used to be a spiritual holiday but now it's becoming a commercial one."

He secures the bandage with small metal clips, opens a nearby cupboard to retrieve a pack of pain killers, and hands them to me.

"So you don't think I need crutches?"

He shakes his head. "Walking is good. Better for circulation."

I stash the tablets in my backpack, then set about pulling my filthy running shoe over the grotesquely swollen appendage. It's not a fun experience. When I finally stand, the pain is blinding, and leaves me on the verge of seeing stars. Gritting my teeth, I search for some inner Diwali light to dispel the encroaching darkness. The process is no fucking holiday, that's for sure.

After several deep breaths, I manage to steady myself and thank the doctor for his care. Then I strap on my backpack, step through the clinic door, and walk into the madness beyond.

In an instant, I am swept up in a torrent of humanity surging through the street. Every step sends a fresh protest through my foot as I struggle against the push and pull of the crowd. Finally, I can endure no more. Seeking refuge, I veer down a narrow alleyway—just as a group of adolescent boys sprint past and toss several firecrackers at my feet. I can hardly walk, let alone run, so I cover my ears and brace for the blasts. The explosions reverberate through the confines of the passageway, hammering my skull. When the ringing in my ears fades, I hobble onward, funneling myself deeper into alleyways that reek of sewage.

Then I hit a roadblock.

A cow.

The animal's resting flank almost fills the entire width of the alley, leaving little room to pass. I approach cautiously, hoping she'll move. She doesn't. I weigh up my options—either pass her horned head and risk a goring, or squeeze by a rear-end that is caked in cow shit. Neither option appeals. So, instead, I try nudging her with my backpack.

"Come on, old girl," I implore. "Move your ass."

The cow watches me, unbothered, her dark orbs meeting mine with a look that begs to be left in peace. I know those eyes. They remind me of an unforgettable moment in my youth; a time when I tagged along on a feral pig hunt with a couple of childhood friends. Their father, a retired crocodile hunter, bundled us into a four-wheel-drive, and drove us to a remote cattle property, where waterholes held porky promise.

I was a pre-teen with zero killing instinct, but I was thrilled with the prospect of tailing a few tuskers through the bush—which is exactly what we did when our long corrugated drive in, coincided with a small mob of pigs crossing the dirt track.

Rudy hit the anchors, and his mate, Laurie, launched out of the passenger door with a large-calibre rifle. Us kids bailed out next. We vaulted from the Toyota's steel tray-back and tore through the scrub barefoot, hot on his heels.

After ten minutes, the pigs did us in and we regrouped at the four-wheel-drive, panting but exhilarated. Fueled by testosterone, we clambered back into the tray, eager for more adventure. Rudy drove us to a landlocked waterhole ahead, killed the engine, and warily led us on foot around the body of murky water, in search of fresh pig tracks.

What we found, instead, was an imprint left by a giant saltwater crocodile.

The old croc-shooter ordered a retreat, directing all of us to safety on the other side of the billabong. Filled with terror, we skirted the waterhole, stopping only when we came upon a bulky object squatting low on the muddy bank.

A cow.

A proud Brahman, sunk to her belly in the muck, her dark hide almost camouflaged against earth of similar hue.

We approached the old girl slowly, not wanting to spook her. As we neared, her survival instinct kicked in, and her legs pistoned, desperately trying to find purchase in the soft silt to make good an escape. But it was a futile effort. She was stuck fast, unable to break free, or charge us.

As we came within touching distance, her nostrils flared, and she snorted audibly in rapid fearful breaths. Her coffee-colored eyes darted restlessly, felled by the adrenalin percolating within.

We debated what to do next.

Finally, the six of us locked onto her horns and heaved with all our strength. The cow, desperate to escape us, marched on the spot but couldn't flee her earthy captor. Exhaustion overwhelmed her, and us, and we took a time out.

Rudy vowed one last try. He grabbed a rope from the Toyota and looped the thick nylon braid around the cow's horns. We all latched on, and with shouts and hollers, put our backs into it. Once again, the cow dutifully stampeded but could only rise inches above the surface of the slop.

And that's when we saw it.

The reason for her predicament.

There was another rust-colored hide. Beneath her.

A calf.

Pinned under her bulk. Motionless.

The young poddy had probably ventured down for water. Inevitably, the animal had become stranded as its spindly legs needled deep into the silt. The mother, no doubt drawn by maternal instinct, had likely walked down to nudge her calf to safety. But with her offspring against her flank, she too had become trapped. Eventually sinking, until she collapsed onto her own offspring, effectively terminating its short life.

The realization gutted us.

The misfortune crushed our hearts and eroded our masculinity. A silence fell over each of us and I fought back tears.

With renewed intent, we tried again to free the mother. My motivation was obvious, I wanted to lift her from the fragile body with splayed limbs that she'd lost. I wanted to release her from that inescapable rut.

I wanted to save her.

Until the time came when I didn't.

As our options ran out I became overwhelmed by the mother's loss. And, suddenly, I wanted her to die. Just as I would have wanted to die if faced with the same despair. I wanted to extinguish her pain, erase her unbearable memory of loss, and thwart the primal grief that I knew would arise from the deep to consume her like the prehistoric monster that would inevitably crawl from the waterhole beside her.

A decision was made.

It was unpleasant and unavoidable.

Laurie retrieved his rifle.

We took several steps back as he raised the barrel to a cowlick of hair on the mother's forehead. Then we waited for the gruesome end each of us wished we didn't have to witness. Moments before we all felt like men. Brave and capable. But now we were all boys. Anguished sons. Of mothers. Whom we loved.

The gunshot split the air.

And just like that, hope deflated before our eyes as Laurie's bullet brought a final surrender that the heavy burden of motherhood would never allow. Around me, the scent from the spent cartridge lingered momentarily, then vanished like an unseen ghost; a wispy reminder, floating into an eerily quiet wilderness that suddenly seemed to be observing a moment's silence for a mother brought to her knees.

By life. By circumstance. By us.

We trudged back to the four-wheel drive, and I consoled myself that there'd been no other option. There was no hope of a happily-ever-after ending. No saving the mother. Her baby was dead. And she was doomed. The right choice had been made. There was no turning back.

A hard road ahead was all that remained.

I blink back to the present, to the dark-eyed Varanasi cow staring at me. The childhood memory sits heavy in my chest, so I abandon any attempt to shift her. Pressing my chest against the sandstone wall, I squeeze past her shitty hindquarters, and continue hobbling through the twisting alleys of the ancient city. Better to keep moving.

Because some burdens are immovable.

Chapter Fifty-Four

MY TRAVEL ALARM buzzes me awake an hour before sunrise. The air is cool and still in the pre-dawn darkness, and the city has yet to stir. The relentless Diwali celebrations—and the resultant night of broken sleep—has left me feeling like death warmed up. Which is fitting, given that Varanasi is synonymous with dying. People from all over India journey to this holy city—and its sacred Ganges river—to die. Their goal: to break free from samsara and escape their endless cycle of life and suffering. Their quest: to find Nirvana.

Today, I plan to see how they do it.

I swallow three painkillers for my foot, then venture into the pitch-black alleyways and limp toward the river. Outside, a chill wind drifts from atop the dark water, prompting me to zip up my dorky jacket. I follow the breeze to its source and emerge at the shoreline, where a course of concrete stairs descends to the Ganges.

Across the river, the bald dome of a rising sun breaks the horizon. Its muted morning rays struggle to pierce a thick fog that creates an eerie, other-worldly atmosphere.

Alongside me, the evidence of a city stirring appears.

A steady procession of people, indifferent to the brisk morning chill, gather on the cement stairs and wade semi-clothed into the murky river. Cupped hands spill water over bowed heads in some spiritual cleansing ritual that is far beyond my understanding.

The personal ceremonies are an intriguing sight (and kinda nuts, given that the Ganges is one of the most polluted rivers on the planet), but they're not why I've come to the river. I'm here to cross off a specific item on my travel bucket list. A kind of Grim Reaper tour. And to take it, I need a boat.

Thankfully, a small flotilla of ramshackle wooden vessels cater to such adventures, many of which are moored along the shore. An aging oarsman beckons me from one of them. With pinched brow, blazing eyes, and leathery skin stretched taut over bone, he bears a striking resemblance to the boatman in Michelangelo's painting *Last Judgement* —the demonic figure tasked to ferry the damned to hell.

"Manikarnika Ghat?" I ask, trying to mask any trepidation.

He answers with a curt nod, and invites me aboard with a calloused hand. We settle on a price with murmured numbers. Then, with a deft push of an oversized oar, the craft slips from the shore, and we silently drift down the river. The current carries us past the old city, and as pre-dawn turns to sunrise, I marvel at buildings daubed in ochre, saffron, and indigo hues. The colors spread to the shoreline, where they are mirrored on the hulls of boats, and the saris of hundreds of women who are waist deep, mid-worship.

For ten minutes, we float like debris on the water's surface, the gentle slap of oars a rhythmic backbeat to the sounds of the city's awakening. Dogs bark. Bells toll. Horns blare. The din is in sharp contrast to the hush on the water. Out here, the quiet is interrupted only by muted conversations from tourist-laden boats. As they draw level, then veer away, I catch the nervous anticipation in voices. Every murmured word carries an undercurrent of apprehension, because we all know what lies ahead.

The burning ghats.

Finally, the funeral pyres come into view. A weathered temple-like structure appears first, looming in the distance. Then, timber barges stacked high with massive piles of lumber, gridlocked near the shore. As we drift closer, a run of concrete steps emerges—rising from an ash-covered river bank to the temple. Scattered fires, in furious blaze or dying glow, flank the stairs. Suddenly, I realize what macabre fuel is giving them life.

It's the dead.

A shiver grips me—this truly is a journey to the underworld.

Without a word, the boatman steers towards the fires. I glance back in concern—I only wanted to *see* the ghats. Not *visit* them.

But it's too late.

The boat nudges the shoreline mere inches from a semi-submerged body at the water's edge. Wrapped in pristine white linen, the dead man's lifeless form is adorned with garlands of red and yellow marigolds—symbols of purity, strength, and new beginnings. His family stands in the shallows beside him. Grief-stricken, they ferry handfuls of the spiritual Ganges into his mouth to ensure he reaches Nirvana.

I watch in stunned silence. The scene is grim yet captivating. Caught between two worlds, I can't decide whether to avert my eyes in shame or acknowledge their sorrow. I feel like the ultimate trespasser. An unwelcome intruder.

Unexpectedly, the boatman motions for me to disembark. I glare at him in wide-eyed protest, but he insists. Thoroughly confused, I step onto the shore. I take in the surroundings once more, unsure of where to go. Life on the ashen river bank is surreal, there are sleeping dogs, cows eating discarded marigolds, and workers tending woodpiles. And, of course, there is a dead man in the water near my feet, and half a dozen other bodies on fire close by.

Unsurprisingly, my presence attracts attention immediately.

Within seconds, a wiry man dressed in filthy clothes strides toward me. His sinewy hand clamps my arm.

"Sir, come, please," he says, eagerly. "I will show you fires."

He has the unmistakable geniality of someone ready to relieve me of my concerns…and money. I pull away, fearful of any scam that may follow.

"Is fine," he assures me. "I am not guide. I work here. Come. Please. I will tell you what is happening. You can take photo. Ten rupee. But pay later, yes?"

I shake my head. "I'm not taking photos."

"Okay, no photo, no problem. Come, sir, please."

I reluctantly follow. His path takes us past bonfires of burning flesh and smoldering bones.

"You are how long in India, sir?"

My mind can't comprehend what I'm seeing. "Umm…three months."

"In Varanasi?"

"Two days."

"You are leaving when after two days?"

"Sorry, what?"

"Leaving Varanasi."

I struggle to focus. "Tomorrow."

"Kolkata or Delhi?"

"Agra."

He smiles in delight. "Ah, Taj Mahal, yes?"

It seems absurd to be having a casual chat while people are in flames alongside us.

"Yeah, Taj Mahal."

"Then home?"

"Thailand. Then home."

"Very good. Very long holiday for you, sir. Very good life for living."

He waves me on, then points to a dilapidated, multi-story building bordering the ghats.

"Come, I will show you hospice for dying."

I stop in my tracks. "No. I'm fine, thanks."

"Please, is all right. So many sick peoples for dying. From all over India. Waiting."

"To die?" I ask.

"Yes, for dying and to stop more living."

I look up at the derelict hospice. Its severe state of disrepair obviously of no concern to the unfortunate inside. They're not here to stall death. They're here to escape rebirth.

"Varanasi is very best place to die," he continues. "And Diwali is very best time. These are very lucky peoples. Please, come."

I refuse to move. "Look, I don't want a tour of the hospice."

"Okay. No problem, sir. Maybe a donation for these poor peoples, yes? For wood."

The key word gives away his scam.

"How much of a *donation*?" I ask.

"Whatever you think is right, sir. You see this wood?" He points to the timber-laden barges floating offshore. "Very expensive. Many suffering peoples with no monies for wood."

I pull fifty rupees out of my wallet. The man looks at it unimpressed.

"Please, sir, many woods is needed for burning."

"That's all I'm giving."

The man takes the notes, quickly buries them in a pocket. "Come, I will walk you to the street."

There are many routes to take, but the man chooses to lead me between the pyres. The heat is intense, and the smell of roasting wood and acrid burnt flesh assaults my nostrils. My guide points to an untouched body, buried beneath timber logs.

"This man is Brahmin," he says matter-of-factly. "High caste. Sandalwood fire. Very expensive."

I look at the man's partially obscured face and decorated burial garment. I'm unsure if the sight is tragic or beautiful. I glance at the other bodies in various stages of cremation around me, then back to the grieving family at the river's edge

I have so many questions.

Who *are* these dead people? What is their past? Were they rich, poor, loved, loathed?

Of course, in the end, none of it matters. Who they are, what they had, and where they came from means nothing. Because they all ended up here, almost within arm's reach of one another, with no earthly riches other than family, and soon to be separated from that precious wealth. Sent where I don't know.

Where do the departed actually go? I wonder.

The ones we love.

The ones who break our hearts and slip from grasp.

Is it heaven or hell? Is it earth or ether?

And what of the broken-hearted they leave behind? Where do they go? Do they find the antidote to grief on a church pew or temple, a whiskey bottle, or a mediation retreat? And if comfort can't be found there...where to next?

Do they lose their mind and fall apart?

Or do they run away to heal their heart?

Chapter Fifty-Five

I CLIMB into the auto rickshaw.

"How much to the Taj?" I ask.

"Taj is closed today, sir," the driver says.

I clench my jaw in frustration. I'm so sick of this shit. So tired of the constant hustling and lies. Like many rickshaw drivers in India, this man's job is, literally and figuratively, taking tourists for a ride. It's a business I have no patience for today.

After a run-in with a pickpocket on the overnight trip from Varanasi, I'm sore, irritable, and exhausted from long-distance travel. I also hate Agra. The *Lonely Planet* devotes over fifteen pages to the city, but they could have saved ink and just printed: *Agra is the asshole of India*.

"I can take you some place else," the driver offers.

He suggests several attractions that apparently rival the majesty of the Taj Mahal. His recommendations include a tailor, a jewelry store, and a shoe shop—all owned by relatives who can offer me a *very cheap deal*.

I'm here for one reason—to see the Taj Mahal—so I repeat my request. The driver, ignores my wishes once again, and persists with his alternatives. My frustration grows, and, for the first time in India, the rage that consumed Marten, the Dutchman, begins to spark inside me. I try to extinguish it to maintain composure.

"Just take me to the Taj, *please*."

"Sir, this is not possible," he insists. "Taj is closed."

I know he's lying because the opening hours are printed on a tourist pamphlet I have in my daypack. I take a deep breath and try again.

"Just drive me past it, okay?"

The driver sighs, exasperated. "Sir, I tell you already—"

Suddenly, a switch flicks inside me.

"Jesus fucking Christ, do you pricks ever let up?!" The words roar out of me, raw and furious. "I am so fucking sick of this country. Stop fucking me around and take me where I want to go. *Right. Fucking. Now.*"

The driver recoils and shrinks in his seat. Then, without a word, he turns to the front, throws the auto into gear, and screws on the throttle.

Anger and adrenalin course through my veins as we drive on. Nothing I see from my seat impresses me. Agra is ugly. It's hot and busy. The streets are choked with refuse and an unpleasant scent of sulfurous egg farts permeates the polluted air. I can't find a single redeeming feature at any turn.

Filled with resentment for all things Indian, I glance up at the driver's rear-view mirror, willing the man to challenge me with a wayward glance so I can vent my seething displeasure and unleash a demonic wrath on him once more.

Finally, the moment comes.

The driver looks up and our eyes meet. But it's not the reflection of a defiant combatant I see. It's the face of a man full of hurt and hate. The vision instantly snuffs out the fire inside me. I look away, in contrition, knowing I crossed a line.

Why did you push me? I silently ask.

Why do you people always have to push me?

Minutes later, the majestic outline of the Taj Mahal appears. Unsurprisingly, the tourist attraction is open. I shake my head in disbelief—at the driver's lies and my hostile reaction. I feel both justified and ashamed. My usual emotional extremes.

The driver stops near the entry gate. Guilt gnaws at me, so I pay him double the fare. Neither of us acknowledges his deception or my outburst. We exchange nothing but money. Then he drives away, leaving me to reflect on my behavior. Despite three months of travel, I've gone nowhere. Nor have I changed. The three buddhist poisons still course through me. I feel neither windswept, nor interesting, just selfish, misunderstood and full of fury.

Swept along by a river of tourists, I enter the Taj compound, and soon find myself funneled into a human bottle neck at a colossal archway. The momentum of the crowd slows at the sandstone aperture, then immobilizes one and all, as a mesmerizing view of the world's greatest monument to love is revealed. I stare in awe because the Taj Mahal is impossibly perfect.

The majestic mausoleum rises at the end of a long reflection pool, appearing as a vast and luminous destination of ivory white columns and marble walls—a masterpiece of design and construction. Acres of manicured grass and gardens, fan outwards from the central pool, like a royal carpet. The symmetry and balance are flawless. The impact absolute. Everything about the Taj is overwhelming—it commands attention, reverence, and silent contemplation all at once.

I stand utterly still as a single minute stretches into an eternity. The sight stirs waves of emotion deep within, and, instinctively, I know my journey is nearing its end. Choosing to delay my walk to the tomb, I sit at a vacant garden bench and take in the breathtaking surroundings.

This is what love can build.

If you give it a chance.

I pull the tourist pamphlet from my bag and read its pages.

Four hundred years ago, an emperor, paralyzed by grief, built this monument for a wife he lost in childbirth. It took twenty years to construct. Shortly after completion, the emperor's own son imprisoned him in his palace, granting him only a distant view of his beloved's tomb. When death came, the emperor was laid to rest beside his wife, and the eternal love story of the Taj Mahal infused itself into a nation's psyche.

The tale cracks open a door in my own heart too.

And, suddenly, Claire walks in.

I NOTICE the changes as she steps into my grandparents' house. Her hair is shorter, her skin glows, and her eyes are clear—a picture of good health. She walks upstairs to the second level of the home I've been entrusted to house-sit, then catching sight of the view, makes a bee-line for the verandah. I hear the inevitable exclamation of *wow* as she takes in the vast hinterland outlook that stretches to the coastline. She steps onto the decking and leans against the railing. The image reminds me of our day at the fire tower—a flashback to a carefree figure set against a never-ending view, alabaster skin luminous in the sunshine.

I follow Claire's footsteps and stand beside her. Our forearms touch, accidentally on purpose. A silent language. Electricity shoots through me. I feel it in Claire too. Our fingertips brush, wordlessly asking for permission to revisit our past—our beginning. They intertwine firmly in answer.

Time rewinds.

And we kiss.

The view is forgotten and we only have eyes for each other.

Claire leads me inside to a spare bedroom and I lie on the mattress. She removes her top, steps out of her shorts, then stands proud and tall. Her ivory white lace underwear draws my gaze first, then the symmetry of her face and, finally, the arresting beauty of her figure.

Claire is a wonder of the world.

She kneels down and pulls a baby blue silk scarf from the pocket of her discarded shorts. Then, in a routine I've seen many times before, circles it twice around her waist, concealing her ostomy bag with a practiced ease. A bow is tied in the front, cute, delicate, feminine.

She climbs onto the mattress, straddles my hips and we kiss once more. Her hand reaches between her legs, guiding me past her warm thighs and between her swollen flesh. Our bodies gently move in unison, as if the story of us was never forgotten.

I miss this. I miss Claire. I miss us.

Suddenly, my lover sits upright.

Fingers splayed against my chest, she studies me. Nothing is said, but she can see the pleasure on my face—the joy of connection. My eye-line falls to her protruding stomach. Claire is so beautiful.

Carrying child.

"What's this little tummy doing here?!" I tease, resting my hand on the bulge.

My words are accompanied by a lighthearted smile but it's also a legitimate question because I know she is delaying her decision.

"Don't worry about it," she says, casually. "I'm going to sort it out."

"You sure?"

Claire nods. "I just need some more time."

I hide my concern as best I can. I'm still broke and unemployed, and I know neither of us is ready for a child. And yet, some part of me has entertained the idea.

"Have you been writing?" Claire asks, changing the subject.

"Yeah. Almost finished my TV script."

She sighs. "See what you can do when I'm not around to hassle you."

"Bub, you weren't a hassle."

Claire laughs. "You don't have to lie."

I want to tell her that it's not a lie. Not now. Now that she's the old Claire again—relaxed, independent, self-assured.

"The medications and my illness messed me up," she adds.

"It wasn't just you," I say. "I was in a rut and needed a change."

She runs her fingers through the hair on my chest. "Well, this might be the change that makes you."

I trace the curve of her belly with my fingers. "And this?"

Claire glances down, expression unreadable. "This might be what makes me."

And in that instant, I know her destiny.

Claire's going to give birth to our child.

A TEARDROP FALLS onto my yellow Taj Mahal pamphlet and I wipe my damp eyes with the sleeve of my shirt.

Why do I keep doing this to myself?

This trip was supposed to fix me. I was supposed to get better. Not worse. I was supposed to move on. But I'm still so fucking lost.

I stare at the towering tomb born from grief and love—built by a madman who was imprisoned by his child—and contemplate whether I can walk the distance and enter it.

I look at the pamphlet again. The emperor's translated poem is inked before me.

Should guilty seek asylum here,
Like one pardoned, he becomes free from sin.
Should a sinner make his way to this mansion,
All his past sins are to be washed away…

I stop reading.

The emperor's words are worthless. More Indian lies. When does freedom come?

When are the sins washed away? When will I be pardoned and forgiven?

Not now. Not ever.

I fold the pamphlet on itself.

I can't live like this anymore. I can't go on. I'm done. With everything. Done with Emma. Done with Claire.

Done with India.

Chapter Fifty-Six

AFTER TWENTY-FOUR HOURS IN BANGKOK, I'm ready to fly back to Agra.

Despite its Buddhist traditions, Bangkok feels shiny and superficial in comparison to India. The evidence of this worship of base pleasures is nowhere more apparent than in the red-light district of Patpong Road. Here, spiritual callings have been traded for carnal ones.

Along the street, bikini-clad hostesses loudly beckon passersby with promises of salvation from boredom via dancing girls, sex shows, and cheap drinks. Their neon-signed temples of flesh—drawing a wanton congregation of tourists—are adorned with names like Thigh Bar, Lipstick, and SuperPussy, which is ironically located near an STD clinic.

Patpong Road isn't solely a sex tourism hotspot, however. Stretching alongside the go-go bars is a bustling night market crammed with hundreds of stalls peddling name-brand fashion, handbags, shoes, watches, and electronics—all counterfeit.

Passing one of the stalls, I catch my reflection in a full-length mirror. The sight is unsettling. My khaki cargo shorts, frayed and stained, hang loose on my hips, my blue hibiscus-print Hawaiian shirt screams *sleazy tourist*, and a pair of knock-off Birkenstock sandals blister my dirty feet. My physical state is even more alarming. One heavily veined hand grips a Marlboro, the other a Red Bull can. I'm skeletal from weeks of battling Indian stomach bugs, and my brown eyes—deep-set in tired, dark sockets—look vacant and lifeless. I'm a shadow of my former self.

Or am I now the *real* me?

As I process that disturbing thought, my reflection shifts, and I see another man's face. I see his hollow cheeks, angular jaw, and sharp chin. I see the wiry arms that cradled a baby in the old Kodak photos. I see the man I always feared I'd become. I see my biological father.

"You see sex show?"

The question jolts me back to reality.

"What?"

A hostess smiles and points to the go-go bar behind us.

"Ping pong show. Dancing girls. Cheap drinks." Her tiny fluorescent bikini sticks to her frame like cling wrap. "Very sexy."

I politely wave her away, but she pouts and grabs my arm.

"Just one drink. Patpong best price."

She pulls me toward the entrance. Instead of resisting, I let her lead me, but I'm unsure whether it's because I'm curious or if I'm on a path to self-destruction.

Inside the bar, a dozen lithe women dance on a narrow, elevated central stage. Their matching bikinis glow phosphorescent under pulsing ultraviolet light. The strobe effect flattens their features, reducing them to faceless, interchangeable objects of fantasy.

My hostess leads me to a small stainless-top table, introduces herself in halting English, then orders me a drink.

"I dance up here now," Pim says, gesturing at the catwalk. "You watch and wait, okay? I come back soon."

I sip my watered-down whiskey and scan the room. The space is alternately spot-lit in neon reds and columns of intimate darkness. A bolstered diner-like seat, upholstered in scarlet vinyl, wraps around the club's perimeter walls. The clientele is mostly graying Western men whose appeal seems inversely proportional to the dancers' youth and beauty. Tainting the air, the musty scent of a thousand spilled drinks and god knows what else.

I turn back to the stage, and watch a dozen bored and listless girls half-heartedly sway to music. Finally, Pim returns and slides next to me.

"See me dance?"

"Yeah."

"You like?"

I nod. "You were great."

"Want private show?"

I look at her, wondering if she means a lap dance or sex.

"Promise you good time," she adds. "Very cheap."

I smile weakly at the clichéd spiel. "No, thanks."

She traces a slow line up my thigh with a hand. "You sure?" Her fingers glide up the zipper of my shorts. "If you want, you can fuck me."

Our eyes meet and I feel my moral fortitude being compromised by a desperate need for affection.

"How does this work?" I ask.

"However you want."

"I mean, where do we go?"

"You pay drink tab," Pim explains. "And bar fee. Because I take away customer. Then we go to hotel."

"So, I pay for my drinks *and* a bar fee just so you can leave?"

She nods, indifferent, leaving me to wonder why I am even considering this. But it's not the head on my shoulders doing the thinking, of course. It's the head that is being expertly massaged by Pim's right hand.

"Okay," I say, draining my whiskey in an attempt to swallow the unpalatable fact that I'm even contemplating doing this.

Pim leaves briefly and returns with the bar tab. I peel off some cash and hand it to her—my shame and self-loathing, now heavier than ever.

Grabbing my hand, Pim leads me outside.

"Where are we going?"

"Just follow me," she says, directing us towards a towering hotel in an adjacent street.

We pass through the polished chrome entrance and Pim points at the reception.

"You pay for room there."

"What do I say?"

"Don't worry. They know. Just pay."

I nervously approach the reception desk, walking past several adolescent Thai boys who are accompanied by tourists who could pass as grandfathers. I quickly pay for the room then meet Pim at the lift.

Surely I'm not going to do this? I think to myself.

But I probably will. Because the only shit I ever follow through with in life is the dumb shit.

Pim unlocks the door and we enter the hotel room.

"Shower first," she says.

I kick off my shoes and remove my shirt. Pim strips naked in front of me, then moves in close to carefully unzip my cargo shorts. She removes them, along with my underwear.

"Mmm..." she moans, eyes appraising me. "Nice body."

I cringe at the compliment because I know it's just an act on her part—she wants a fast start and a fast finish.

"Too skinny," I state flatly.

"No. Good body," she says, pressing against me. "Very nice." Her hand drifts to my groin, stroking me. "This nice too."

I laugh. "Now I know you're lying."

She removes her hand, gently grabs my wrist, and leads me to the ensuite. We shower, towel off, and move back to the queen-sized bed.

With practiced ease, she unrolls a condom, her gaze meeting mine, almost lovingly. Suddenly, Pim ceases to be a prostitute to me. She's now a lover...who I desperately want to please. And even though I'm paying for our connection, I want Pim to like me so much that she would sleep with me for free.

Because I'm worth it. Because I'm worthy.

I roll her onto her back, then glide my hand over one of her legs from thigh to hip. My fingertips trace over Pim's waist and stall at a point below her belly button. I rest my palm on the warm skin of her stomach, and a momentary memory plays out. After a lingering beat passes, my hand retreats back the way it came. When it reaches her knees, I direct my touch to her inner thigh and edge slowly toward her heat until my thumb gently brushes against the folds of her sexual flesh. Pim flinches and I see her small breasts rise with a sharp intake of breath. I repeat the caress—teasing, attentive. Loving. I want her to remember me as a selfless lover. A good lover. A man full of love.

I stop, draw my head level with Pim's, and kiss her lips. She makes no attempt to disengage. Instead, she pulls my body in tight and wraps her legs tightly around my thighs. Rocking her hips into position, she expertly takes me inside her.

After a few short minutes, and a series of desperate thrusts, I climax. Then, in a ludicrously naive display of masculinity, I try to bring her pleasure. It's a futile effort—given that Pim has probably slept with several men tonight already—and before long I am so flaccid that the condom falls off. I withdraw in a cold dread and voice my concern.

Pim retrieves the rubber with a practiced indifference, then retreats to the bathroom. Left alone on the bed, feelings of guilt and regret set in. As does the fear of contracting HIV from a Bangkok hooker. I close my eyes in self-loathing, then raise both hands to my head in disbelief.

Why do I always think sex is the answer?

My god, I truly am a dumb fuck.

As if to underscore this truth, the very next thought I have is this:

I need to find Emma.

Chapter Fifty-Seven

MY SISTER EXITS PASSPORT CONTROL, lightening my mood the instant I see her. She greets me with a hug and kiss, then takes a step back to size me up.

"Holy shit, you're so skinny."

"New cleansing diet," I say with a touch of irony in my voice. "You can eat as much as you want. As long as you eat it in India."

As a reward for surviving the first year of art college in a rural university town, my sister has booked a cheap flight to tag along on my final month of vacation. Unbeknownst to my youngest sibling, my travel itinerary consists of just one destination: Phuket. Also unbeknownst to her, is the purpose of my trip—to make Emma's bikini prophecy of love come true.

I heave Aleta's heavy backpack off her shoulders, and carry it to the bus bound for Khao San Road. She settles into a window seat and takes in the view. Like a seasoned traveller, I watch on, anticipating the culture shock that will widen her eyes as we venture into the city.

When we reach Khao San Road, the sensory assault visibly overwhelms her. But any apprehension is quickly extinguished upon realization that the kaleidoscope market street that is filled with global travelers, is actually spiritual nirvana to a fashion-loving, party-girl. We navigate the bustling thoroughfare, bypassing the numerous shopping opportunities, and veer down several alleyways until we reach the relative calm of my guesthouse. I allow my sister one whole minute to settle in before unpacking my own baggage.

"So…" I begin tentatively. "You'll never guess what I did last night."

Aleta stops all activity and gives me a wary, but knowing, look. "Please don't tell me you slept with a prostitute."

I remain silent and let her conclude for herself.

My stiff lipped response causes Aleta's forehead to pinch and her jaw to drop open in disbelief.

"Are you serious, Christopher?" Her tone befits a parent berating a child—a really stupid child. "Do you know how many sex workers have HIV in Bangkok?"

"Tens of thousands," I reply. "I checked it online."

Her eyes plead for the impossible. "Please tell me you're joking."

I shake my head, sheepishly.

My sister sighs in exasperation. "What the hell is wrong with you men? Why do you always think with your dicks?" She spots the pack of Marlboros by the bed. "And why are you smoking?"

"I'm not. I just quit." I note her skeptical expression. "It's true. Turning over a new leaf as of today."

"Bit late, don't you think? Couldn't do that yesterday, *before* you risked your life for sex?!"

I can only offer a shrug in defense.

She picks up the smokes, turns them over, then a mischievous glint flashes in her eye.

"So can I have one of these then?"

Her unexpected request breaks the tension and we both laugh at our respective idiocy and lack of will power.

For a much younger little sister, Aleta is a pretty cool chick to hang out with—she's smart, funny and sincere, and possesses an innate talent for art, academics, social awareness and virtuous conduct that clearly wasn't passed on to me.

"Grab the whole pack," I say. "And I'll take you for a proper tour of Khao San Road."

Out on the street, Aleta is in her element. She greedily scans every restaurant, tattoo parlor, hair-braiding stall, and hot young male backpacker that we pass. I try my best to live vicariously through her excited eyes, but the upbeat vibe of Khao San Road is in direct contrast to the heavy low I'm feeling inside. The street's relentless energy presses in, amplifying my inner exhaustion, and every burst of music and shoulder bump from a backpacker grates on my raw nerves.

"What next?" my sister asks, as we reach the end of the road.

"Internet cafe. So you can tell Mum you arrived safely."

We find such a cafe nearby. It's crammed with backpackers. Aleta claims the only available computer terminal and I pull up a spare chair beside her. As she logs in to her email account, I glance at the clientele. None of the travelers look like me. Their faces are relaxed and their skin glows with sun-kissed health. Unchecked optimism and youthful enthusiasm sparkles in their eyes. This isn't my tribe. I don't belong here, which is fine because I'm only here in body. In my mind, I'm in Patpong Road playing sexual Russian Roulette, I'm in Agra staring solemnly at the Taj Mahal, I'm in Sydney crying on a first date dinner, I'm in Brisbane destroying lives.

Aleta slides her chair out.

"Finished, already?" I ask.

"Nothing much to say yet," she says. "By the way, Claire's online."

A jolt, like an electric current, shoots through me at the mention of her name.

"We were chatting," Aleta adds. "But it keeps dropping out. My account is still open if you want to try her again."

She vacates her chair and I slide into it.

"How long do you think you'll be?" Aleta asks.

"Couple of minutes."

"Okay, I'll be outside."

I grin knowingly. "Having a cigarette?"

Aleta laughs. "Yep."

I watch her leave, then turn to the computer monitor. Ever the snooping big brother, I check her *sent* folder to see what words went home, just in case it's some lie about me sleeping with a Thai sex worker. I open her most recent emails. One is a short update to our mother and the other is to her old high school art teacher—a woman, around my age, who I once tried talking to in the vain hope of getting laid. The moment stuck with me because the imprint I made was so insignificant that her face looked like a blank canvas until she found someone more colorful to chat to.

Neither of Aleta's emails has any mention of prostitutes, so I log out of her account and check mine. As I do, I spot Claire's avatar in my sidebar contact list. I notice the green dot next to it, which means one thing.

Claire is online.

UPRIGHT – Time for absolution. Rise up for rebirth. Reveal yourself.

REVERSED – Refuse to self-examine and your just desserts will be served.

Chapter Fifty-Eight

I OPEN a new chat window and begin typing.

Chris: Hey, Bub

The icon alongside Claire's avatar immediately turns red, indicating she is now offline. I refresh the page, hoping her disappearance is just a poor Internet connection and not deliberate.

Finally, her avatar returns—green-lit.

Chris: Are you mad at me?

Several dots pulse on the screen. Claire is typing.

Claire: Internet keeps dropping out
Chris: Oh, ok. I was about to email you
Claire: Why?
Chris: Thought you logged off because you hate me
Claire: Ha. I do hate you ;-)
Claire: Where did your sister go?
Chris: Outside … having a cigarette!
Chris: and no, it wasn't my idea

Claire: You are such a bad influence. That really annoys me. I bet you're smoking too
Chris: Nope. Just stopped ;-)
Claire: For how long? Until your next whiskey?
Chris: No, time to get healthy. Time to reboot my life. Starting a massage course tomorrow. Need to change. I want to be a better man.
Chris: And, yes, I can hear you laughing!!
Claire: Why are you doing a massage course? New skills for seduction?
Claire: Actually, forget it. Don't answer. I don't want to know.
Claire: By the way, how come I had to beg to get a massage from you?! ;-)
Chris: Yeah, I know. Sorry about that.
Chris: Pretty useless, hey?
Chris: Don't want to be like that anymore.
Chris: Gotta learn to give a bit
Claire: Everything ok? You sound down
Chris: All good. Just stuff
Claire: Travel stuff?
Chris: Life stuff
Claire: You weren't completely useless, Chris. You just sucked at following through on promises. Actually, you suck at following through on anything!! ;-)
Claire: But you're not all bad.
Claire: Lies and manipulations are a different story though

I stop typing, unsure of how to reply because I know she's right.

Chris: I really want to be a loving partner and a good dad someday.
Chris: I know I can be. Just gotta sort through some baggage first
Chris: BTW, I didn't mean to be a prick
Claire: I know you didn't, which kind of makes it worse. Because people keep trying to reach out to you but you keep hurting them.
Claire: I'm not perfect either, but I can't forgive you for not giving me a chance. Nor can I forgive myself for losing who I am

Claire: Or for not being stronger.
Claire: Blah, blah, blah…
Claire: Same old, same old. Let's not rehash things neither of us really needs to go over again
Claire: So… are you enjoying Bangkok?
Chris: I get stressed when I think about you, Bub. I get scared that me going back home will drag us back to the past
Claire: You don't need to worry because I'm never going back to that past. I'm only going forward.
Chris: Why did you decide you wanted out again?
Claire: When?
Chris: The other week. You sent that email after my episode went to air.
Claire: I decided long before that
Claire: Because I'm really messed up. And I don't want to be anymore. The TV show was the final straw.
Claire: I felt so betrayed
Chris: Why betrayed?
Claire: I watched the episode after yours. The one she wrote
Claire: Emma
Claire: It was about relationships
Claire: And abortion

The last word sucks the air out of my lungs. I knew this moment would come. I deliberately didn't warn Claire about the love triangle and abortion storyline in Emma's episode because I didn't want to hurt her. Again. Suddenly, the tarot reader's advice makes sense.
You must not hurt this woman.
Maybe the cards meant Claire. Not Emma. How could I not see that before now?

Chris: That storyline didn't come from me
Chris: They already had it planned. I hated it because it didn't ring true. I got upset about it and Emma asked me what was wrong
Chris: So I told her about that day
Chris: At the clinic
Chris: But she brushed me off like it was nothing and they went

and made up some manipulative storyline because they didn't want to leave a 'dry eye in the audience'.
Chris: Their words, not mine.
Claire: I felt betrayed because of the subject matter
Claire: And who wrote it.
Claire: And because you fell in love with Emma immediately after me. Then you just wrote me out of your life
Claire: And I couldn't understand why you chose her and not me
Chris: You hated me, Bub. So I shared my secrets with her
Claire: NO…!!
Claire: You shared MY secrets with her
Claire: then SHE wrote about them
Claire: And by the way, I know why you went overseas. I've always known.
Claire: You were chasing her
Claire: And I know you lied about the other girls.
Claire: The ones you slept with in Sydney.
Claire: And you lied to me so I'd sleep with you before you left for India.
Claire: And I stupidly believed you
Claire: And now I'm not even sure I was the only girl you were with all those years we were together.
Claire: Which sucks, because I've never lied to you, Chris. EVER. Not once. And now I feel betrayed because I know you've slept with other women in India too
Claire: And I know I don't have any right to be hurt by your private life but I still am. And I don't want to be.
Claire: I can't trust you.
Claire: I can't trust ANYONE anymore. Because of YOU
Claire: And I'm so angry at myself because of that
Claire: And because I still can't hate you

I stare at Claire's avatar, wondering how I can defend myself.

Chris: I just wanted some attention, Bub. From someone who actually 'liked' me
Claire: I asked if you had been with anyone and you told me 'No'

Chris: I said 'yes'
Claire: You did not!! You said NO
Chris: When? In Brisbane or Sydney?
Claire: I would never have slept with you again if I'd known you had been with other women
Claire: In Sydney
Claire: Forget it. It doesn't matter anymore. None of this matters

I pause to get my head straight. Everything is starting to unravel but Claire's status remains green. We're still in dialogue. But I know our connection is tenuous at best.

Chris: We're not going to keep in contact are we?
Chris: Claire…?
Claire: No
Claire: I don't want to do this anymore. I want to be me again.
Chris: Bub, you're all I have.
Claire: Are you still in love with her?
Claire: Did you travel because of her?
Claire: Why did you sleep with me before you left?
Claire: Why, Chris?
Chris: Because I'm still in love with you.
Claire: No. You're not
Claire: You love me … but you've never been *in love* with me.
Chris: That's not true
Claire: Did you ever cheat on me?
Claire: When I was at work? Or when you were out with the boys?
Claire: Answer me
Chris: You were never there for me
Claire: WHAT?!!!
Chris: I needed someone to make everything feel better
Claire: I WAS ALWAYS FUCKING THERE FOR YOU
Claire: You wouldn't even go to a party with me.
Claire: You didn't want to travel with me.
Claire: But you went backpacking straight after we broke up!!
Claire: You went halfway around the world for HER

Chris: I went backpacking because I had a fucking breakdown, Claire
Chris: I needed a new beginning
Chris: because you couldn't see that I was hurting too
Chris: You didn't understand what I was going through. And Emma didn't understand.
Chris: No one understands

I stop writing and stare at the keyboard. Spent. Defeated. By myself. Because it's all a lie. All a manipulation. I did this to us. Not Claire. *My* fingerprints are all over this—*my* insecurities, *my* decisions, *my* actions. It was me who always wanted *more*, until that moment when more instantly became less. That moment when I realized what I had sacrificed in the pursuit of more—realized *who* I had sacrificed.

I look back at the computer monitor. Claire is still online. Still riding out the turbulence.

Chris: Sorry, Bub.
Chris: I wish my life could have encompassed just you but I was so lost
Chris: I fucked up, okay? I truly fucked up
Chris: Are you all right?
Chris: Hello…??
Chris: Claire?
Chris: Come on, Bub, talk to me
Chris: Please…?
Chris: I just wanted someone to save me
Chris: Because you were too busy saving you.
Chris: Claire?
Chris: Bub…???

Claire's dismissive silence reminds me of the same treatment she gave me a year ago. I try to put that particular day out of my head, hoping the Internet connection has simply dropped out again. But deep down I know it hasn't. Because I know exactly where Claire is right now. She's trapped in our inescapable past. Revisiting that same unforgettable day. The one I keep reliving.

The one I keep running from.

My insides churn as I watch Claire park her Subaru across the road from the abortion clinic. Her sister, Louise, is in the passenger seat, acting as support. A role I once played, badly.

I climb out of my old sedan, and tentatively walk over to meet them. Louise acknowledges my arrival with a cursory glance. Claire, face expressionless and guarded, refuses to acknowledge me at all. And for good reason, because today is the tomorrow we never really planned for.

Today is Judgement Day.

Filled with trepidation, we cross to the building and ride the lift to a lifeless corridor two floors above. We follow it to a plain reception desk. Claire and Louise approach the female receptionist, and after a subdued exchange, we are directed to a waiting room decorated with sober beige walls, grey carpet, and a long row of apricot-colored chairs. I discreetly scan the transparent souls seated around us. There's a silent twenty-something couple, a teenage girl with her mother, and a middle-aged woman on her own. Some seem confused, some vacant, some relieved. But all seem outwardly calm as they wait to terminate…

Terminate what?

A mistake, a complication, a responsibility?

A life?

Is that what it is?

My mind scrambles in confusion and my heartbeat quickens as a panic attack begins to rise and engulf me. I feel faint. Nauseous. I hang my head and take several deep breaths in an attempt to regain control of my senses.

Forget it. Forget it.

Just forget it.

I take another long deep breath.

I know what it is.

It's Damon.

That was the name I suggested to Claire if it was a boy.

Damon.
D-A-M-O-N.
Nomad.
Spelled backwards.

A life without limits. A traveller on an endless wheel of life adventure. A perpetual wanderer on an eternal journey. A journey that I convinced Claire to end.

But she wouldn't end it.

Couldn't end it.

All Claire managed to abort was appointments. She'd drive past the clinic with me, stall in the car park opposite and break down. In tears. Fueled by fear, guilt, and confusion. Consumed by endless concerns about her health, my selfishness, and our uselessness. On and on it went, until, eventually, all that was terminated was any communication between us. We were on different journeys. Claire was going in circles, while I was on the road to success because a television network had called about my writing. There was no room in my life for Claire, let alone a child.

"How you doing?" Louise asks, her female intuition sensing my inner torment.

Despite the loathing Claire's younger sister must hold for me, her concern seems genuine.

"Getting there," I reply, pretending I'm not falling to pieces.

She questions me no further, so I sit in silence until Claire's name is finally called. She stands and begins her journey. Every fiber of my being tells me that this moment is the biggest turning point of our lives. Every part of me wants to stop time, pause the drama, rewind the movie of us back to the beginning, so I can rewrite the scenes—edit the arguments, erase the abuse, delete my selfishness, and add the one single line of dialogue I wish I could tell her before it's too late:

Bub, let's keep it.

But I don't say anything. Because, in my gut, I know Claire wants to excise every trace of me from her life. She wants freedom from my lies and manipulations. And now she will get her wish, because for the first time in our relationship, Claire is the one in control, and I am finally neutered.

Filled with anguish, I watch Claire approach the hallway that leads to the surgery. My anxiety builds because this is my last chance to give voice to something that is more important than me. All I have to do is stand up and be accountable.

I stay seated, and Claire turns the corner.

My head involuntarily tilts towards the floor as she disappears from view, and I feel the universe swallow me.

After an eternity, she returns. Was it ten minutes? Sixty? I have no idea. She walks past, eye-line fixed on her feet. Her face is white with shock and shame. Louise receives her quietly, then leads her outside, leaving me in the waiting room. Finding my feet, I approach the receptionist and charge my credit card with a personal debt I know I'll forever pay. Then, like an automaton, I exit the building, aware that a little piece of Claire and me has been left behind. And although her and I are pro-choice, the moment—at least for me—feels unmistakably like several lives have been lost. I'm aware something else has been lost too.

My masculinity.

Every inch of my so-called manhood and its ever-present bravado has been eroded and stripped away. I am no longer a man. I am a helpless child in need of someone to hold. A feminine touch to soothe me. From anyone. I look to Claire for support. But she's been violated.

By the doctor, by life, by me.

I ask Claire how she feels, but she refuses to acknowledge me. There's no relief on her face. Just hurt. And something more. Something I've seen a thousand times before—heartbreak. Suddenly, the horrible consequence of all my actions and inactions dawn on me and I see an obvious truth I've been blinded to.

Claire wanted this child.

Which doesn't make sense, because if Claire wanted it... and now I want it... why did we—

Oh God... what have I done?

My hands fall to the computer keyboard in front of me. Claire's avatar is still online. Hanging on. Waiting.

Chris: Claire?
Chris: Please
Chris: Just one letter of acknowledgment.
Chris: Please...

The dots finally appear. Claire is replying. I self-consciously glance around the cafe, wishing I was anywhere but here. I don't want to be around happy people who are plotting their next nomadic adventure, their next party, their next hook-up. I hate them all because no matter how hard I try, or how far I travel, I can't be like them.

Finally, Claire's message arrives.

Claire: Do you have any idea what you have done?

Her question skewers me because it's the first time she has ever inferred that I am to blame. Claire has made her judgement.

I am guilty.

And I truly am. From our awkward first embrace to our final clinical separation, I've controlled Claire's mind, constantly eroding her choices to cement in mine.

I read her words again, knowing no amount of apologies will ever be enough.

Do you have any idea what YOU have done?

I type my response.

Chris: Yeah, I do know, Bub
Chris: I ruined your life. I knew that a long time ago
Chris: I killed your dreams
Chris: I killed your love
Chris: I killed

Claire's green light turns red before I can finish my message. I click on her avatar but there's no response. Our connection is cut. I stare at the screen, wondering how my life came to this. How did I become nothing of the man I wanted to be and everything of the one I didn't? I am my namesake. I am the son of my biological father. A man who hurt his partner and didn't want his child.

Just get up and run, you dumb fuck…
Run…

I heed the voice in my head, but my body refuses to obey the command. I'm crippled by self-loathing and paralyzed by the reckoning that I can feel coming once again. Just like that day when Claire was in ICU. Just like that day at the clinic. Just like that day in the restaurant with Emma. Just like the day in front of the Taj Mahal. And just like so many other days since that one singular day.

And then it arrives.

Please, no…

The inescapable truth that is impossible to run from.

Please, not here… not in public… not again.

But it's too late.

My façade of strength fractures and the wall of masculinity I've built to protect myself begins to crumble. In an instant, the all too familiar waves of guilt and regret rush in and flood my body. The hurt and anguish rise inside me until, finally, the dam breaks. And as my whole world slips under once again, I begin to slowly drown in deep sorrow. Then, in silence, I begin to cry.

For Claire. For me. For he or she.

I'm so sorry, Bub. Please forgive me.
Please, please forgive me…

Chris: I killed our child.

UPRIGHT - The cycle of life, karma, destiny, fate. Your new beginning.
REVERSED - Shitty luck if you resist change. Break the cycle or else.

New Beginnings

DÉJÀ VU...

The internet cafe looks the same—the computers, chairs, tables, even the backpacker clientele. It's as if time has stood still. But time hasn't stood still. Three years have passed since I was last here typing those fateful words to Claire. A lot has changed since then.

My last Thailand trip with my sister was a blur of backpacker clichés—we ate, drank, stayed in cheap bungalows, and lounged on pristine beaches.

I didn't seek out Emma.

After a month of travel, we returned home—Aleta to her university town, and me to the mining town I'd come from pre-Claire. My future didn't look bright. The contract on my TV series expired, and I was never invited back as a writer. I had burned bridges, isolating myself from agents, executives, and every opportunity I once thought I deserved. I was a destroyer, not a creator. With all chances at redemption severed, I retreated back to a familiar life of failure. My brief television career was over. I was thirty years old, single, unemployed, and still lost.

Then Claire called.

A tragedy had impacted her family, so I returned to Brisbane to offer support. Inevitably, our romance rekindled, and the movie of us spooled up again. For a year, we acted out scenes that had no direction —we made up, made do, broke up, broke down. Take after take. Rinse and repeat. The storyline went nowhere, and we couldn't move forward. There would be no happy ending to our sequel. And no absolution in our resolution.

The end credits rolled.

And we faded out.

I cast an admiring glance at the person sitting at the computer next to me and take in the fair-skinned face that is framed by striking curls of henna red.

It isn't Claire.

Or Emma.

Or my sister.

Janine's gaze shifts from her monitor and meets mine. Then, with a twinkle in her eyes, she pokes out her tongue. I smile brightly because my sister's old high school art teacher is a whirlwind of cheerful chaos. She's a year older than me, but has the boundless energy and attention span of a toddler—a toddler with ADHD.

We've been living together in London for the past year and now we're returning to Australia. Eighteen months ago, we were chatting in a Brisbane pub while Janine caught up with my sister. She had flown in from London, where she lived, to see her sick father. We shared a few laughs and talked about life. She knew my family and had lived and worked in the same mining town. It was easy, fun, which was the opposite of my life.

When she went back to the UK we swapped text messages and chatted on the phone. Our connection eventually drew her back to Australia to see if I was the 'One'. I followed her overseas, once again traveling for love. But this time, it was reciprocated.

"I'm done," Janine says, closing her internet browser. "How long will you be?"

I hold up a couple of fingers. "Two minutes tops."

Janine can't sit still for two consecutive breaths, let alone two minutes. "I'm going to get a banana pancake," she says. "Meet you outside."

I watch her depart, then return to my email.

To: Aleta
Subject: Thai surprise

Currently in Bangkok. Trying to get to Koh Tao in time for Janine's birthday. Cutting it fine. I'll let you know how it goes.

I log out, pay up, and walk outside to find Janine near a food stall, scoffing a banana pancake. She grins childishly as globs of chocolate sauce threaten to stain her shirt while she ferries portions to her mouth. A few years ago, a woman like Janine would have unnerved me. She's vivacious, social, optimistic, carefree and fun, which is everything I'm not. Her kind of boisterous confidence and spirited independence would have been a challenge to my masculinity, and heightened my insecurities—she's more educated than me, more worldly, more experienced. But these days, none of that makes me feel less, in fact, being around Janine brings balance.

But it didn't come easy.

Initially, the excess baggage from my past threatened to ground us. I missed Claire deeply. I craved for the very things I once hated—the plants she had bought, the music she listened to, the way she shelved her books. I ached for the familiar: the scent of her skin, her quiet bookish demeanor, and the deep intimacy we shared. I felt nostalgic for her creativity: the books she handmade at the table, her elegant strokes of calligraphy on Japanese paper, the artistic love letters she wrote to me. I missed Grace and Trevor. Even the cantankerous cat that ruled the house, became a yearning for a safe haven that now ceased to exist. I mourned the loss of those blue Mondays, pined for the movie nights, and, inexplicably, I grieved for the absence of our endless shared lows.

I refused to let Claire go.

But Janine refused to let go of me. She weathered testing days of second thoughts, then stood like a beacon of hope while I navigated inner storms. Finally, the clouds parted, the skies turned blue, and we found clear altitude.

Following the lazy trail my sister and I took three years earlier, Janine and I bus down the east coast of Thailand in a race against time to reach a small island renowned for its diving. We catch a midnight ferry from a mainland port, and arrive at Koh Tao as day breaks. It's Janine's birthday. And I intend to make it memorable.

An overland journey to a remote hideaway follows, and by midmorning, a run-down resort set into a hillside that overlooks a rocky bay comes into view. We check in and find our bungalow. Its furnishings are spartan and cheap: double bed, fan, mosquito net, basic bathroom, and a balcony with a worn timber bench seat. The ocean outlook, however, is truly spectacular.

"Happy birthday, babe!" I say, gifting Janine a broad smile.

With clear water and blue skies beckoning, we shed our clothes for swimmers, and descend a steep set of stairs past a rustic, open-walled restaurant. The path snakes over a rickety walkway towards a jetty that juts into azure water. Gliding languidly in the shallows are several snorkelers. We watch as the marine explorers duck-dive intermittently in search of tropical color.

The birthday girl and I cautiously slide into the liquid blue. The temperature is perfect, much like a cool drink after mowing the lawn on a summer day. Beneath us, vibrant fish dart around our bodies. Janine pulls a pair of lap swimming goggles over her eyes, takes a deep breath, and disappears in pursuit. I do the same, but my intent isn't to chase tiny sea creatures. I have a bigger catch in mind.

Trawling over several submerged boulders, I search for the perfect spot from which to reel in my intended trophy. Finding a suitable rock, I stand on it, allowing my head and shoulders to protrude above the waterline. Janine pops up nearby, de-mists her swimming goggles, then promptly disappears again. I extend an arm into the pocket of my board shorts, extract her birthday gift, then anxiously wait for her to resurface within reach. When she finally does, I quickly hook my hands around her waist. My girlfriend thrashes like a spawning salmon, laughing underwater as I haul her in.

"Stop tickling me," she gasps, trying to release herself from my grasp.

I latch on tighter. "Just wait a second."

Janine wriggles some more.

"Stop," I continue. "I need to ask you something."

Janine stops thrashing and gives me a frustrated look that belongs, once again, to that of a toddler—a toddler denied whatever shiny object they are fixated on.

"But the fish?" She playfully pronounces the last word as '*feeesh*'.

"The *feeesh* can wait," I say. "I've got something important to say."

"*Ooooh*," she mocks. "Okay, Mr. Serious, what's so *important*?"

I pull her closer so her feet can find the rock. Her bright blue swimming goggles with their bright blue tinted lenses are still covering her bright blue eyes. It's a vision of cuteness that makes my heart burst. I gently pull the nose bridge of the goggles away from her face and relocate them to her forehead. Her brow wrinkles in an over-exaggerated frown. I swear today could be her third birthday the way she acts, not her thirty-third.

"I need you to stay still." My own eyebrows rise as my facial expression turns serious. "Please? For one minute?"

"Why are you shaking?" she asks.

"I'm cold," I lie, trying to hide my nervousness. "Look, there's a reason why I was so desperate for us to get—"

"I know, I know. Because it's my birthday."

"Yeah, but there's a reason why I wanted to get *here*, specifically."

Janine stares at me, unsure of what I'm hinting at.

I push on. "You know I love you, right?"

Suddenly, her expression becomes grown-up, as does her tone. "Why are you being freaky?"

"Because I want you to know that I love you." I see the escalating concern in her eyes. "And that you've made me happier than I've ever been in my life. And that there's only one thing that could make me any happier."

Janine looks perplexed. "Right, please stop," she demands. "You're acting really strange now. And I don't like it."

But I can't stop. Because it's true that I've never been happier. I'm neither depressed nor sad. Nor am I lost. Despite having no money, no career and no success, I feel pretty content.

"Will you marry me?" I ask earnestly.

From beneath the water, I reveal her birthday gift.

Janine looks at the oversized, 100-carat diamond ring that's the size of a baby's pacifier. Her face is expressionless, and not just because the ring is made out of confectionery.

"Are you kidding?" she asks. Her eyes beg for clarification.

"No, I'm serious."

Her bottom lip twitches nervously. "You are not."

"I am, Babe. I want to marry you." I hold the lollipop up, a silly grin on my face. "I spent 25 pence on a ring for Christ's sake."

"Really?" Her head is above water but she is clearly drowning. "But why?"

"Because I want to be with you forever."

Her eyes study my face in silence, weighing up her future.

"So…" I say quietly. "Will you marry me?"

Janine waits a brief moment, then nods her head emphatically. "Yes." A wide smile fills her face. "Yes, yes, yes!"

I slip the lollipop ring on her shaking finger and suddenly the gravity of the moment overcomes Janine and she begins to laugh. And cry.

"Are you sure?" she asks, her voice betraying doubt that someone would actually propose to her.

Her query makes my heart hurt, because I know most men don't see her strong personality as marriage material.

"I'm one hundred percent positive, Babe."

Janine hugs me, then wraps her legs around my waist. We kiss, goggles on foreheads, fish around our feet. The moment lasts a full thirty seconds—which is a lifetime for Janine—then she disengages as a sudden realization hits her.

"We need a photo," she proclaims with a degree of urgency in her tone.

Immediately, she drags me off the rock and we swim back to the jetty where our belongings are. I follow her up the ladder and we find ourselves face-to-face with an attractive woman who is watching the snorkelers. Janine proudly raises her ludicrous lollipop ring to show the girl.

"We just got engaged," she says excitedly. Her beaming smile makes her look unspeakably gorgeous.

The traveller glances at the novelty ring, unimpressed. "You must be so proud," she says, her European accent laced with sarcasm.

There is a stark contrast between the two women in front of me. One is a sultry, olive-skinned, lithe-bodied brunette, who is modeling Gucci sunglasses and a designer black bikini that highlights her assets. The other is an upbeat, lily-white limbed, flame-haired force of nature, who is wearing excessive amounts of suncream, an old sports top and a pair of oversized board shorts.

There's no doubt in my mind that my fiancé is infinitely more attractive…on every single level imaginable.

I grab the camera from beneath our towels, pull Janine tight against me, and capture our special moment for posterity in a selfie. I give my wife-to-be a quick kiss then absorb the scene around us—I'm on an island, in Thailand, standing beside the woman I want to marry. I can see a bikini, but just like in Emma's fortune-teller reading, my true love isn't wearing it.

Everything feels right. All of it. I'm not lost anymore.

I'm exactly where I'm meant to be.

Happy Endings

RELATIONSHIPS ARE LIKE PLANE FLIGHTS.

Well, that's my theory.

Sure, it's a crap theory, but in my mind, it's a series of journeys—some are no-frills and turbulent, others first-class and trouble-free, but most are in between. There are domestic separations and long-distance frustrations. We plan flight paths. We make diversions. Trips are missed. Connections cancelled. We pack baggage. We get lost. But we eventually reach our destination.

This is the journey we're all on.

It's been over twenty years since Janine and I got engaged in Thailand. I'm not in my thirties anymore. I'm a middle-aged man with thinning hair and even less motivation. My life hasn't been perfect. Instead, it's been a normal existence filled with the usual highs and lows of births, deaths, marriages, graduations, and seemingly endless obligations. There's been boredom, depression, and financial distress, but there's also been contentment, adventure, and a soundtrack of laughter that, these days, I measure as success.

All these moments were shared with an amazing partner.

Who became an amazing ex.

Janine and I separated three years ago. Like many long-term relationships, the demands of domestic life, child-rearing, and career, gradually dissolved our connection. The very differences in our personalities that had initially brought balance eventually disrupted equilibrium. Our needs and dreams were mismatched, and the older we got, the more important it was to be ourselves, rather than constantly compromise or reinvent. We loved each other, but we were no longer in love with each other. Sometimes that's the evolution of relationships. It's not right or wrong, it's just life and it's many manifestations. Fortunately, we reached that conclusion together, which allowed us to move on, proving the cliché that life is an unfolding journey, not a predetermined destination.

Or is it?

I PARK the truck at the depot. It's the end of my Saturday shift working in the world's best job. I'm one of four truck drivers who provide a library service to a dozen coastal and hinterland communities scattered across one of the most picturesque places in Australia.

Our trucks magically transform into physical libraries, complete with slide-out office pod, networked computers, air-conditioning, and, of course, wall-to-wall shelves that house thousands of books for young and old. Once open for business, I also transform—from truck driver to librarian. I move from place to place each day—a nomadic job—connecting people to stories. My role is grounded, without turbulence. It's calm in my space, meditative, but I never enforce quiet. I read to toddlers, I laugh with parents, I tease retirees and they stir me back. It's a wonderful experience, more a vocation than a job—and perfect work for a middle-aged book lover who has a truck license from a past life. Once again, I'm one of those lucky bastards who actually love going to work on Mondays.

I turn the ignition off and the library truck shudders into silence.

Ordinarily, I'd spring from the driver's seat at shift end and make preparations for the following day's run, but today I'm happy to sit for a moment and catch my breath.

Earlier in the morning, one of my lively regulars asked if I could recommend any memoirs that were a bit *rawer* than the standard fare. I saw the cheeky twinkle in Moureen's ninety-year-old eyes, and grabbed a book from the shelf behind her.

It was called *Happy Endings*.

"Here you go." I handed her the memoir. "Bella Green. She's a comedian—and a sex worker."

Moureen's eyebrows rose. "That's more like it."

"Beware the *Brown Shower* chapter," I warned. "It'll make your toes curl."

"Takes a lot to shock me, Christopher."

I didn't doubt it because Moureen is quite the character. She looks mild-mannered and innocent, but she's a firecracker with the kind of quick, bawdy wit that would make a construction worker blush. I love her dearly for that.

"When do I get to read your book?" she asked.

"Trust me, it's not your thing."

"I'll be the judge of that," she countered. "You just don't want me to read it."

The truth is, I don't want Moureen to read it, because I'm not proud of the things I've done. But I also don't want to bore her with a complicated one hundred thousand word love letter, that's masquerading as a convoluted confessional about a past I'll never get a chance to apologize for.

"I haven't finished it yet," I said, giving her my usual evasive excuse.

"Well, bring it in when you do. And don't forget, you cheeky bugger."

And with that Moureen dashed out the door, set on a course to meet the world head-on with her trademark good humor and refreshing directness. Her departure, prompted thoughts of another resilient matriarch who I owed some words—an octogenarian who I've maintained secret contact with for two decades.

Picking up my phone, I ready myself to make the long overdue call. Scrolling through my contacts, I find the number for the woman who has administered her maternal care via an annual email and phone call.

Her name is Grace.

Claire's mother.

Concern creeps into my mind because these calls occasionally unsettle me. When Grace talks about her family I feel love and joy, but it's tainted with guilt and remorse. I know details about Claire's life from social media: relationship status (unmarried), career (professional), travel (frequent), family (childless). Without fail, I construct my own narrative to explain that last fact. In my mind, Claire isn't a mother because of me, and she travels the world to escape the trauma I created. Grace has dismissed my narcissistic assumptions time and again, crediting her daughter with having more agency over her life than I choose to believe.

My phone chimes a message notification as I'm about to make the call. The alert is from a telco company informing me that half our monthly family data limit has been used—in the space of a week. I shake my head in exasperation, then find the guilty family member's last message in my phone, and compose a frustrated text about phone addiction. It's a pointless exercise because I receive the same data alert from the telco every single month, and the same teenager receives the same frustrated message from me.

Daughters.

I always wanted daughters because I knew I wouldn't be a good father to boys. I was too soft, too emotional, and I lacked many of the alpha male traits they would need to survive in a masculine world. I liked cars, four-wheel-drives, motor racing, and contact sports—the stereotypical boy stuff—but I also loved film, theatre, musicals, and books. I was built to be a feminine father so I hoped for daughters.

Fate gifted me two sons.

I send the message to my youngest, Matt, aka Mr Mobile Data Depletion. Then I scroll up the message thread to a recent interaction. It's an essay-length birthday text I sent, followed by his barely two-line reply. I read both, as I do regularly, since he is no longer in my care full-time.

> Dear Matty, I want to tell you a story about an incredibly handsome, emotionally available, highly intelligent human. I met him exactly sixteen years ago. Right from the moment I saw him, I knew he had everything at his disposal to be anything he wanted

to be. In those early years, I could see that he was funny, talented, loyal, entertaining, and considerate. He was also tapped into a consciousness that operated on a higher plane. He was an unusual soul, in so much that he seemed instinctively connected to a deeper subtext in life—he saw and felt dimensions of emotions that most of us aren't privy to.

When I realized that fact, I understood that this amazing human was a communicator—a writer, singer, musician, actor. An artist. A creator. So his mum and I deliberately set him on a path that could lead him to the summit of his passions and talents. I had no idea if he truly had the skills to realize his dreams, because I wasn't sure if my judgement of his innate gifts was sound or whether I was clouded by parental pride. Turns out his mother and I were right—this kid was talented. Right from the start. He was born to do the things he loved. And he was good at doing them.

I was moved to tears when I saw you act in *Medea*, MattyMoo. And your mum was too. It reminded me of the end scene in the movie *Billy Elliot*, when Billy's father finally watches his son dance in *Swan Lake* on stage. Billy leaps into the air and, in that moment of personal victory, he steels his father's heart. For both characters the journey has been long and arduous to get to that point, but in reality, Billy's journey is truly just beginning. The world awaits, and Billy is about to soar. I saw this in you too, Matty, when you were on stage. I saw you embody and bring life to a fictional character who was created on a page 2500 years ago. You made that character real, identifiable, tangible. And in doing so you put breath into your own life. And mine. I watched your soul soar. And I felt an undeniable connection to the miracle I witnessed on stage before me, just as Billy Elliot's father did.

You're an incredible son, Matthew. A beautiful boy who has many traits of my own. The exception is that you have the talent and ability that I lacked. Plus you're far more intelligent and far more well-rounded than I ever was! I've always been hugely impressed by you. I never cared if you did or didn't do well at school or sport or anything else. I've only ever cared about you being true to yourself.

I'm someone who has relied upon artists to keep me alive at various points in my life, particularly in my younger years. I needed writers, actors and musicians to soothe me, to create moments of resonance and understanding during times when I felt isolated, lost, and misunderstood. These people were my sun, my air, my sustenance—my saviors. They were my cosmic connection to the universe. They allowed me to believe I belonged somewhere.

These creatives were important to me, as they are to millions of other people like me—the empaths who are lost in a seemingly insensitive world. I needed, and have always needed, those people to fill my life with joy and hope, with connection and love. You're one of those creatives, Matthew. You have the power and talent to positively touch countless lives. Your skills and personality can save people. Literally keep them alive. It's not an insignificant thing. It's a superpower. It makes you a very unique individual. Which is simply confirmation that I was right all those years ago when you first came into my world. I knew you were special then. And I know that fact to be true, still, to this day.

I'm incredibly proud of you, Sweetheart. And I always will be. Happy birthday, mate. Love you forever and hope you have a wonderful day, beautiful boy.

I read Matt's short reply, hoping his response is genuine.

Thank you so much, Dad. I'm crying from that. You truly are the best dad anyone could ask for. Love you too.

His words prompt me to read another essay-length birthday message I sent five days earlier to his older brother, Nick; a child who somehow managed to best his younger sibling in the brevity stakes by returning just a single-line reply to his father's overemotional and overwritten ruminations. I find the message thread and read it, recalling the day my life utterly changed.

> Dear Nicky. Eighteen years ago a little boy came into the world with great difficulty and drew his first breath. He found his voice in that first cry, and with a bruised and battered head was whisked away from an exhausted mother who had endured a long, painful, and arduous labour. While his mum was recuperating, I visited the little boy in the pediatric ward. He was alone, isolated, sore and restless. The back of his head was black with deep bruising from the forceps used to remove him from his Mummy's womb.
>
> Swaddled in cotton wraps, the little boy was handed to me by a nurse as I sat in a chair. He settled. His crying stopped, and he fell asleep in the crook of my arm. I hummed a song to him as I looked down upon his angelic features. In that moment, I felt an indescribable and unconditional love that I knew would forever rule my world. I instinctively knew there would be moments of pride, of fear, of joy, of hurt, of celebration, and, I also knew, there could be moments of insurmountable grief if that little boy ever left the world before me. My life changed in that instant. There was no 'me' anymore. I wasn't 'Chris'.
>
> I was 'Nicholas's father'.
>
> My role in life had altered. My purpose became clear. I would never leave your side. I was Saint Christopher from that moment. The protector of the heavenly child who lay swaddled, Christ-like in my arms.
>
> I spent forty-five minutes staring at this perfect little life in my arms that day. And since then I've spent almost ten million minutes more admiring your soul. You are, without exception, one of the finest beings to have ever been created, Nicholas. I swore I would love and protect you for the entirety of your life. At any cost. And I still adhere to that lifelong contract I silently made to

you, and the universe the day you were born. You are a wonderful human, made in perfect form for this world. A delightful son for your mother and me. A caring and concerning brother for Matthew. A sensitive and fun lover for those who are lucky enough to receive your romantic affections. And a supportive, understanding peer for your friends. You're also now, in the eyes of the law, an adult. Unbelievable as that is!!!

Eighteen years has passed since I fell deeply in love with you, Noodle. It's been a joyful eighteen years. You changed my life. You allowed me to be a dad, and gave me the freedom to be the man I always wanted to be. It was an amazing gift. And I'll forever be in your debt for being the son you are. Never change to be anyone else, NickyNoo. Always be you. Unapologetically you. Forever. Happy birthday, Sweetheart. Love you heaps.

I read his reply. All thirteen words! Tellingly, both boys have written all the words a father will ever need to read.

Thank you so much dad, I love you. You're the best dad ever.

I'm not the best dad ever, of course. No one is. All parents learn as we go.

Several years ago, my biological father passed away from cancer. He hadn't seen me since I was a toddler, and wanted to find me before he died. I was several weeks too late for that. Eventually, I met his wife and two daughters. Despite his earlier mistakes, Chris became a loving husband and a good father. His story was one of redemption and rebirth.

Of new beginnings.

I press the dial icon on my phone and hear the ring tone pulse through the speaker. My heartbeat rises in nervous anticipation because this is the last call I will ever make to Claire's mother. I want to set her free from the obligation of looking after me. I also want to set myself free, because for twenty years I've harbored a naive and unhealthy fantasy. I dreamed of Grace giving me her daughter's phone number. I dreamed of calling Claire and saying 'I'm sorry' for all the pain I caused.

I dreamed of forgiveness, closure and release.

The irony is that the relationship and obligations I sought to run from back then stayed with me for over twenty years. Claire was always on my mind. Since then, I've carried a burden of guilt and remorse for my actions that has kept me imprisoned, and in desperate need of pardon.

I'm finally ready to let go of those poisons.

I'm ready to forgive myself and accept who I truly am: a devoted father, a caring ex-husband, a loving son. I'm a family man, and that role is more than enough. Getting to this destination has been a long road and a hard lesson. Sometimes the path to true love is closer than you realize, but the journey of self-love is further than you ever imagined.

The phone stops ringing and suddenly I'm connected.

My heart beats faster, fueled by the ever-present fear that Grace will, today, finally blame me for hurting her daughter.

Then I hear a sound that finally ends my story...but begins a new chapter.

"Hello," says the familiar voice. "Claire speaking."

- The End -

Acknowledgments

I have the good fortune of being blessed with the ability to fall hopelessly in love with strong, intelligent women. Unfortunately for some of these women, that trait has brought this book to life. So, right off the bat, I would like to apologize to the real-life versions of any past loves portrayed within these pages, and assure them, and readers, that any events and conversations documented in this book are based on my own recollections, imaginings, and need to create melodrama. As such, any perceived faults of character can only be attributed to me. Without exception, I remember the real-life cast of players in this story as decent, loving, compassionate people. And, obviously, mildly insane for putting up with me!

I'd also like to thank the people I met in India, some of whom found themselves with walk-on roles in a story that wasn't always kind to their country. My interactions on the subcontinent were memorable and, sometimes, life-changing.

A huge thank you to my mother who always encouraged me to finish the story, no matter what people thought. And also to my family who have maintained the misguided belief that I can write readable sentences.

And lastly, books don't just appear magically—although I wish they did. In fact, if you surveyed the partners of writers on how much of their life is spent placating all the author angst and self-doubt, you'd wonder how it is that books are even completed at all. So, at the risk of bastardizing writing and marriage quotes, I would like to acknowledge the infinite sacrifices made by my long-suffering benefactor, sounding board, and ex-partner in crime, Janine, and suggest the following as a truism: An author lives one word at a time…while their partner lives an eternal sentence.

About the Author

Chris Bates has been a failed TV writer, a failed magazine publisher, and a wildly successful procrastinator.

Lost In Transit is his first book…and probably his last.

www.ingramcontent.com/pod-product-compliance
Lightning Source LLC
Chambersburg PA
CBHW020515080526
44583CB00013B/604